On the Brink
The US, China and the Nuclear War Shadows

On the Brink

The US, China and the Nuclear War Shadows

Musa Khan Jalalzai

Vij Books India Pvt Ltd

New Delhi (India)

Published by

Vij Books India Pvt Ltd
(Publishers, Distributors & Importers)
2/19, Ansari Road
Delhi – 110 002
Phones: 91-11-43596460, 91-11-47340674
Mobile: 98110 94883
e-mail: contact@vijpublishing.com
www.vijbooks.in

Copyright © 2022, *Musa Khan Jalalzai*

ISBN: 978-93-90917-20-4 (Hardback)
ISBN: 978-93-90917-27-3 (Paperback)
ISBN: 978-93-90917-43-3 (ebook)

Contents

Introduction

The United States military and economic power is in decline. Its political and military body has broken. The majority in the EU and Asian leadership had delighted at Joe Biden's victory on the pipe-dream that he will bring roasted Gallus-Gallus to Europe and Asia, but they shortly became hopeless about his slow and contended approach to global challenges. The European, Asian and African attitudes towards his crumbling leadership massively changed. They think that the US military and political system has broken and cannot trust his vanquishing leadership. As a matter of fact, the Joe Biden government received a fragmented and fractured body of the American state from the Trump administration together with politicized intelligence infrastructure and domestic turmoil. The politicization of intelligence infrastructure and war of strength between CIA, Pentagon and FBI caused internal political turmoil. Uttermost inequality, already a distinguishing feature of the United States, worsened during the pandemic. Poverty and alienation are on the rise. Expert and analyst, Richard Wolff in his *Asia Times* analysis (Why the troubled US Empire could quickly fall apart: For the first time in more than a century, the United States has a real, serious, ascending global competitor - 31 October 2021), has noted causes of US decline:

> "There is no way for the United States to change China's basic economic and political policies since those are precisely what brought China to its now globally envied position of being a competitor to a superpower like the US. Meanwhile, China is expected to catch up to the United States with the economic size before the end of this decade. When empires decline, they can slip into self-reinforcing downward spirals. This downward spiral occurs when the rich and powerful respond by using their social positions to offload the costs of decline onto the mass of the population. That only worsens the inequalities and divisions that provoked the decline in the first place... Decline provokes more hiding, and that in turn worsens decline. The downward spiral is engaged. Moreover, attempts to distract an increasingly anxious public — demonizing immigrants, scapegoating

1

China, and engaging in culture wars – show diminishing returns. Empire decline proceeds but remains widely denied or ignored as if it did not matter".[1]

American intelligence agencies, the army and political leadership, were dancing to different tangos during the Trump era, and still changing their positions in the field of intelligence and politics. War of strength and political affiliation of intelligence agencies have badly damaged the image of the so-called superpower in and outside the country. Officers of CIA, FBI and policing agencies are openly criticising democratic leadership and supporting leaders of their choices. John E. Mclaughlin, in his paper, (Four Phases of Former President Trump's Relations with the Intelligence Community. International Journal of Intelligence and Counterintelligence, Vol. 34, No. 4, 787-794, 2021), has noted the relationship between intelligence agencies and the Trump administration: "The relationship then descended to a low point when, on 6 January 2017, the DNI released a declassified report affirming that Russia had interfered in the election— and adding that Moscow's aim was indeed to help Donald Trump. The CIA and Federal Bureau of Investigation expressed "high confidence" in the judgment regarding Trump, with the National Security Agency (NSA) opting for "moderate confidence. "The politicization of intelligence, phase four of Trump's engagement with the profession, came increasingly into public view as Trump neared the end of his term, particularly in the run-up to, during, and in the aftermath of his first impeachment in February 2020".[2]

The current US intelligence infrastructure and its management has ultimately politicised by adopting the role of ISI in Pakistan's politics. During the Obama era, without acknowledging the President's office and CIA, State Department was begging for funds for the ISIS terrorist groups in Iraq and Syria. Former CIA analyst and expert, John A. Gentry in his research paper, (Trump-Era Politicization: A Code of Civil–Intelligence behaviour is needed. International Journal of Intelligence and Counterintelligence-2021) has documented politicisation of civilian and military intelligence agencies during President Trump's era: "As intelligence officers have made public statements and signed letters (I signed the letter protesting the decision to lift John Brennan's clearances), I have seen something of a cleavage between civil and military intelligence officers. The cleavage is not absolute but, on the whole, retired senior military intelligence officers appear to have been more reticent about criticizing President Trump. The military oath differs from the civil oath. Military personnel also swear to obey the orders of the president and officers appointed by him. But neither group takes an oath of loyalty to the president. The very concept reminds me of the Fuhrer oath taken by the German military, pledging "unconditional obedience" to Adolf Hitler. I assume this is not what my colleagues mean when they talk of loyalty to the president. In US usage, such a concept simply does not exist."[3]

The United States has labelled China as a strategic competitor and a serious threat to U.S. national security. The military confrontation between the United States and China has put in danger the territorial integrity of Littoral states in the South China Sea. In 2009, China made a state-of-the-art territorial claim on the region through different actions, such as militarization in land and sea. In the recent past, the Chinese government created two more districts to strengthen its political and military position viz-a-viz the United States-asserted that intelligence gathering in the region was illegal. Political and military confrontations continue to mount in the South China Sea, but the international community views things differently. In July 2020, the US Secretary of State warned that most of China's claims to offshore resources in the South China Sea were unlawful. The United States, during the past two years, mishandled the issue and created more tensions by extending its naval power to keep igniting the fire of trade war. Having kept the pot boiling, the Biden administration managed a nuclear alliance of the US, UK and Australia to challenge the naval power of China in the South China Sea. This trio alliance known as AUKUS has raised denunciation in the region.

South-East Asian states understand that they are part of the game and want China and the United States to ask their association to enter military confrontations. On 10 August 2021, Associated Press reported a clash between China and the US in the Security Council meeting. Secretary of State Bliken warned: "would have serious global consequences for security and for commerce. In the South China Sea, we've seen dangerous encounters between vessels at sea and provocative actions to advance unlawful maritime claims. The United States has been clear in its concerns regarding actions to intimidate and bully other states unlawfully to access their maritime resources." He said. On 06 October 2021, Congressional Research Service presented a report (U.S.-China Strategic Competition in South and East China Seas: Background and Issues for Congress) to Congress on US position and interests in the South China Sea. In this report Chinese claim on the South China Sea has been negated:

"China has maintained ambiguity over whether it is using the map of the nine-dash line to claim full sovereignty over the entire sea area enclosed by the nine-dash line, or something less than that. Maintaining this ambiguity can be viewed as an approach that preserves flexibility for China in pursuing its maritime claims in the SCS while making it more difficult for other parties to define specific objections or pursue legal challenges to those claims. However, it does appear clear that China, at a minimum, claims sovereignty over the island groups inside the nine-line segments. China's domestic Law on the Territorial Sea and Contiguous Zone, enacted in 1992, specifies that China claims sovereignty over all the island groups inside the nine-line segments. Whether and how to compete strategically with China in the SCS and ECS is a choice for U.S. policymakers to make, based on an assessment of the potential benefits and costs of engaging in such a competition in the context of overall U.S. policy towards China, the Indo-Pacific, and the U.S. foreign policy in general. Competing strategically with China in the SCS and ECS formed an element of the Trump Administration's confrontational overall approach toward China and its efforts for promoting the FOIP construct. A key issue for Congress is whether and how the Biden Administration's strategy for competing strategically with China in the SCS and ECS is appropriate and correctly resourced, and whether Congress should approve, reject, or modify the strategy, the level of resources for implementing it, or both".[4]

China, the United States and Russia have already exhibited their military strength in the South China Sea and Black Sea, while these developments forced the UK to respond with a strong venture. The Integrated Review of Security, Defence, Development and Foreign Policy elucidated the UK intention to make more nuclear bombs and assert itself as a strong and indomitable state on international forums. The Prime Minister Johnson administration abruptly reversed its disarmament policies and announced a significant increase in nuclear weapons production up to no more than 260 warheads. Arms Control Association in its recent report, noted the UK intention of producing more weapons in the near future: "The UK currently has about 195 nuclear warheads, (Kingston Reif and Shannon Bugos- April 2021) of which 120 are operational, according to an estimate by researchers at the Federation of American Scientists. The UK deployed its entire nuclear arsenal aboard four Vanguard-Class Submarines, each of which is armed with Trident II D5 submarine-launched ballistic missiles. At least one submarine is always at sea on deterrence patrol. London maintains that a submarine on patrol would require several days' notice to launch a missile".[5]

The Integrated Review of Security, Defence, Development and Foreign Policy featured a change in the policy of warhead stockpile to the evolving security environment, including the developing range of technological and doctrinal threats. Wyn Rees and Azriel Bermant (Why does the UK want more nuclear weapons? – 20 May 2021) have noted some aspects of these recent developments in the UK nuclear warhead expansion to compete in the sea and land warfare. They also noted technological developments and the emergence of Russia and China as superpowers generated more challenges. China has been increasing its nuclear capabilities and hostility towards Taiwan:

"The size of the UK's deterrent has been gauged in concert with the much larger US capability. The UK and its allies have historically been concerned that the US might be reluctant to use its nuclear forces in defence of its allies and have believed it necessary to possess a 'second centre of decision-making' in which their own weapons could be used in a supreme national emergency. The British government says the decision to expand its nuclear stockpile is driven by a deterioration in the strategic landscape and technological threats. Russia has been overhauling its nuclear forces since 2007 and investing in new technologies such as underwater nuclear drones and hypersonic missiles. China has been increasing its nuclear capabilities and its current hostility towards Taiwan increases the risk of a China-US confrontation. In addition, the UK is mindful of the need to deter newly proliferating countries as well as novel threats such as cyberattacks. The UK has committed to replacing its four Trident submarines with a new generation of vessels to preserve its deterrent into the 2050s. The surprise for some is that Russian improvements in missile defences have played a key role in the UK's decision".[6]

Security concerns, technological developments, and the emergence of Russia and China as new superpowers have forced the Johnson administration to redesign nuclear strategy and increase the production of more warheads. This new policy will enable the country's army to defend its territory. Responding to emerging threats, the UK government needs to introduce security sector reforms to make law enforcement agencies competent and high-spirited. In his article, (UK Nuclear Weapons: Beyond the Numbers - 06 April 2021), Heather Williams has highlighted concerns of the Boris Johnson government that how to respond to emerging security threats and how to protect national interests abroad:

"There are indeed plenty of causes for concern both in the security environment and with regard to technological developments. In particular, advances in Russian missile defence may be concerning to countries with smaller nuclear arsenals, such as the United Kingdom. The S-500, which Russia announced will be introduced later in 2021, is expected to be capable of intercepting ballistic, cruise, and, potentially, hypersonic missiles. (To be clear, the S-500's full capabilities are unknown, and some experts have suggested that Russia's anti-access area denial capabilities are "woefully overhyped.") Other concerns include the breakdown of the Intermediate-range Nuclear Forces Treaty, and Russian advances in dual-capable shorter-range systems like the 9M729, which the United States alleged was in violation of the Intermediate-range Nuclear Forces Treaty. Many of these concerns resonate with a 2019 inquiry by the House of Lords, which concluded that nuclear risks were rising because of inter-state competition, technological developments, and nuclear doctrines and declaratory policy. These arguments, of course, will not persuade all experts, but the Integrated Review's explanation is nonetheless plausible".[7]

Its domestic political turmoil and emergence of Russia and China as superpowers forced the Biden government to manage a nuclear alliance against China. Now, as the country is struggling to regain its world superpower status, President Joe Biden is planning to support India and Australia against China. In Afghanistan and Pakistan, Taliban and the ISIS adorned their forces with sophisticated weapons and deployed suicide squads on China-Afghan and China-Pakistan borders. The Pentagon allowed its proxies such as Taliban, ISIS, Al Nusra, and Lashkar-e-Taiba to capture Afghanistan, challenge Russia, Tajikistan and India, but never tried to manage the poverty and security of the poor country. The US army has committed war crimes by establishing criminal militias to kidnap, and kill women and children, and plunder their houses. The NATO states have been collaborators and co-conspirators in this business since the 2000s. On 15 September 2021, an agreement was signed between Australia, US and UK to supply nuclear-powered submarine and underwater-drone technology to Australia.[8]

Australian and American governments deployed advanced military technology for keeping China under surveillance in South China Sea and the Indian Ocean. Mark Valensia (*Asia Times*, 07 October 2021) noted: "The alliance leader announced that their shared commitment to peace and stability in Indo-Pacific regions will help to sustain Pakistani Generals think they defeated US and NATO forces in Afghanistan, but they generated more troubles for their country by supporting terrorist Taliban, al Qaeda and the ISIS terrorist networks to kill Afghans, and destroy their country's national critical infrastructure".[9] Former CIA Station Chief in Pakistan, Robert L. Grenier, warned: "Pakistanis should watch what they wish for. "If the Afghan Taliban become leaders of a pariah state, which is likely, Pakistan will find itself tethered to them.

After abandoning Afghanistan, and shamelessly destroying Airports of the poor country, the Pentagon and Joe Biden's jihadist forces now want to return to Afghanistan for further destruction, or they may well use the country against China. The fact is, Biden has no specific strategy for Afghanistan to build the state, its economy and armed forces. The US army shamelessly killed innocent children before leaving Afghanistan and plundered natural resources to finance its war crime business. If they come back with new destructive strategies and new jihadist ideologies, this will cause more suffering and misery of the people of Afghanistan. The AUKUS agreement (Mark Valensia – *Asia Times*, 07 October 2021) "has certainly ruffled Australia's relations with South China Sea littoral countries. Some view it and the Quad as further undermining the Association of Southeast Asian Nations' "centrality" in regional security affairs. They think the agreement may even drive some Southeast Asian countries away from the US for fear of further angering China. Malaysia is concerned that the agreement could lead to more conflict and an arms race in the region".[10] The agreement cannot contain China and Russia's technological development and prevailing influence in Asia and Africa. Analyst and researcher Elie Perot (The Aukus agreement, what repercussions for the European Union? August 2021) in his article highlighted some aspects of the AUKUS agreement and suggested that this agreement was not against the interest of European Union states:

"The AUKUS agreement is not in itself fundamentally opposed to the objectives and interests of the European Union and, in particular, of France - the Member State that had been until now most strongly engaged in the Indo-Pacific in response to the Chinese challenge. Yet the announcement of the trilateral partnership between Canberra, Washington and London led to a particularly severe crisis with Paris, with France losing a major deal with Australia since 2016 for the supply of 12 conventionally powered (diesel-electric) submarines. With the telephonic exchange between Presidents Joe Biden and Emmanuel Macron on 22 September 2021, during which it was acknowledged that "the situation would have benefitted from open consultations among allies on matters of strategic interest to France and our European partners", it is possible that the worst of this diplomatic crisis is now over. The question now is whether this sequence, which at first sight was played out at the bilateral level between France and the three AUKUS states, could have wider and longer-term repercussions at the EU level. With this in mind, this paper first proposes to understand the new AUKUS agreement in its proper perspective, since above all, it signifies a reinforcement of military-industrial cooperation between Australia, the United Kingdom and the United States rather than a true diplomatic revolution concerning China".[11]

There is a perception that China will first use nuclear weapons against the United States and Britain if they attacked its military installation, but Admiral Charles A. Richard, the head of the U.S. Strategic Command, told Senate Armed Service Committee that China will not use-first its nuclear weapon for the reason that its assessment is based on very shallow information. The Chinese leadership is mature and understands the consequences of nuclear war with the United States. During the last two decades, Australia has been struggling to modernise its armed forces, retrieve modern technology and recruit more soldiers for its armed forces. Perhaps, it will come to be a historic milestone for the Indo-Pacific region and the new Cold War, now waged between Washington and Beijing…..Under AUKUS, they are planning to openly share information and technology, "bringing together sailors, scientists and industries to maintain and expand [their] edge in military capabilities and critical technologies, Gregory Kulacki noted ."[12]

The AUKUS pact, (BBC – 16 September 2021) 'which also covers AI and other technologies, is one of the countries' biggest defence partnerships in decades. China condemned the agreement. Foreign Ministry spokesman Zhao Lijian said it "seriously undermines regional peace and stability and intensifies the arms race". China's embassy in Washington accused countries of a Cold War mentality and ideological prejudice. The three countries were "severely damaging regional peace and stability, intensifying arms race, and damaging international nuclear non-proliferation efforts," Zhao told a regular press briefing. BBC noted. The AUKUS agreement that elucidates the provision of eight nuclear-powered submarines to Australia through technology transfer by Britain and the US, uses a rarely utilized loophole in the nuclear Non-Proliferation Treaty[13]

International humanitarian organizations have been struggling to intercept nuclear war since 2001, but major terrorist groups trained by the US, UK and Pakistan are now seeking nuclear weapons against their targets. Groups based in Syria and Iraq have been transporting their fighters to Afghanistan since 2020 to strengthen the military position of Daesh against Taliban. The ISIS, al Qaeda, Kashmiri and Chechen groups have already made efforts to retrieve nuclear weapons, material of dirty bombs and nuclear explosive devices from states where the security system is weak. Analyst and expert, Evan Braden Montgomery in his recent analysis (Understanding the threat of nuclear terrorism, The Centre for Strategic and Budgetary Assessments, 02 April 2010), has documented dimensions of nuclear proliferation and nuclear non-proliferation, and supply and demand:

"There are two major dimensions of the nuclear terrorist threat: the "supply" side of nuclear proliferation and the "demand" side of violent Islamist extremism. Over the past decade, longstanding concerns over proliferation have become increasingly acute in light of several worrisome developments, including the status of India and Pakistan as overt nuclear-weapon states, North Korea's two nuclear weapons tests, the international community's failure to restrain Iran's nuclear ambitions, and the fear that an Iranian nuclear weapons program could spark further proliferation throughout the Middle East...In recent years, analysts have increasingly come to view this scenario as the most plausible route for terrorists seeking nuclear weapons for two main reasons. First, large stockpiles of fissile material can be found throughout the world in the military as well as civilian facilities, some of which are inadequately monitored and protected. Second, building a crude nuclear device once a sufficient amount of this material has been obtained, although not an easy task, is certainly within the realm of possibility. Here, the principal challenge for terrorists would involve the trade-off between the quantity of fissile material required for a weapon and the type of weapon that could be built".[14]

States and international bodies have tried to stop the smuggling of nuclear and biological material, but in some states, radicalized elements within armed forces are making things second-rate. The main objective of all states is to reduce the risk of nuclear theft and terrorism to the lowest possible level. As discussed earlier, a professional approach to the security of nuclear sites requires achieving effective and lasting security for all nuclear weapons and weapons-usable nuclear materials. As we experienced in Belgium, where terrorists strived to retrieve nuclear weapons by force while the incident of Fukushima in Japan, where a dirty bomb attack forced major evacuation. Matthew Bunn Martin B. Malin Nickolas Roth William H. Tobey (Project on Managing the Atom Preventing Nuclear Terrorism Continuous Improvement or Dangerous Decline? Belfer Centre for Science and International Affairs Harvard Kennedy School-2016) in their detailed research paper have raised questions of nuclear material security:

"Indeed, in the low-security scenario, there would be a very real possibility that by 2030, a nuclear sabotage causing a "security Fukushima"; a dirty bomb attack forcing the evacuation of many blocks of a major city; or even the incineration of the heart of a major city in a terrorist nuclear blast would already have occurred. The dangers of the low-security scenario are real and affect every country—though some (Particularly the United States) are clearly more likely to be targeted than others. The countries of the world must continue to work together to stay off the low-security path and move toward the high-security one. Despite significant progress over the past two decades, some nuclear weapons materials remain dangerously vulnerable to theft—and incidents such as an IS operative's intensive monitoring of a senior official of a Belgian facility with significant stocks of HEU highlight the continuing threat.........In November 2015, Belgian police discovered that some IS operatives involved in the Paris attacks had taken hours of surveillance video at the home of a senior official of SKN-CEN, a Belgian nuclear research centre with a substantial amount of HEU on-site. Investigators have not managed to confirm what the terrorists were seeking to accomplish through this monitoring. One possibility—and it is only a possibility—is that they envisioned kidnapping the official or his family in an effort to force him to help them gain access to the nuclear facility and its materials. This focused, extended monitoring of a nuclear official at a sensitive site is the most worrying indicator of IS nuclear intent to date".[15]

Stories of nuclear smuggling in major Indian newspapers caused consternation when police arrested seven smugglers and recovered 6 kgs of Uranium from them following raids at different parts of India. Police said the accused-suspected of being part of a national gang involved in the illegal uranium trade. Indian authorities arrested individuals on charges of illicit trading in uranium. The incidents raised concerns about what appears to be a growing nuclear security risk in the region. On 07 May 2021, Dawn reported a statement of the Indian anti-terrorism squad that the confiscated material was worth around $2.9 million. "We had received information that one person identified as Jigar Pandya was going to illegally sell pieces of uranium substance, a trap was laid and he was arrested," the Maharashtra police said. "Investigation into the case revealed that another person identified as Abu Tahir gave him these pieces of uranium." It is the second time in India that such a highly radioactive substance has been seized by police in recent years. In 2016, police seized almost 9 kg of depleted uranium in the Thane area of Maharashtra. Dawn newspaper reported.[16]

In 2021, adventures of uranium smuggling in India reported in newspapers and electronic media prompted consternation and fear that terrorist organizations may use it in their bomb-making process, or may possibly further smuggle to African and Central Asian terrorist groups. Indian police seized uranium in different quantity from different provinces of the country. Pakistan's Foreign Office called for a thorough investigation into such incidents. Considering the nature of these reports, the international community remained silent. An EU spokesman when questioned about the possible proliferation activities said that the bloc "is aware of the information and understands that the Indian authorities are investigating". Dawn reported.[17]

The future of illicit trade of nuclear materials in South Asia by non-state actors and terrorists may further jeopardise security of the region. Problem of this trade appears to be growing worse as technologies proliferate. With the global spread of technologies and rapid illegal sale of uranium and plutonium, traffickers could find it easier to expand their dangerous trade. If the tension between India and China escalated, the possibility of nuclear war cannot be dismissed because China continues to demonstrate aggressively. India has developed more than 140 nuclear weapons, while China has developed all but 290 nuclear bombs and 320 warheads. Nuclear head-to-head and ruckus between Russia, China, US, India and Pakistan has jeopardized stability and prosperity of South Asia, where India has been contesting Chinese military power, and Pakistan encounters India. Misinterpretation of each other's motives has also caused misunderstandings. They threatened each other with nuclear bombs and then assessed its consequences and fatalities.[18]

The international community has been facing difficulties in dealing with the threat of a dirty bomb, Improvised Nuclear Device and smuggling of nuclear technology since years, but after the Paris, Pakistan, Brussels and Pulwama attacks, experts and military commanders realized need for a joint fight against the evolved threat of nuclear terrorism. Security experts within the Council of Europe said that terrorists assessing the impact of coronavirus, would now recognize the fact that they could use biological weapons to inflict a major blow on Western countries. According to these experts, the virus has exposed vulnerability of modern societies.[19] After the Chinese army attacked Indian army soldiers in a hand to hand fight that left 20 Indian soldiers dead, Prime Minister Modi warned that the sacrifice made by the soldiers would not go in vain. Minister of External Affairs S.Jaishankar spoke to his Chinese counterpart Wang Yi. Former Congress president Rahul Gandhi, meanwhile, said the country needed more clarity on what was happening. India and Pakistan also developed advanced missile technology and tested short and long-range nuclear and non-nuclear missiles.[20] Research Affiliate at the Strategic Vision Institute (SVI), a Non-Partisan Think-Tank based out of Islamabad, Pakistan, Sher Bano (16 June 2020) has reviewed rapid modernization of India and Pakistan, and noted their frustration and fear of each other military build-up:

"The rapid modernization of strategic weapons in South Asia has become the cause of increasing rivalry between India and Pakistan. With India's quest to achieve a nuclear triad that includes the development of submarine launched ballistic missile, land based ballistic missiles and fighter bomber aircrafts; it aspires to attain the global power status. India in order to strengthen its nuclear force is rigorously working on building a strong naval force and is also developing short range ballistic missiles that are nuclear in nature. India is also expanding its capabilities in outer space by developing its fleet of satellites and is building anti-satellite missiles that can be used for both military and civilian purposes. This shift in India's nuclear posture along with strategic modernization will pose a huge threat to Pakistan's nuclear threshold and will increase the risk of nuclear escalation in South Asia. On January 8, top Government officials of India said "The BMD program has been completed". Under this program India has developed home-grown ballistic missile defence (BMD). DRDO and IAF are now looking for the government's approval in order to activate and install the system. But according to the sources the complete installation of the system will still take three to four years".[21]

The United States has been interfering in Taiwan since the 1980s, where modern military technology is being sold on cheap prices. In the 1980s, China agreed on a one country-two system proposal in order for Taiwan to gradually become part of China, but things shaped differently with increasing interference of Western nations. In 2000, with the establishment of a new government in Taiwan, China felt danger when Taiwanese President supported the movement for an independent state. In 2004 and 2008, relations between Taiwan and China deteriorated. In 2016, President Tsai Ing-wen was elected. She leads the Democratic Progressive Party (DPP), which leans towards eventual official independence from China. After Donald Trump won the 2016 US election, Ms Tsai spoke to him on the phone. China, however, struggled to bring the strategically and symbolically important island back under its control, but failed to convince Taiwan's leadership that the country will not interfere in its internal affairs.

Conversely, the United States provided military and financial support to Taiwan to increase military influence in the Indo-Pacific region. On 24 October 2021, the Independent newspaper reported: "The U.S. Defence Department's recent report to Congress noted that in 2000, it assessed China's armed forces to be "a sizable but mostly archaic military" but that today it is a rival, having already surpassed the American military in some areas including shipbuilding to the point where it now has the world's largest navy".[22]

As relations between India and China deteriorated after the Chinese interference in the Ladakh region, Indian leadership became more close to the United States to get sophisticated military technology, but the US leadership never realized the importance of its allies. Notwithstanding the US negligence, India entered an economic and technological agreement with Taiwanese government. Analyst and expert, Arjun Gargeyas has documented in his article (Why India, Taiwan should strengthen ties: Taipei and New Delhi could collaborate in several areas, including the semiconductor supply chain, *Asia Times*, 19 October 2021) relationship of India with Taiwan, and also noted Taiwan's relations with South-East Asian nations: "It was reported in October 2021 that Indian and Taiwanese officials met to discuss a possible collaboration on building a semiconductor manufacturing facility in India. An investment of US$7.5 billion was reportedly offered by Taiwan in exchange for liberal trade tariffs on semiconductor manufacturing materials to build a state-of-the-art fabrication facility in India. With the Quadrilateral Security Dialogue focusing on securing the semiconductor supply chain, Taiwan's expertise in that domain could serve as a base for developing a robust technological partnership with India".[23]

Musa Khan Jalalzai

November 2021, London

13

Chapter 1

New Cold War, Military Showdown between China and the United States in Taiwan and the South China Sea

Over the past 20 years, China has emerged as a world technological superpower to dethrone the United States as a global power. Since 2018, US policymakers adopted an anti-China policy by imposing different types of restrictions and sanctions to handle its economic rise. Research scholar and expert, Akriti Vasudeva (US–China Strategic Competition and Washington's Conception of Quad Plus. The Journal of Indo-Pacific Affairs, Vol.3 No.5 special issue, 2020) views the Trump administration policy towards China as adversarial: "The Trump administration's policy toward China can be described as adversarial, with the 2018 National Defence Strategy naming Beijing as a "strategic competitor" that aims to achieve "Indo-Pacific regional hegemony in the near-term and displacement of the United States to achieve global pre-eminence in the future."[1] China has asserted a number of islands in the South China Sea region, where the PLA established naval bases, and modern surveillance system to oversee activities of the United States. President Trump ran after the Chinese President-thinking that his friendly strategy could domesticate China's economic challenge. When failed to intercept China's technological development, he declared trade war against China. To challenge China's military power in the South China Sea, the Pentagon established five military bases in the Philippines (Antonio Bautista Air Base, Basa Air Base, Fort Magsaysay, Lumbia Air Base, and Mactan-Benito Ebuen Air Base).

Military confrontations between China and Taiwan were exacerbated after the President of Taiwan, Tsai Ing, authenticated the presence of US forces in her country on 28 October 2021. The US supported Taiwan with arms sales to protect the country from Chinese aggression-deployed forces in Taiwan to fight the country in the South China Sea more firmly. Her revelations sparked criticism against the Pentagon deployment in Chinese media, which indicated that the US army crossed the bottom line. "Our support for defence relationship with Taiwan remains aligned against the current threat posed by the People's Republic of China," US defence spokesman John Supple explained his country's position. On 26 May 2021, BBC noted in its commentary strained relationship between Taiwan and China: "Throughout 2018, China stepped up pressure on international companies, forcing them to list Taiwan as a part of China on their websites and threatening to block them for doing business in China if they failed to comply."[2]

However, on 01 October, 2021, on China's national day, the PLA military planes flew over the Southern parts of Taiwan, which enraged the country's entire population that this demonstration of China was a clear violation of international law. Experts and analysts, Carla Freeman and Andrew Scobell (What's next for US-China Relations amid Rising Tensions over Taiwan: Chinese provocation in Taiwan Strait prompts U.S. and Chinese officials to discuss fraught state of bilateral affairs. October 9, 2021) have documented continuity of US support to Taiwan: "Washington has offered more muscular support for Taipei on a number of fronts in recent years. The Trump administration integrated the island into its Indo-Pacific strategy, expanded arms sales to Taiwan and took other steps that expanded official contacts between Washington and Taipei. The Biden administration has affirmed its own commitment to Taiwan, making clear that it not only supports strengthening Taiwan's defence capabilities but would like to see Taiwan play a larger international role".[3]

In his election campaign, President Biden had told Americans that his country would lead the world again, but the world has changed, and two more superpowers emerged. Moreover, US public opinion toward China was trending down and there were vocal critics of various stipes in Congress. All of this suggests that the United States is no more a great superpower to decide the future of Asia. In March 2021, the Chinese government began to launch a global campaign to repair its damaged image, rewrite the narrative of the crisis, and position itself as an emerging leader in the international community. Analyst and expert Robert R. Bianchi (China-US rivalries after the Afghan war-August 24, 2021) in his paper noted some aspects of US-China rivalries after the US withdrawal from Afghanistan:

"The outline of the script for confrontation is already taking shape before our eyes. American strategists claim that letting go of albatrosses in Afghanistan and the Middle East gives them greater freedom to block China's assertiveness in more critical regions, particularly in South Asia and the newly-dubbed Indo-Pacific. Winding down yesterday's wars against jihadists will pave the way for redeployment to future conflicts where even greater resources need to be concentrated with the aid of democracies in India, Australia, and Japan. At the same time, however, Chinese commentators insist that America's credibility is so shattered that no U.S.-led coalition can appeal to Asian neighbours who value their independence and freedom of manoeuvre. In this view, the string of broken promises in Iraq, Syria, and Afghanistan will make even the Taiwanese lose faith in Washington's staying power. Under different circumstances, the path ahead for Afghanistan and its neighbours would seem straightforward. The country abounds in untapped resources, both natural and human, that can fuel post-war recovery while spurring development in surrounding regions and far beyond. Its vast and varied mineral wealth is a prize for any multinational mining company and a potential lifeline for battered supply chains struggling to support factories and construction sites on every continent. Along with Pakistan, Afghanistan lies at the intersection of at least two planned energy corridors that can carry oil and natural gas from Iran to China in one direction and from Turkmenistan to India in another. Transit fees from these routes alone could transform Afghanistan's economy and society within a single generation. On top of this, there is a future role for Afghanistan as a land bridge linking the commerce of the Indian Ocean with Central Asia and, from there, to growing transcontinental railroads and highways reaching all the way to the Atlantic and Pacific coasts".[4]

The rise of China and humiliation of the United States on the international stage has generated potential challenges to the US interests in Asia, Middle East and Africa. Internal political turmoil, politicization of state institutions, and divided communities have smudged its image, while China is leading the world in cutting-edge technologies. During the past two decades, innovation of modern technologies has changed the world. The world is now at the crossroads of power competition. Chinese assertiveness in the South China Sea might prompt regional rivalries with littoral states. Analyst and expert M Matheswaran (US-China Strategic Competition in the Asia-Pacific. M Matheswaran, 04 August 2021) noted causes of concerns of the Biden administration that his government was worried about the disintegration of power and influence, which is indicated by the passing of the recent bill–Strategic Competition Act of 2021:

> "The US initiated the trade war against China in 2017, citing a massive trade imbalance and accusation of opaque procedures, technology theft, IP violations, and lack of fair access to China's market. However,

the underlying driver for this clash is the race for global technological supremacy as China leapfrogged into cutting-edge technologies like AI and 5G. Although China is the world's largest exporter of high-tech products, at US $733.4 billion in 2020, it is critically dependent on imports for most materials and components, including semiconductor chips mainly from the US and the West. China's share of global semiconductor demand is 35 percent. Its share of the world's integrated device manufacturers, capable of designing, manufacturing, and selling integrated circuit products, is less than 1 percent. As a result, when the US initiates technology and export control measures in the name of national security, it causes serious disruptions for Chinese companies like ZTE and Huawei. The 'Made in China 2025' (MIC 2025) policy, a 10-year plan initiated in 2015, focused on creating self-sufficiency and technological innovation capacity in robotics, AI, and energy-efficient cars. This policy expands on the earlier SEI (Strategic Engineering Industries) policy, prioritizing seven critical high-tech industries. MIC 2025 calls for utilizing indigenous patents against imports and has aimed to increase production of domestically designed components to 40 percent by 2020 and 70 percent by 2025. The 'MIC 2025 industrial upgrade strategy,' with exclusive support to domestic industries, is seen as a serious threat to the US and Western competitiveness in high-tech sectors. To counter American-led trade and technology sanctions".[5]

A Chinese hypersonic missile test demonstrated that China can deliver nuclear weapons from space. The US President lost his political and military vision, and is now looking for a competent foreign policy to meet challenges of China and Russia's growing influence in Asia and Africa. The Trump and Obama administrations kept their allies in the dark by invading Iraq and Afghanistan on the pretext of so-called war on terrorism and weapons of mass destruction. After 20 years of killing, kidnapping and torturing Iraqis and Afghans, the US and its allies tired of their dirty business. The Biden administration supplicated Congress back, now controlled by invisible stakeholders, which never allowed his government to manage the looming crisis. Analyst and expert, Daniel Williams in his article (Bumbling Biden heads to Rome and Glasgow: US president badly needs a foreign policy win but without clear support for his domestic agenda his international credibility is fading -29 October 2021), highlighted compulsions and desire of the Biden government. He also noted danger of domestic turmoil of his administration to manage political confrontation, Chinese technological war and Russia's exacerbating influence in Europe, and Asia·

"His chief National Security Advisor Jake Sullivan also suggested that foreign leaders are eyeing Biden's domestic abilities. "They'll say, 'Is President Biden on track to deliver on what he said he's going to deliver?' Sullivan conjectured. "Our allies are making their judgment," Heather Conley, director of the Europe, Russia and Eurasia program at the Centre for Strategic and International Studies in Washington, told Politico online. "Can the president deliver? They're not sure. They see the domestic agenda— very difficult—and they see the sporadic, uncoordinated processes that affect their security, and they're not sure." So far, no good. His own party continued to wrangle over social programs that were excised from the original social spending package, which had been whittled down from $3.5 trillion. Biden got on a plane and left for Rome without a vote. He may not get one until next week—if at all".[6]

Hands of the President have tied and is unable to control rising rebellion in Congress against his crumbling government. He wants to return to Afghanistan by different means and strategies-settling military confrontation between Taliban and Daesh to constitute a strong army consisted of all terrorist groups for fight against China and Russia in the near future. Expert Richard Jawad Hedarian (28 October 2021) also noted his old wine in a new bottle technique: "Taiwan Straits have become openly apparent as tensions have risen in the maritime regions. A US-China conflict over either would inevitably redound on peripheral Southeast Asian states. So far, the Biden administration has simply continued its predecessor's regional strategy, which relies heavily on necessary but ultimately insufficient Freedom of Navigation Operations (FONOPs) to check China's maritime ambitions."[7] Lecturer of international policy at Stanford University and a former Christian Science Monitor foreign correspondent, Daniel Sneider (Biden's China trade policy is old wine in an old bottle: Administration's promised 'new approach' to China trade relations leaves in place Trump's ineffective and short-sighted policies-28 October 2021) noted his government's failure to work with allies: "The absence of a global, or even a regional, trade strategy based on working with allies and partners was particularly disturbing to some observers. In the policy speech, there was only a brief mention of working with European allies in the US-EE Trade and Technology Council to combat "non-market practices," but no mention at all of working with Japan, South Korea and others on technology security and supply chain management issues. The emphasis instead was on building domestic industrial competitiveness and defending industries such as steel and solar panels from foreign competitors".[8]

The army, Navy, politicized intelligence infrastructure, and a divided government of democrats have been unable to meet growing national security threats. His government has also failed to tackle modernization of nonstrategic nuclear weapons, hybrid warfare, cyber-attacks, and other subversive activities of extremist and terrorist organizations based in the country. Russia and China have become superpowers by their innovations of modern military technology, building competent armies and tactical nuclear weapons. Strategic Studies Quarterly (An Air Force–Sponsored Strategic Forum on National and International Security-fall 2021, Vol.15, No.3) in its foreword analysis noted concerns of US allies about the emerging US national security threats: "The US and allied states are increasingly concerned about these emerging threats and the challenges they pose to US and international security. These apprehensions have reignited debates about the role of nuclear weapons in the US and NATO deterrent strategies. Many in the US have proposed modernizing the US nuclear triad, extending its life service, and modernizing nuclear-capable aircraft. Ground-Based Strategic Deterrent (GBSD) missiles are under development to replace Minuteman III missiles. Still, whether these efforts will address and deter today's threats remains to be seen".[9]

The danger of war between US, NATO and Russia still exists as Russian officials in October 2021, held an urgent meeting with the German Embassy's military attaché in Moscow, expressing concern at a series of comments by the country's Defence Minister. On 25 October, 2021, RT reported a statement of the German Defence Minister articulated on radio Deutschlandfunk that nuclear weapons could be deployed over the Baltic nations that border Russia. According to her statement, "we must make it very clear to Russia that we are ready to use such measures as well, so that it would have an early deterrent effect." This, she said, "is in response to the current behaviour of Russia."[10] However, Moscow regretted and said: "such statements provoke increased tension in Europe and are not conducive to the normalization of the situation." Responding to the claims, Kramp-Karrenbauer's Russian counterpart, Sergey Shoigu, said that "security in Europe can only be collective, without infringement on Russia's interest." However, he went on, "currently NATO is the party that's not ready for equal dialogue on this issue. Amid calls to deter Russia militarily, NATO is consistently building up its forces near our borders. The German foreign minister must know quite well how such actions have ended for Germany and Europe previously," Shoigu added, in a remark widely interpreted as a reference to WWII. RT reported.[11]

Moreover, on 24 October, 2021, RT reported NATO's new secret plan for nuclear war and space battles with Russia. Expert of Russian affairs and Professor at the University of Ottawa, Canada, Paul Robinson urged in his article: "Tensions between Russia and NATO are at an all-time high. But instead of seeking a way off the ladder of escalation, the US-led bloc's new plan for hybrid war risks accelerating an already dangerous lethal arms race with Moscow. There's a concept in international relations, almost one of the first that students learn, called the 'security dilemma'. It's hardly rocket science, but it's something governments and armed forces planners seem to consistently forget when it comes to making policy. The dilemma is that if you do nothing to strengthen your defences, you'll be insecure, but if you do something you'll end up worse off because of the counter-measures the other side will take. What do you do?"[12]

Nuclear security experts have warned that Nuclear Weapons Free Zone arrangements were urgent as nuclear proliferation regime becoming strong. In the North East Asian region, some states such as North Korea have been testing nuclear weapons and nuclear missiles since the 2000s. The United States and China are part of the game as they have also deployed nuclear forces in the region, and threaten each other with using nuclear weapons.[13] The United States total warheads are currently 3,800 of which 1,750 have been deployed-including air-launched Cruise Missiles and gravity bombs at US bomber bases.[14] "China, against whom the US nuclear encirclement is primarily oriented, has steadily increased its nuclear weapon stockpile in yesteryears. China has deployed 240 nuclear warheads for delivery in sea and land based ballistic missiles, and 90 ICBMs in both land silos and on road-based launchers, with ranges of up to 12,000 km".[15] However, China's threat to Taiwan have impacted security of regional states. They are now seeking Washington's protection. Expert and analyst Bertil Lintner in his recent analysis (US encircling China on multiple new Cold War fronts: US-Australia nuclear submarine deal is part of a wider alliance-based strategy to counter and contain China's rise and ambitions, Asia Times, 20 September, 2021) highlighted some aspects of Indo-Pacific cold war, which has been heating up since 2000:

"The Indo-Pacific's Cold War is heating up as the region splits ever more decisively into opposed camps with a loose alliance of US-led democratic powers on one side and authoritarian China and its aligned satellites on the other. And the first economic salvos of the contest launched by Donald Trump's trade war are becoming more militarily provocative under Joe Biden. The escalating contest took a game-changing turn last week when the

US and Britain announced they will provide Australia with the technology and capability to develop and deploy nuclear-powered submarines in a new trilateral security arrangement that will put more pressure on China's contested claims in the South China Sea and other maritime theatres. The nuclear submarines will tilt the region's strategic balance and potentially cause China to concentrate more of its security energies closer to home and less so on far-flung theatres. From that perspective, the submarine deal is part of a coordinated encirclement strategy that Beijing will certainly view as a threat to its plans to increase and strengthen its presence in the Indian Ocean region. Meanwhile, the US and India signed a new agreement on July 30 to jointly develop Air-Launched Unmanned Aerial Vehicles (ALUAV). The deal is the latest under the Research, Development, Testing and Evaluation Memorandum Agreement between India's Ministry of Defense and the US Defense Department first signed in 2006 and renewed in 2015".[16]

Historian at Koç University in Istanbul, working on Russia, Ukraine, and Eastern Europe, Tarik Cyril Amar has highlighted (NATO's bullish new plan to fight Russia on the seas, the skies and in space could backfire, igniting a catastrophic nuclear conflict, RT, 25 October 2021) NATO's new strategy to fight Russia across the width of Europe–from Baltic to Black Sea: "As you would expect, NATO insists that this cross-continental strategy will serve only defensive purposes and the US-led group has also emphasized that it does not believe that Russian attacks are imminent. In other words, NATO presents this initiative as an act of due diligence: preparing for the worst imaginable scenario, while helping to avoid it ever becoming a reality by deterrence, as German Minister of Defence Annegret Kramp-Karrenbauer has duly underlined. When it comes to why the measures are necessary, NATO, of course, blames Russia. Specifically, it claims Moscow has a recent record of militarily challenging the status quo in Georgia and Ukraine and probing the bloc's capabilities in the Baltic and Black Sea areas. Moreover, this story goes, Russia has generally beefed up its military capabilities and the entire continent should apparently be worried. Moscow, of course, sees things differently. In the Kremlin's view, it is NATO that is encroaching on its security in its immediate neighbourhood, especially by expanding its activities in Ukraine and offering the latter full membership, in principle if not – yet – in reality. Russian Deputy Foreign Minister Alexander Grushko has warned that what he describes as NATO turning "the Black Sea into an arena of military confrontation" is "an extremely dangerous path fraught with the risk of military incidents and escalation."[17]

In view of deteriorating relationship with Russia, the US Army and Navy successfully tested three hypersonic weapons in October 2021. But testing cruise or hypersonic weapons cannot be viewed as an alarm that Russia and China must prepare themselves for a nuclear war. In October 2021, China had also tested hypersonic missiles to exhibit the military power of communist regime. Both the US navy and army expected to conduct a flight test of the completed weapon at some point in future. RT news reported Chinese denial of US accusations that it had conducted a test of nuclear-capable hypersonic missiles in August 2021. Russia tested its own Tsirkon hypersonic missile, successfully firing the high-tech projectile from a nuclear submarine. Moscow also confirmed another successful test of a missile capable of carrying hypersonic warheads. RT reported. On 25 October 2021, RT reported Ukrainian President Zelensky's warning to Russia. Expert Jonny Tickle in his column (Missiles 'aimed at Moscow': Adviser to Ukraine's Zelensky warns Kremlin that war with Kiev would spell 'end of Russia' & its army-25 Oct 2021) noted Kiev's long-range missiles programme:

"Speaking to the Dom TV network, Alexey Arestovich warned the Kremlin that his country would soon have the ability to hit the Russian capital with its missiles. Arestovich serves as an adviser to the office of Ukraine's leader Volodymyr Zelensky. "Putin will get to the point, in the foreseeable future, where Ukrainian missiles will be aimed at Moscow, and for one simple reason: we are working on a missile program," he explained. "And our operational-tactical missiles will be able to reach Moscow." In Arestovich's opinion, the Russian Army is already aware of Ukraine's military capabilities, and the heads of the armed forces are telling the Kremlin that an attack on Ukraine "would be the end of the Russian army and the end of the Russian Federation". "This is an absolutely losing option. They cannot fail to understand that," he added. "And when they scare us with an invasion, an expansion, a hint of threats – it's a bluff." In recent times, the Ukrainian leadership has brought up possible war with Russia on numerous occasions, despite Moscow's insistence that it has no desire for any conflict. Commander of Ukraine's Special Operations Forces Grigory Galagan called for "all regions" of the country to have their defences bolstered, claiming that there is "no guarantee Russia won't invade and subsequently escalate."[18]

After the US and NATO withdrawal from Afghanistan in August 2021, relations between US and EU remained exhausted. The United States demanded more financial and military contribution in the NATO alliance, but the EU is reluctant to further the US hegemonic agenda with its own resources across the globe. The EU has also exhibited reservations on nuclear submarine agreement signed by the US, UK and Australia, and its trade relations with China. Moreover, the EU also wants an equal share in the distribution of plundered resources from Afghanistan. Because the EU was a collaborator and co-conspirator with the US and UK in war crimes in Iraq, Syria and Afghanistan. Professor at the University of South-Eastern Norway and an editor at the Russia in Global Affairs journal, Glenn Diesen in his analysis (Beset by flagging economies, rising debt & defeat in Afghanistan, US-led West is lashing out at Russia and China in desperation-RT New, 25 October 2021) noted the US deteriorating economic situation, rising debt and defeat in Afghanistan:

"Western unity is fragmenting as the EU stumbles from crisis to crisis, NATO is struggling to recover from its rout in Afghanistan, and US President Joe Biden has apparently turned his back on America's endless foreign adventures. That was the backdrop to this year's annual Valdai Discussion Club conference, held in Russia's southern city of Sochi and attended by President Vladimir Putin and other top dignitaries. The theme, fittingly, was 'Global Shake-Up in the 21st Century: The Individual, Values and the State', and the question attendees were grappling with was how Russia should respond to the rapid transformation of the world. The modern capitalist system, as Putin put it, "has run out of steam" – it is under immense pressure because Western states are overburdened by debt, the stock market has decoupled from the real economy, and the concentration of wealth is intensifying and destabilizing society. As a result, inflation is likely to soon ravage the world economy. Among other manifestations of 'woke' ideology, the West is also seemingly in the midst of a cultural revolution in terms of liberating itself from its own past by purging its own history, culture, values, and biological reality. Moreover, the historic principle of free speech to ensure an open society is being replaced with unprecedented censorship in the US and elsewhere. Meanwhile, power continues to shift to the East, and the West does not know how to respond to falling behind. Its mentality has been shaped by 500 years of supremacy, meaning its armoury is stocked with counter-productive actions such as sanctions, a reluctance to abide by international agreements, provocative military posturing, and the demonization of adversaries".[19]

In dealing with Russia and its military and technological capabilities, the US policy comes to nothing. President Joe Biden want to do everything of his choice immediately, but he needs to concentrate at his country social and political divisions, restore the US trust in Europe and the Muslim World. It must be crystal clear that the United States is no longer a superpower. It is only an American power. President Biden needs to adopt a friendly policy towards Russia and China to make the US economy and the army competent, but his intransigence has generated troubles. Analysts and experts, Eugene Rumer, and Richard Sokolsky, (Grand Illusions:"The Impact of Misperceptions about Russia on U.S. Policy. The Carnegie Endowment, 30 June 2021) have noted the reason behind the degeneration of relationship between NATO and Russia:

"Although Russia's resentment of and opposition to NATO expansion had been known from the earliest days of the discussions about admitting new members, the perception that it was unable to stop this became so entrenched that Russian actions to do so came as a shock to Western diplomats and policymakers. The pivotal point was Putin's speech at the Munich Security Conference in 2007, in which he warned the United States against pursuing its policy of expanding NATO, which he claimed would destabilize Europe and threaten Russian security. The sequence of events that followed Putin's Munich speech is well known. The allies largely dismissed his blunt warning as retrograde rhetoric that belonged in the past. At the 2008 Bucharest summit they made a vaguely worded pledge to Georgia and Ukraine to admit them to the alliance at some point in the future; the announcement was a compromise that resulted from a last minute lobbying campaign by an outgoing U.S. president George W. Bush, and strong pushback by Germany and other NATO members".[20]

On 04 October 2021, the National Interest Magazine published an article of analyst and expert David T. Pyne, in which he has documented the strength of Russia's army and danger posed by US national security. In his recent article, he noted that when Russia amassed more than 100,000 troops along the Ukraine borders, President Joe Biden immediately invited President Putin in Geneva for a meeting to discuss future relationship and cooperation in different fields. In fact, President Joe Biden deceived President Putin by false commitments of cooperation and, hinted at continuing anti-Russia policy.[21] Analyst and expert, David T. Pyne also noted authentication of the commander of U.S. Strategic Command, Admiral Charles Richard, to the Congress in April 2021 that the United States can face Russia and China on three fronts:

"In March-April 2021, Russia reportedly massed 100,000-150,000 troops along Ukraine's northern and eastern borders poised for a possible invasion. In response, the United States raised its alert status to Defence Condition

(DEFCON) Three for the first time since September 11, 2001. Moreover, the U.S. European Command raised its watch level to "potential imminent crisis" in fear that a Russian invasion of Ukraine might be followed by a Russian attempt to overrun frontline NATO states including the former Soviet republics of Estonia, Latvia, and Lithuania. It was this crisis that caused President Joe Biden to propose the June 2021 Geneva summit with Russian president Vladimir Putin to reduce tensions and improve U.S.-Russian relations, which were then at their worst since the end of the Cold War. More disturbingly, Russia's achievement of nuclear supremacy over the United States could potentially enable it to coerce or blackmail U.S. leaders to do its bidding and unilaterally disarm or, far worse, launch a catastrophic attack on the U.S. homeland with a comparatively low risk of effective U.S. military retaliation. Such an attack would essentially have the effect of erasing the United States from the geopolitical map much as the Allies did to Germany at the end of World War II. The commander of U.S. Strategic Command, Admiral Charles Richard, testified to Congress in April 2021 that the United States might well face a two-front or even a three-front war if Russia were to invade Ukraine and/or other Eastern Europe nations, China were to attack Taiwan, and North Korea were to attack South Korea simultaneously and in coordination. Adm. Richard testified that the United States currently has no contingency plans for how to confront two allied nuclear superpowers in a future war. Thus, the ability of the United States and its allies to survive, let alone win, a war fought with such powerful, unconventional weapons against our enemies remains very much in doubt".[22]

President Biden grilled the Trump administration for his controversial nuclear policies and warned that "the sole purpose of the U.S. nuclear arsenal should be deterring—and, if necessary, retaliating against—a nuclear attack". In March 2021, White House released national security guidance, which stated that US administration would seek to re-establish its credibility as a leader in arms control. In yesteryears, Russian President Putin was forced by the US offensive policies to expand his country's nuclear weapons deployment.[23] He has been proclaiming new systems that have been unique, like the nuclear weapon delivery system known as the Burevestnik nuclear-propelled cruise missile. According to the State Department calculation and Arms Control assessment (26 October 2021), "Russia declared 1458 deployed warheads, 527 deployed launchers, and 742 total launchers. In March 2021 the numbers were 1456, 517, and 767, respectively. The U.S. numbers in September 2021 were 1389 warheads, 665 deployed and 800 total launchers".[24] Navy of the Russian Federation continues to develop and deploy strategic weapon–a bus-sized torpedo tipped with a nuclear warhead. Russian nuclear arsenal have been estimated as 6,375 warheads, of which 4,315 are operational. Experts and analysts, Hans M. Kristensen and Matt Korda in their research paper on Russian nuclear weapons (Bulletin of the Atomic Scientists, 2021, vol. 77, no. 2, 90–10818 March, 2021: Russian nuclear weapons, 2021) have highlighted deployment of nuclear weapons by Russian Federation across the country:

"As of early 2021, we estimate that Russia has a stockpile of nearly 4,500 nuclear warheads assigned for use by long-range strategic launchers and shorter-range tactical nuclear forces. This number is a little higher than last year due to the addition of the fourth Borei-class nuclear-powered ballistic-missile submarine (SSBN) and an increase in non-strategic warheads. At the same time, we have lowered the estimate for strategic bomber weapons to better match the number of operational bombers. Of the stockpiled warheads, approximately 1,600 strategic warheads are deployed: just over 800 on land-based ballistic missiles, about 624 on submarine-launched ballistic missiles, and 200 at heavy bomber bases. Another 985 strategic warheads are in storage, along with about 1,912 nonstrategic warheads. In addition to the military stockpile for operational forces, a large number – approximately 1,760 – of retired but still largely intact warheads await dismantlement, for a total inventory of approximately 6,257 warheads. Russia has significantly reduced the number of warheads deployed on its ballistic missiles to meet the New START limit of no more than 1,550 deployed strategic warheads. Russia achieved the required reduction by the February 5, 2018 deadline, when it declared 1,444 strategic warheads attributed to 527 launchers (Russian Federation Foreign Affairs Ministry 2018). The most recent data, declared on September 1, 2020, listed Russia with 1,447 deployed warheads attributed to 510 strategic launchers (US State Department, Bureau of Arms Control, Verification and Compliance 2020a)".[25]

Nuclear and missile technology are playing crucial role in modern conflict. The Afghan war authenticated the US use of nuclear and biological weapons against civilian population. The former Soviet Union used biological weapons against Afghanistan as well. In future, experts have made predictions about the use of nuclear weapons if NATO, or the United States attacked Russia. President Joe Biden's resentment towards Russia, and his new jihadist strategy indicated that Pentagon's intentions were dangerous. Relations between Washington and Moscow are defined by a strategic balance characterized by a high degree of mutual vulnerability.

Russia captured Crimea but didn't use nuclear weapons, controlled Eastern Ukraine, but never deployed nuclear forces, or missiles.

Conversely, the United States is talking about nuclear weapons use, modernizing its nuclear infrastructure and deploying nuclear missiles in sea and land. Who can de-escalate the ongoing standoff with Moscow and who will mediate to prevent a longer-term hardening of animosity? This question needs answer from EU and the Muslim world. In the case of war against Russia, Moscow has no option but to use nuclear weapons against intruders. President Joe Biden's jihadist agenda faces grim criticism from global community. In October 2021, Russia and China simultaneously tested nuclear missiles that threatened Taiwan and South China Sea. The possibility of escalation to nuclear use will cast a shadow over any military confrontation between Russia and NATO. Experts and analysts, Clint Reach, Edward Geist, Abby Doll, and Joe Cheravitch in their joint research paper (Competing with Russia Militarily Implications of Conventional and Nuclear Conflicts, RAND Corporation, June 2021) have explained prospect of nuclear war between the NATO and Russia:

"Western discussions of possible Russian limited nuclear use tend to assume that it will follow Schelling's logic that the purpose of limited nuclear use is to convince the enemy "that the risk of general war is great enough to outweigh their original tactical objectives, but not so great as to make it prudent to initiate it pre-emptively." But it is not obvious from Russian doctrine or public statements that policymakers conceptualize limited nuclear use as what Schelling dubbed a "competition in risk-taking." Instead, they might regard their NSNW as a usable military instrument that can be used to attain military objectives. This would be in keeping with what is known about Soviet-era planning for NSNW employment. Moreover, achieving military objectives and coercive bargaining can complement each other. The case can also be made that the political efficacy of limited nuclear employment would be improved if it produced significant military benefits: as Bernard Brodie commented in 1964, "a demonstration use has to be militarily effective or it is likely to demonstrate the wrong things." In any case, NATO should take steps to minimize Russian perceptions that limited nuclear use could produce either exploitable military advantage or coercive political leverage......Russia's status as a nuclear great power acts as an amplifier for Russia's limited conventional military capabilities in a sustained great power conflict."[26]

Terrorist organizations adopt several measures and strategies against states. They detonate Improvised Explosive Devices constituted from material obtained from different means. They also destroyed nuclear weapon sites, and dispersed radioactive material by dirty bombs. Terrorist groups of South and Central Asian states attempted to retrieve nuclear weapons-usable materials. They attacked Pakistan, Russia and Brussels nuclear plants but failed to retrieve materials of dirty bombs. In some cases, seized material was described as a sample of a larger quantity for sale. In the 2000s, terrorists attacked Russian nuclear plants, while newspapers documented monitoring nuclear weapon transport trains by two terrorists. Some states of weak nuclear security measures, and their links with terrorist organizations, create a strong opportunity of retrieval to fabricate, transport, and detonate a nuclear explosive device, sufficient nuclear material or a weapon had been stolen. Experts and analysts, Matthew Bunn. Nickolas Roth. And William H. Tobey in their research paper on nuclear security and nuclear terrorism (Revitalizing Nuclear Security in an Era of Uncertainty., Project on Managing the Atom. Belfer Center for Science and International Affairs Harvard Kennedy School- January 2019) documented incidents of nuclear weapons theft and future of nuclear terrorism:

"It is now seven years since the death of Osama bin Laden, and many see al Qaeda as too damaged to have any hope of obtaining fissile material and fabricating it into a workable nuclear bomb. In recent years, there has been little evidence of core al Qaeda actively directing even much simpler large-scale conventional attacks against the United States, as opposed to merely lending its brand and advice to regional affiliates that are now more powerful. As for the Islamic State, with its geographic caliphate in Iraq and Syria largely defeated, some see it as not capable of implementing attacks that go much beyond suicide bombings or driving vehicles into crowds of people. As far as is publicly known, the Islamic State never did anything with the dangerous radiological sources in the territory under its control (which have since been recovered), even as it manufactured both conventional and chemical weapons.......Since the 2016 Nuclear Security Summit, countries have continued to take measurable steps to improve nuclear security, from requiring protections against cyber-attacks to launching programs to strengthen security culture in nuclear organizations. But momentum is slowing, raising serious doubts as to whether national leaders are fulfilling their commitment to continue to make nuclear security a priority. High-level political attention to nuclear security and overcoming obstacles has largely faded, international mechanisms for fostering nuclear security action and cooperation have not managed to fill the gap created by the absence of nuclear security summits, and political disputes continue to impede efforts to sustain or expand cooperation in crucial areas. At the same time, stockpiles of nuclear weapons and materials in unstable regions continue to grow and to shift in directions that increase risks. Terrorist threats and important nuclear security weaknesses exist that must be addressed. Additionally, rapidly evolving technologies such as cyber and drones could increase adversary threats to nuclear facilities and stocks in the years to come. If nuclear security improvements do not keep pace, the risk of nuclear terrorism is likely to grow".[27]

Chapter 2

Nuclear Jihad against China, South China Sea, Taiwan and the Underwater Nuclear Drones

The recent test of Chinese hypersonic missile (September-2021) is a barefaced torment for the US, UK and Australia who formed a nuclear alliance against China to establish permanent military bases in the South China Sea and South-East Asian region. China had sternly reacted to this alliance by testing hypersonic nuclear missiles and exhibited its military strength on surface and sea. The missile circled the earth at low orbit before speeding towards its target. Pentagon spokesman John Kirby said: "We have made clear our concerns about the military capabilities China continues to pursue, capabilities that only increase tensions in the region and beyond. That is one reason why we hold China as our number one pacing challenge."[1] The lack of clarity about China's nuclear intentions and capabilities, combined with the increased risks that Beijing's arsenal will pose to the United States. In 2020, Pentagon published a report on Chinese military capabilities indicating that China maintains 200 nuclear warhead stockpiles, but the US intelligence failed to assess the whole military and nuclear strength of China and disregarded China no first use policy China will respond with nuclear missiles if attacked.[2]

China and Russia are cooperating in the field of military technology to counter the US technological power. Russia has also tested a Hypersonic Cruise Missile, which caused torment for the Biden administration. Russian President Vladimir Putin said the new hypersonic missile, Zircon, was "part of a new generation of missile systems. The Russian Defence Ministry in a statement authenticated the missile was fired from the Admiral Gorshkov frigate. Russia has a strong military power that cannot be challenged by the US and its allies. The Russian President announced in 2018 that his country was developing nuclear missiles, including Avangard. Analyst and expert, Rajeswari Pillai Rajagopalan in his analysis (Russia Tests Hypersonic Zircon Missile: Growing geopolitical rivalries will continue to drive the development of hypersonic and other lethal weapons systems. The Diplomat-July 22, 2021) highlighted developments in Russia's hypersonic nuclear missiles:

"Some of Russia's hypersonic missiles are already claimed to be deployed with its armed forces. According to Russian media reports, the government has "deployed two interceptor jets capable of carrying the hyped Kinzhal hypersonic missile for war games in Syria." Russia's defence ministry is quoted in the same report as saying that "a pair of MiG-31K aircraft with the ability to use the latest hypersonic missiles from the Kinzhal complex flew from Russian airfields to the Russian airbase Khmeimim in Syria for exercises." Russia is not alone in these efforts. China has been making consistent efforts at developing hypersonic weapons. In 2019, at the military parade on the occasion of the 70th anniversary of the founding of the People's Republic of China, China showcased the DF-17 missile for the first time. Even though the U.S. has known about the DF-17 prototype for close to a decade, Mike Griffin, the U.S. undersecretary for research and engineering at the Department of Defence, in 2018 revealed that China had done "20 times as many hypersonic weapons tests as has the United States over the last decade." Like Russia, China's pursuit of hypersonic missiles appears to have been spurred by U.S. missile defence developments, which could potentially neutralize the traditional ballistic missiles that Russia and China possess".[3]

The United States has already established a sophisticated system to counter cruise and ballistic missile attacks but not satisfied with how and when the US army would be able to contain China. China has been aggressively developing nuclear technology to effectively respond to US missile attacks. The Pentagon failed to get advance information about the Chinese hypersonic nuclear missile. The US intelligence groups, Pentagon brass, and perhaps even the White House itself received a sobering shock to hear about the test of Chinese missiles. Financial Times also reported that China clandestinely tested a nuclear-capable hypersonic missile. This test of the PLA left US intelligence officials at the Pentagon stunned China has been consecutively modernising its nuclear weapon and missile systems since the 1990s. Beijing could also be moving beyond its long-standing "minimum deterrence" nuclear doctrine. Over the next decade, China will become the world strongest nuclear power. With its announcement of a new nuclear-capable strategic bomber, China will soon field their own nuclear triad. By hearing the Chinese test news, US, UK and Australia expedited efforts to work together to build their nuclear and missile capabilities.

The US allies are reluctant to trust Pentagon and CIA capabilities after they committed war crimes and left Afghanistan without informing the NATO alliance. While competition between China and the United States has grown, nuclear issues have not become a driving element of that competition relative to other issue areas, but China views US missile developments and its missile defence system as a threat to its national security. Expert and analyst Michael Mazza in his paper noted nuclear dynamics surrounding Taiwan (Three scenarios for China's evolving nuclear strategy: Implications for the Taiwan Strait. Global Taiwan Institute – 14 July 2021) and highlighted Chinese modernization:

"A comprehensive assessment of nuclear dynamics surrounding the Taiwan Strait would consider nuclear force modernization efforts and doctrinal revisions in both China and the United States, and perhaps in Russia and India as well. Such an assessment would likewise take account of changes in conventional force structure and posture, missile defence capabilities, and conventional threats to strategic forces. This type of wide-ranging evaluation is not possible here. Instead, the analysis below will focus on one pillar of China's nuclear approach and three scenarios for how it may evolve in the coming years: China's "no first use" policy. For the United States, having to grapple with nuclear strikes on assets in the region would present a significant challenge. The use of nuclear weapons against US bases in allied countries, for example, could trigger "nuclear umbrella" commitments, and the United States might struggle to settle on a proportionate response (or a disproportionate one) to nuclear use against naval forces at sea. This would be a potentially very different fight for Taiwan than the one often imagined, and one in which there could be substantial pressure for the United States to employ counterforce capabilities and resort to the first use of nuclear weapons. China might think such an approach is far more likely to convince America to leave Taiwan to its own devices and more likely to ensure victory if America does intervene. After all, quick nuclear strikes on US regional assets could devastate America's ability to operate in the western Pacific, presenting Washington with a menu of unappetizing choices (to put it mildly). But, of course, things might not play out as Beijing might imagine. If the United States did come to Taiwan's defence in these circumstances, Beijing and Washington might find themselves performing a high wire act to avoid a nuclear exchange".[4]

Today's China is too big and strong economically and militarily to be contained. The United States with its fractured political body and failed strategies, cannot contain China and Russia, for the reason that most of the allies have set apart to support its cause. The United States has lost confidence of the Muslim world while Pakistan, India, Bangladesh and Central Asian states are dancing to different regional tangos. Expert and analyst Doyle Mcmanus in his article (A new military alliance, a summit meeting: The U.S.-China face-off is looking like the Cold War, *Los Angeles Times*, 26 September, 2021), has highlighted the Biden administration's Quad policy and the growing Chinese economic and military developments. He also noted the attitude of the AUKUS alliance towards China:

"Biden and his fellow Quad leaders never publicly uttered the word "China," but the Quad is all about containment. It seeks to blunt China's growing influence, deter it from launching military adventures and prevent it from muscling the United States and other countries out of Asia's growing markets. The Quad isn't a military alliance — formally, at least. A Biden aide who briefed reporters before the summit took pains to make that point three times in 20 minutes......In Australia, the muscle China used was economic: After Australia called for an investigation of the origins of the coronavirus, Beijing retaliated by cutting imports of Australian beef and called on the Canberra government to stifle "anti-China statements" from members of Parliament and the media. The naked pressure backfired; the Aussies got their backs up and decided to move closer to the United States. One result was Aukus, the new military partnership of Australia, Britain and the United States, whose first big project was building nuclear-powered submarines for the Australian navy. Between the Quad and Aukus, "we're seeing the emergence of a new security architecture," Bonnie Glaser, a China expert at the German Marshall Fund of the United States, told me. "It sends a signal to Beijing that other countries are willing to stand up together and defend a rules-based international order."[5]

The Indo-Pacific cold war has been heating up since 2020, when Trump's administration adopted an anti-China policy. As we all know, the US, UK and Australia nuclear submarine deal is part of a wider alliance-based strategy to counter and contain China, but the growing altercation took a new turn when the US and UK declared to provide Australia with nuclear technology for countering China. Analyst Bertil Lintner (US encircling China on multiple new Cold War fronts, Asia Times, 20 September 2021) views these developments in different perspectives:

"Meanwhile, the US and India signed a new agreement on July 30 to jointly develop Air-Launched Unmanned Aerial Vehicles (ALUAV). The deal is the latest under the Research, Development, Testing and Evaluation Memorandum Agreement between India's Ministry of Defence and the US Defence Department, first signed in 2006 and renewed in 2015. A September 3 statement describes the deal as yet another step towards "deepening defence technology collaboration between the two nations through co-development of defence equipment." Needless to say, the target of the deal is China. Just as provocatively, US ally Japan is now staging its largest military drills since 1993, separately but hardly by coincidence at the same time, Taiwan launched a new major military exercise known as Han Kuang to strengthen combat readiness in the event of a Chinese attack. China considers self-governing Taiwan a renegade province that must be "reunified" with the mainland, a seizure Chinese President Xi Jinping has indicated is a near-term priority. Taiwan's incorporation into the mainland would undermine the US' strategic advantage in the Indo-Pacific, making the island a strategic centre point of the new Cold War".[6]

China has claimed over the region where 11 billion of oil and 190 trillion cubic feet natural gas existed. Moreover, this Chinese claim antagonized competing claimants Brunei, Indonesia, Malaysia, the Philippines, Taiwan, and Vietnam. Analyst and expert, Ralph Jennings in his VOA news article (27 August 2021) has highlighted the presence of competing powers in South China Sea, and noted China's claim on 90% area of the sea:

"An increase in world naval activity in the disputed South China Sea will prompt the strategic waterway's largest claimant, Beijing, to send more of its own ships as a way of showing others it won't retreat, experts say. Two Indian navy warships and a Vietnamese navy frigate held exercises there that started at a port in Vietnam and extended into firing drills and helicopter moves further at sea, the Indian Defence Ministry said on its website. It said the exercises were "in continuation with ongoing deployment of Indian Navy ships in the South China Sea" and "would be another step towards strengthening India-Vietnam defence relations." Among other exercises in or near the sea, a Royal Canadian Navy warship joined Australian, Japanese and U.S. naval vessels for a coordinated workout in January. Ships from Australia, India, Japan and the United States scheduled their annual Malabar exercises near Guam – the U.S. territory closest to Asia – for August 26-29. Since about the start of 2021, warships from eight countries with no actual maritime claims have passed through or near the South China Sea. China claims about 90% of the 3.5

million-square-kilometre sea, overlapping waters five other governments also claim. Chinese officials point to maritime documents dating back to dynastic times as support for their claim. The others cite a United Nations convention on sea usage. Officials in Beijing have indicated they hold exercises largely in response to U.S. movements. The People's Liberation Army Southern Theatre Command "will always remain on high alert" and "resolutely safeguard" China's sovereignty, a senior colonel said in August last year after it had "warned off" a U.S. guided-missile destroyer. China fears the dispute is becoming more "internationalized" because of the spike in foreign navy operations and that it has lost its clout to discuss sovereignty disputes one-on-one with other Asian states, said Yun Sun."

As noted earlier, the South China Sea has been an important gateway for trade and is an important economic and strategic region. The Lowy Institute is an Australian think tank in its recent commentary on the South China Sea has highlighted its geographical location that has bordered with Brunei, Cambodia, China, Indonesia, Malaysia, the Philippines, Singapore, Taiwan, Thailand and Vietnam: "Japan and South Korea rely heavily on the South China Sea for their supply of fuels and raw materials and as an export route, although the availability of diversionary sea lanes bypassing the South China Sea provides non-littoral states with some flexibility in this regard. The South China Sea also contains rich, though unregulated and over-exploited fishing grounds and is reported to hold significant reserves of undiscovered oil and gas, which is an aggravating factor in maritime and territorial disputes.....Australia has been conducting its own airborne surveillance operations in the South China Sea and Indian Ocean, called Operation Gateway, since 1980. These patrols are conducted by P-3 Orion maritime aircraft and some of them have been verbally challenged by China".

The U.S. Naval Institute News, in its commentary (Report on U.S.-China Competition in East, South China Sea. 10 September 2021) documented the importance of the South China Sea that emerged as an arena of U.S.-China strategic competition. The report noted the construction activities of Chinese naval forces, their operation. The United States is supported by Australia, Britain, Philippines, and Germany, while China received great support from neighbouring states. Both the US and China are struggling to control the South China Sea, but the rising military, nuclear and missile power of China has changed the competitive environment. The US army want to disrupt every development project of China, for example, the CPEC project that ruined Pakistan economy.

"Construction activities at sites that it occupies in the Spratly Islands, as well as actions by its maritime forces to assert China's claims against competing claims by regional neighbours such as the Philippines and Vietnam—have heightened concerns among U.S. observers that China is gaining effective control of the SCS, an area of strategic, political, and economic importance to the United States and its allies and partners. Actions by China's maritime forces at the Japan-administered Senkaku Islands in the East China Sea (ECS) are another concern for U.S. observers. Chinese domination of China's near-seas region—meaning the SCS and ECS, along with the Yellow Sea—could substantially affect U.S. strategic, political, and economic interests in the Indo-Pacific region and elsewhere. Potential general U.S. goals for U.S.-China strategic competition in the SCS and ECS include but are not necessarily limited to the following: fulfilling U.S. security commitments in the Western Pacific, including treaty commitments to Japan and the Philippines; maintaining and enhancing the U.S.-led security architecture in the Western Pacific, including U.S. security relationships with treaty allies and partner states; maintaining a regional balance of power favourable to the United States and its allies and partners; defending the principle of peaceful resolution of disputes and resisting the emergence of an alternative "might-makes-right" approach to international affairs; defending the principle of freedom of the seas, also sometimes called freedom of navigation; preventing China from becoming a regional hegemon in East Asia; and pursuing these goals as part of a larger U.S. strategy for competing strategically and managing relations with China".

On 24 October 2021, Pakistani newspaper Dawn reported the statement of Khalid Mansoor who accused the United States of conniving in cahoots with India against the economic lifeline of Pakistan. "From the point of view of the emerging geo-strategic situation, one thing is clear: the United States supported by India is inimical to CPEC. It will not let it succeed. That's where we have to take a position," Mr Mansoor said. He said the Western powers view CPEC as a symbol of China's political ambition. "That's the reason CPEC is seen suspiciously by both the United States and Europe… they view CEPC more as a move by China to expand its political, strategic and business influence," said Mr Mansoor, noting that China has been able to manage that apprehension "to a great extent". The United States is now "taking stock of the economic and political consequences" of withdrawing from the region, he said. "I had a very detailed discussion with the American embassy people. I told them CPEC is available for them as well. They have also expressed their wish that they would like to develop some kind of involvement and see how it can be beneficial for both countries." Dawn reported.

Analyst Mark Valencia in his analysis, (Mixed military messaging in the South China Sea: US-led joint naval effort to contain China in contested waterway is being diluted by the participants' own national agendas. 13 August 2021) has noted activities of the UK, Germany, France and India which deployed warships that transited or will transmit the South China Sea: "The confusion stems in part from the United States' disingenuous conflation of freedom of commercial navigation with its military priorities there – freedom to probe China's defences and to attempt to intimidate it into abandoning its claims......In September 2020, France, Germany and the UK jointly submitted a note verbale to the United Nations emphasizing "the importance of unhampered exercise of the freedom of the high seas" in the South China Sea. Given this context, the deployments certainly send a collective political and strategic signal – the latter intended or not. Beijing perceives the South China Sea as being well within its "sphere of influence." For China, it is a historically vulnerable underbelly that must be turned into a "natural shield for its national security."

India and China has become permanent competitors in South Asia and the Indian Ocean due to their association with different ideological blocks. India is dancing on behalf of the United States, while China wants to establish its military and political influence as a superpower in the region. India's political and military stance is fluctuating by trying to keep two watermelons in one hand. Its inclination towards both Russia and the United States made the country untrustworthy. After the withdrawal of US and NATO forces from Afghanistan when Pakistan distanced from the US so called war on terrorism, India affixed with the US confrontational strategy to threaten China in every front. In 1988, when India attacked Maldives, there was no harsh reaction because it was a surgical strike against terrorists, but in the 1990s, India established a friendly relationship with Maldives. Indo-Maldives strategic relations have also gone through substantive changes. The Congressional Research Service report (China-India Great Power Competition in the Indian Ocean Region: Issues for Congress, April 20, 2018) has highlighted competitions between China and India and their rivalry in the Indian Ocean:

"Competition between China and India is driven to a large extent by their economic rise and the rapid associated growth in, and dependence on, seaborne trade and imported energy, much of which transits the Indian Ocean. There seems to be a new strategic focus on the maritime and littoral regions that are adjacent to the sea lanes that link the energy rich Persian Gulf with the energy dependent economies of Asia. Any disruption of this supply would likely be detrimental to the United States' and the world's economy. China's dependence on seaborne trade and imported energy, and the strategic vulnerability that this represents, has been labelled China's "Malacca dilemma" after the Strait of Malacca, the key strategic choke point through which a large proportion of China's trade and energy flows. Much of the activity associated with China's Belt and Road Initiative (BRI) can be viewed as an attempt by China to minimize its strategic vulnerabilities by diversifying its trade and energy routes while also enhancing its political influence through expanded trade and infrastructure investments. China's BRI in South and Central Asia and the IOR, when set in context with China's assertive behaviour in the East China Sea and the South China Sea and border tensions with India, is contributing to a growing rivalry between India and China. This rivalry, which previously had been largely limited to the Himalayan region where the two nations fought a border war in 1962, is now increasingly maritime-focused. Some in India feel encircled by China's strategic moves in the region while China feels threatened by its limited ability to secure its sea lanes".[7]

India's military views China as a great enemy, the Indian Army Chief warned. India moved 50,000 troops to its border with China in 2021, with about 20,000 troops in the Ladakh sector, but still not entered a full-scale war with China.[8] China is facing a serious strategic threat from Australia, UK and the US modern nuclear and missiles technology. China decided (China urged to increase sea-based nuclear deterrent amid US Intensified strategic threat. Zhang Hui. (*Global Times*, 18 May, 2021) to increase the number of nuclear weapons, especially its sea-based nuclear deterrent of intercontinental submarine-launched ballistic missiles, to deter potential military action by US warmongers.[9] On 18 September 2021, Al Jazeera reported warning of Chinese President Xi Jinping against "interference from external forces" in the region. In an address to Shanghai Cooperation Organization, President Xi urged heads of states to "absolutely resist external forces and their interference [in] countries of our region at any excuse, and hold the future of our countries' development and progress firmly in our own hands".[10] Expert and analyst, Gerald C. Brown, noted in his article (Understanding the Risks and Realities of China's Nuclear Forces, (Arms Control Today, June 2021) that China's capabilities exhibit substantial threat. In the U.S.-Chinese context, Gerald C. Brown argued that policymakers should be more focused on how conventional weapons and related strategies could impact the nuclear calculus between the two countries".[11] *Global Times* in its editorial comment (US should stop eyeing too much on China's hypersonic missiles and broaden its horizons, Oct 17, 2021) highlighted nuclear development in China, and its resolve to challenge the US military power in Europe and Asia. The newspaper also noted improvement of China's nuclear and missile technology:

"The US is very concerned about China's nuclear development. There is no doubt that China has no plans to build a nuclear force of the same size as that of the US. In other words, we have no intention of launching a "nuclear arms race" with the US. However, China will certainly improve the quality of its nuclear deterrence to ensure that the US completely eliminates the idea of nuclear blackmail against China at any critical moment and its idea of using nuclear forces to make up for the weakness that US' conventional forces cannot crush China. The US is constantly releasing rumours that China is strengthening its strategic nuclear tools, which is believed to pave the way for public opinion in the US to further increase its military expenditure from a high starting point. Perhaps we need to point out that no matter how much military spending the US increases and how much new equipment it procures, it is impossible for the US to continue to enjoy overwhelming military superiority in China's coastal areas. Washington needs to be realistic and rethink its approach to China".[12]

The United States' new cold war (new jihad) against China and Russia will endanger the state's unions of the US, UK, NATO and Europe, as domestic turmoil, poverty and alienation of citizens from the state has worsened and inflamed. China is the biggest economic power while Russia is technologically strong that can inflict huge economic and military cataclysm on UK and US civilian population and military infrastructure. Political differences between the EU and UK may further fatten clefts of unsettled disputes. The United States is also facing economic challenges and regional alienation. Union of the UK (Michael Keating, 23 April 2021) "was never a unified project or ideology but rather a complex structure with numerous strands, which sometimes cohere and sometimes pull apart... Welfare state restructuring has emptied the concept of social citizenship of much of its meaning.[13] Economic disparities have increased in the absence of state-wide policies aimed at spatial cohesion, although the disparities do not map clearly onto the boundaries of the component nations. Devolution has set in train institutional dynamics which critics predicted could lead to the weakening and, eventually, dissolution of the bonds of union"[14]

Fragile peace in Northern Ireland and disaffiliation trends in Scotland and Wales raised several questions, including new waves of sectarian and ethnic violence that challenged the authority of the state. The Johnson administration contributed little to thinking about an energised and viable future for the Union. The Welsh Government has already exhibited dissatisfaction with the centralization of power by the Johnson administration. Former Prime Minister Brown warned: "For too long we have left unstated the shared purpose and values that bind the UK together, Scotland, Wales and Northern Ireland have taken different approaches to tackle the coronavirus, and elected regional mayors in England rowed with the government in London. I think the public is fed up. I think in many ways, they feel they are being treated as second class citizens, particularly in the outlying areas, that they are invisible and forgotten." Brown told BBC.[15]

The Johnson administration abruptly reversed its disarmament policies and announced a significant increase in production of nuclear weapons up to no more than 260 warheads. Arms Control Association in its recent report noted the UK intention of producing more weapons in near future: "The UK currently has about 195 nuclear warheads, (Kingston Reif and Shannon Bugos – April 2021) of which 120 are operational, according to an estimate by researchers at the Federation of American Scientists. The UK deploys its entire nuclear arsenal aboard four Vanguard-class submarines, each of which is armed with Trident II D5 submarine-launched ballistic missiles.[16] The AUKUS agreement (Mark Valensia –*Asia Times*, 07 October, 2021) "has certainly ruffled Australia's relations with South China Sea littoral countries. Some view it and the Quad, as further undermining the Association of Southeast Asian Nations' "centrality" in regional security affairs. They think the agreement may even drive some Southeast Asian countries away from the US for fear of further angering China. Malaysia is concerned that the agreement could lead to more conflict and an arms race in the region".[17]

There is a general perception that extremist organisations in South Asia could use some advanced technologies against civilian populations. If control over these weapons is weak, the possibility of theft increases. Problem of nuclear and biological terrorism deserves special attention from all South Asian states, including Afghanistan, while nuclear weapons, missile technologies and bio-weapons proliferate, there is a grave danger that some of them might fall into the hands of the Pakistani Taliban (TTP), ISIS and Indian and Afghani extremist groups. In South and Central Asia, some states, including Pakistan, have started responding to the threat of nuclear and biological terrorism with technical means. Each state has its own approach towards the threat perception. More recent focus on global terrorism issues is also now sharpening the focus on non-proliferation activities that do not necessarily apply at the level of the state. There are speculations that non-state actors may possibly engage in these activities. The Islamic State that controlled parts of Iraq and Syria established its network in Afghanistan and Pakistan as the region is already dominated by violent terrorist groups.

Pakistan's former Interior Minister, Senator Dr. Rehman Malik (The Nation, 24 September 2020), highlights terrorist activities of the Islamic State (ISIS) in Pakistan and Afghanistan and warned that the group has been trying to establish a strong terrorist network in Punjab. He noted more than eighty thousand (80,000) Pakistanis, mostly from Southern Punjab, have been recruited by the ISIS group, while its women brigade is already operating in Sialkot district of Pakistan that training and purveying to the group young girls fighters.[18] Chechen extremist groups have also consistently expressed the desire to obtain, build, and utilize unconventional devices against selected targets, and have innovated by incorporating hazardous materials into their ordnance. The war in Syria and Iraq significantly altered modern terrorism, with radical Islamic militants from Central Asia being no exception. The terrorists' method for recruiting forces is almost the same in most of the countries in Central Asia.

While the majority of ISIS recruits originate in the Middle East, the Maghreb, and Western Europe. Central Asia is the third-largest source of foreign fighters in Syria. More than 4,000 Central Asian fighters are believed to have joined armed groups fighting in Syria, with an estimated 2,500 arriving there in 2014 and early 2015 alone. Russian President Vladimir Putin once stated that as many as 7,000 fighters from Russia and Central Asia have joined the ranks of the Islamic State.[19] The Chinese government has criticized the US for adopting the Cold War mentality based on zero-sum mindset and ideological prejudice. President Xi warned just days after President Biden's inauguration that "To build small circles or start a new Cold War" will push the world into division and even confrontation.[20]

South Asian states are facing the threat of terrorism and violent extremism. The unending civil war in Afghanistan and Pakistan has destabilised the whole region. Terrorism in Afghanistan affects Pakistan and Iran, its heat touches Iranian borders while its flames are clearly seen in China and Russia as well. As South Asian states have been embroiled in protracted conflicts for decades, the lack of proper strategies to counter the TTP, ISIS and Indian extremism, and the clash of interests, have further aggravated the problem. Extremist and terrorist groups in this region are striving to retrieve nuclear and biological weapons and use them against the government or civilian population, but the issue was further complicated when some secret reports revealed the use of nuclear and biological weapons inside Russia. In November 1995, Chechen separatists put a crude bomb in Moscow's Izmailovsky Park.

The debate about bioterrorism is not entirely new in the region because both Pakistan and India have developed these weapons to use them in a future war. On 03 December 1984, the worst chemical disaster occurred in the city of Bhopal in India, causing the deaths of thousands of people. If a nuclear war were to break out in South Asia, experts believed that it was most likely to happen in India and Pakistan. This kind of war would have dire consequences. In the Seoul Summit, Indian Prime Minister Manmohan Singh warned that South Asia is under threat. Two incidents in Karachi and another in Balochistan proved that terrorists were trying to retrieve nuclear weapons to use them against military or nuclear installations.

The threat of chemical, biological and nuclear terrorism in South Asia also causes deep frustration and anxiety as the region hosts many militant organisations. These groups have already learnt the technique of making nuclear explosive devices and the illegal transactions of poorly protected material. Subcontinent is the most volatile region because India and Pakistan are engaged in a dangerous nuclear arms race. India is enjoying conventional superiority. The addition of a nuclear dimension to this conflict is a matter of great concern. India's National Security Advisor admitted in one of his recent speeches that a fourth-generation war is being fought against Pakistan with different tactics and dimensions. Strategically speaking, India and Pakistan have their own threat perceptions, which are quite similar. India wants to be a strong nuclear state because of its fear of Chinese aggression, while Pakistan also needs nuclear weapons because of its fear of Indian aggression. China helps Pakistan in upgrading its nuclear weapons and provides sophisticated weapons to the country's army, while the US helps India.

This misinterpretation of each other's motives has also caused misunderstandings. First, they threatened each other with nuclear bombs and then assessed the consequences and fatalities. This issue has also been highlighted in a recently published book by Nathan E Busch: "Due to continual mistrust between the two countries, each would be likely to misinterpret military movements, missiles tests, or accidental detonations as an impending attack by the other side. The risks of misinterpreting each other's motives are compounded by the vulnerabilities of their nuclear forces and the short flight times of the forces to key targets." Nuclear trafficking in South Asia was a key concern while the nuclear black marketing networks of Pakistani generals and some mafia scientists were uncovered from Libya to Syria, Malaysia and Afghanistan. Recent media reports identified Moldovan criminal groups that attempted to smuggle radioactive materials to Daesh in 2015. Cases of nuclear smuggling in Central Asia were made in recent cases. Muhammad Wajeeh, a Research Associate at Department of Development Studies, COMSATS Institute of Information Technology, Abbottabad Pakistan, in his research paper (Nuclear Terrorism: A Potential Threat to World's Peace and Security- JSSA Vol II, No. 2) has reviewed a consternating threat of nuclear terrorism in South and Central Asia:

"ISIS is believed to have about 90 pounds of low-grade uranium (which was seized from Mosul University in Iraq are the invasion of the city in 2014) that can be used in the Dirty Bomb's to create serious panic among the public. In 2015 and 2016, ISIS became the leading high profile jihadist group in Iraq and Syria. Moreover, ISIS carried out attacks in Paris on November 13, 2015, killing 130 civilians and injuring more than 100 people. ISIS carried out a series of three coordinated suicide. Bombings in Belgium: one at Maalbeek Metro Station, Brussels and two at Brussels Airport in Zaventem, killing about 32 civilians and injuring 300 people. During the attacks, a G4S guard working on the Belgian nuclear research centre was also murdered and it led the world to believe that ISIS has a potential plot to attack the nuclear facility either to steal the radioactive material for dirty bombs or to release the radioactive material and waste into the atmosphere. These attacks also raised the issue of nuclear security, a discovery made by the Belgian authorities that ISIS has kept an eye on the local nuclear sciences and their families. Moreover, two Belgian nuclear power plant workers at Deol having knowledge of the nuclear sites joined ISIS and could provide assistance to exploit them for terrorist purposes". On March 30, al-Furat, the media wing of ISIS, threatened attacks on Germany and Britain on the eve of Washington Nuclear Security Summit 2016".[21] However, analyst Damon Mehl in his paper (Damon Mehl, CTC Sentinel, November 2018, Volume-11, Issue-10) noted some aspects of the development of ISIS networks in Tajikistan:

"Jamaat Ansarullah, an Afghanistan-based Tajikistani terrorist group, was formed in 2010 with likely fewer than 100 members and has since received support from the IMU, the Taliban, and al-Qaeda. The group's stated mission is to bring an 'Islamic' government to Tajikistan. Beginning with its foundation, Jamaat Ansarullah sporadically published videos and disseminated messages through its website, which has been inactive since 2016. The group's leader Amriddin Tabarov was killed in Afghanistan in December 2015 and Tabarov's son-in-law Mavlavif Salmon was appointed as the new leader by the end of 2016. In 2014, Jamaat Ansarullah sent some of its members to fight in Syria with Jabhat al-Nusra, an al-Qaeda-aligned group now known as Hayat Tahrir al-Sham. At a point in 2014 or 2015, some Jamaat Ansarullah members ended up fighting alongside the Islamic State. The Islamic State subsequently began financially supporting Ansarullah, according to Afghanistan expert Antonio Giustozzi, citing a Jamaat Ansarullah commander. This support reportedly caused fissures between Jamaat Ansarullah and al-Qaeda, and by 2015, Ansarullah received 50 percent of its financial backing from the Islamic State. In October 2014, a Jamaat Ansarullah member going by the name Mansur stated on the group's website that Jamaat Ansarullah considered the Islamic State a jihadi organization, but had paused its decision on whether to accept the Islamic State's claim of being the caliphate".[22]

The CIA and Pentagon spent more than $1 trillion in Afghanistan but couldn't succeed to bring Gallus-Gallus chicken to the White House. According to the Washington Post, the 2,000 pages interviews with more than 400 generals, diplomats, and other officials directly involved in the Afghan war exposed the incompetence of a so-called superpower that killed innocent Afghans with impunity. Many officials described a sustained effort by the US government to hide the truth from the American public. The Post also released hundreds of pages of previously classified memos about the Afghan war dictated by former US Defence Secretary Donald Rumsfeld. Before the rise of ISIS, the Islamic Movement of Uzbekistan (IMU) was the main Central Asian extremist organization in the field. Its base of operations is in Afghanistan and Pakistan. Central Asian fighters linked to ISIS headquarters in Syria also participated in acts of terrorism in other countries. ISIS has previously restrained itself from getting involved in attacks in Central Asia as the group's leadership emphasised that attacking this region was not the highest priority.

In his the-Diplomat analysis (20 September 2016), Uran Botobekov, documented videos and extrajudicial killing in Iraq and Syria by terrorist groups: "Recently, Central Asians saw on YouTube a terrible video of a teenager, Babur Israilov from Jalal-Abad in southern Kyrgyzstan, on his way to becoming a suicide bomber. According to Radio Free Europe/Radio Liberty, Babur Israilov was a member of an extremist group of Uzbeks–Imam Bukhari Jamaat–which fights alongside Jabhat al-Nusra in Syria. Just like the father of the British boy JoJo, resident of Suzak district in the Jalal-Abad region of Kyrgyzstan Tahir Rahitov saw his son Babur via video.[23]

Analyst, Mr. Uran Botobekov also noted the establishment of the group's two important branches to maintain its army: "It is known that KIB has two branches. The group's main fighting force of more than 500 militants, led by leader Abu Yusuf Muhojir today is based in the Syrian province Idlib. Despite the fact that KIB positions itself as an "independent" faction it is closely connected with Ahrar al Sham who has had al Qaeda operatives embedded in its own ranks. The KIB's second branch is concentrated in Afghanistan, which positions itself as an integral part of the Taliban".[24] Chechen fighters have also established networks across Russian Federation and want to retrieve sophisticated weapons. The group in Afghanistan received military training to strengthen its army for the future war against Russia. Pakistan has also trained Chechen commanders years ago, while during their jihad against Russia, some reports confirmed the participation of over 2000 Pakistani jihadists and retired military officers in fighting alongside their fighters against Russia. Analyst and researcher, Mr. Christian Bleuer (Chechens in Afghanistan 1: A Battlefield Myth That Will Not Die-Afghanistan Analysts Network, 27 Jun 2016) noted the presence of Chechen leadership in Afghanistan:

> "Extremist members of Chechnya's rebel movement adhere to ideas tied to jihad and the creation of an Islamist state. Afghan and foreign officials say as many as 7,000 Chechens and other foreign fighters could be operating in the country, loosely allied with the Taliban and other militant groups. Local reporting by Pajhwok News, sourced to the Logar governor's spokesman, was slightly different, naming the targets as "Taliban Commanders Mullah Saber, Mullah Sabawon and Mullah Bashir," but also noting the presence of Chechens–in this case, three Chechen women who were allegedly killed. Khaama Press also reported the incident, noting that "[f]oreign insurgents fighting the Afghan forces is not new as scores of militants from Chechnya and other countries are routinely reported killed during the fight with the

Afghan forces," with the caveat that "[t]he anti-government armed militant groups have not commented regarding the report so far."[25] With the presence of Jihadist Groups and the ISIS in Central Asia, the use of chemical, biological and nuclear weapons cannot be ruled out, the fact is that the ISIS found such weapons in Syria and Iraq. If they used these weapons, the reaction of Central Asia States and Russian would be violent, and they might attack the US and NATO installations inside Afghanistan.

Researchers and analysts Keir A. Lieber and Daryl G. Press (Stets Won't Give Nuclear Weapons to Terrorists-2013) in their paper have warned that if state transferred nuclear or biological weapons to jihadist groups and ISIS in Central Asia, this will change the whole picture of war in Afghanistan:

"The concern that a state might transfer nuclear weapons to terrorists, however, is among the greatest of these worries, and to many analysts it is the most compelling justification for costly actions—including the use of military force—aimed at preventing proliferation. Despite the issue's importance, the danger of deliberate nuclear weapons transfer to terrorist's remains understudied. Scholars have scrutinized many other proliferation concerns more extensively. Analysts have investigated the deductive and empirical bases for claims that new nuclear states would be deterrable; the likelihood that Iran, in particular, would behave rationally and avoid using nuclear weapons recklessly; and the risks of proliferation cascades, "loose nukes," and nuclear-armed states using their weapons as a shield for aggression or blackmail. To the extent that analysts have debated the possibility of covert state sponsorship of nuclear terrorism, however, the arguments have consisted mostly of competing deductive logics—with little empirical analysis. This article assesses the risk that states would give nuclear weapons to terrorists".[26]

If terrorist groups such as ISIS or Lashkar-e-Taiba decide to go nuclear, what will be the security preparations in Central Asia to intercept them? These and other Pakistan based groups can attempt to manufacture the fissile material needed to fuel a nuclear weapon—either highly enriched uranium or plutonium, and then use it. Moreover, there are possibilities that Pakistan, Afghanistan and Central Asia based extremist and jihadist groups can purchase fissile material in the black market or steal it from a military or civilian facility and then use that to construct an improvised nuclear device. US tensions with Russia receded and nuclear strategy came to seem like a relic of a bygone era. ISIS found dangerous weapons in Syria and Iraq and killed thousands of innocent women and children.

In Central Asia and the Russian Federation, there are several extremist and terrorist groups that seek nuclear weapons to use against local security forces. Daesh has reached Moscow. The group (ISIS) will use biological and chemical weapons and will also attack Russian nuclear installations in near future. The group has established networks through different sources and is struggling to expand its network to Central Asia. Chechen extremist groups have also consistently expressed a desire to obtain, build, and utilize unconventional devices against selected targets, and have innovated by incorporating hazardous materials into their ordnance. Information on how to manipulate nuclear material to produce an explosive device—an improvised nuclear device, which would produce a nuclear explosion and a mushroom cloud, or a radiation dispersal device, which would spread dangerous radioactive material over a substantial area—is now available widely.

On 25 March 2016, Daily Telegraph reported militants plan to attack the Brussels nuclear plant: "In the wake of claims the Brussels attackers had planned to set off a radioactive 'dirty bomb', Yukiya Amano, the Director-General of the International Atomic Energy Agency said: "Terrorism is spreading and the possibility of using nuclear material cannot be excluded. The material can be found in small quantities in universities, hospitals and other facilities.[27] "Dirty bombs will be enough to (drive) any big city in the world into panic. And the psychological, economic and political implications would be enormous," said Mr Amano. One security expert suggested that the terrorists could have been plotting to kidnap the nuclear researcher they had been filming to coerce the scientist into helping them make a 'dirty bomb'.[28] The Newspaper reported. State sponsorship of nuclear terrorism in Central Asia is a matter of great concern as some states support terrorist groups such as the ISIS, Taliban, Katibat-e-Imam al Bukhari, Chechen groups, and Lashkar-e-Taiba, and provide dangerous weapons. These states can sponsor terrorist groups to launch nuclear attack inside Russia or Central Asia.[29]

47

Chapter 3

New Cold War, Non-State Actors, and Threat of Biological Terrorism

The credible use of biological and nuclear weapons in Central Asia, Russia and Europe by terrorist organizations will deeply impact the domestic industry, financial market, agriculture and military installations. There are newspaper reports on the contribution of Central Asian States citizens in extremist infrastructure of South Asia and Middle East after the dismemberment of the Union of the Soviet, 9/11, and jihad in Chechnya. They were facilitated by Pakistan and Saudi Arabia to challenge the authority of the state in Russia, Central Asia, Chechnya and Euro-Asia. As far as foreign fighters are concerned, prior to the war in Syria (2011), Central Asian states started investigating their own citizens leaving to fight for radical causes in Afghanistan and Pakistan, but war in Syria, and Iraq, and emergence of ISIS, opened the doors for Central Asians Mujahidin to engage with extremist violence on a much larger scale than before. Mujahidin from Central Asia actively participated in the US war in Syria, Iraq and Afghanistan, and some of their leaders rose to the positions of authority within the ISIS terrorist group and Pakistan based international terrorist organizations. The irony is, the majority of terrorist groups operating in Afghanistan and Central Asia are seeking access to nuclear and biological weapons in order to use that against their targets, but ISIS has already retrieved expertise in constituting dirty bombs. Russia based clandestine networks may target nuclear installations to obtain the material of dirty bombs. The ISIS and Central Asian jihadists are maintaining several networks in Russia.

On 29 April 2020; Voice of America reported reaction of Russian Foreign Ministry to the State Department paper's assertion that the low-yield weapons "reduce the risk of nuclear war by reinforcing extended deterrence and assurance".[1] Moreover, Federation of American Scientists warned (January 2020) that the U.S. Navy had deployed a submarine armed with a low-yield Trident Nuclear Warhead for the first time. The warhead, which was criticised at home and abroad, was estimated to have about a third of the explosive power of the atomic bomb the U.S dropped on Hiroshima.[2] "Any attack involving a U.S. submarine-launched ballistic missile, regardless of its weapon specifications, would be perceived as a nuclear aggression," Russian Foreign Ministry warned. However, on 16 April 2020, Associated Press reported Chinese Foreign Ministry response to the allegations of U.S. State Department report about the country's secret nuclear test: 'China has always performed its international obligations and commitments in a responsible manner, firmly upheld multilateralism, and actively carried out international cooperation,' Foreign Minister Spokeswoman said.[3]

Having quoted Russia's "Military-Political Analytics", Xinhua News Agency in 28 May, 2020 reported biological weapons facilities under the U.S. control, including sanitary surveillance stations in Andijan, Urgench, Fergana and the veterinary centre of Uzbekistan that caused an outbreak of infections in Uzbekistan in places where U.S. military biological facilities operated. In the spring of 2017, a chickenpox epidemic broke out, which affected a large number of adults. Since January 2019, 279 cases of measles have been reported. Also, meningococcal infections were rising in the Central Asian country. Anna Popova, head of Russia's consumer rights and human well-being watchdog Rospotrebnadzor, at a meeting of the heads of the Security Councils of the CIS countries, expressed concern over the outbreaks of previously unknown infections in places where the U.S. military labs had opened. Xinhua News Agency reported.[4] However, Analytical Article (Nurlan Aliyev-November 27, 2018) noted a press conference in Moscow on October 4, 2018, in which Major General Igor Kirillov, commander of Russia's radiological, chemical and biological defence troops, warned that 73 citizens of Georgia had died as a result of medical experiments conducted by a company owned by former U.S. Secretary of Defense Donald Rumsfeld. Expert and analyst, Nurlan Aliyev (Russia's "Biological" Information Operation against the US and Georgia. 27 November 2018, the CACI Analyst) noted the US biological centre in Georgia and Moscow's concerns about the suspected biological activities there:

"Moscow has periodically accused the U.S. and the aforementioned republics of conducting "suspected biological activities" in areas close to Russia's borders. Representatives of the U.S. and other accused states have refuted the allegations, yet the dissemination of negative information has intensified in recent years. High level officials of Russia's MFA have accused the U.S. of violating the Biological and Toxin Weapons Convention, whereas the country's former Chief Sanitary Physician, Gennady Onishchenko, claimed that U.S. military microbiologists in Georgia could purposely infect mosquitoes with the Zika virus. The use of such narratives as a component of information warfare is not new to Russia, but has a strong legacy in the active measures employed by Soviet security agencies against the West during the Cold War. For example, in the 1960s the Soviet propaganda machine embarked on a campaign claiming that the U.S. intentionally infected Eastern Europe with Colorado potato beetles. According to Tamara Eidelman's book "How Propaganda Works," one of the most complex fabrications in this narrative was a massive influx of Colorado potato beetles across the Baltic Sea. In order to strengthen their case, Soviet propagandists "invented" an amphibian Colorado potato beetle. In 2016, several media outlets in Armenia blamed the Lugar Centre in Georgia for the deaths of more than ten people from swine flu (H1N1), yet the absurdity of these accusations was recognized even in Russian media. Recently, a group of Dagestani journalists led by Mukhtar Amirov alleged that the Georgian laboratory had been involved in the use of biological weapons in Dagestan and Chechnya".[5]

In Central Asia, the focus of Jihadists groups has been Tajikistan, Turkmenistan and Russian Federation but it is unclear how many Central Asian fighters will ultimately seek to return to their countries of origin, and if they do, whether any of them will remain committed to the ISIS terrorist group. Before the rise of ISIS, the Islamic Movement of Uzbekistan (IMU) was the main Central Asian extremist organization in the field. Its base of operations is in Afghanistan and Pakistan. Central Asian fighters linked to ISIS headquarters in Syria also participated in acts of terrorism in other countries. The ISIS has previously restrained itself from getting involved in attacks in Central Asia as the group's leadership emphasised that attacking this region was not their highest priority. In July 2018, five Tajik men killed four foreign cyclists in a car-ramming attack, accompanied by an on-foot gun and knife assault in the Khatlon province of Tajikistan.[6] The presence of Daesh in Iraq and Afghanistan, and participation of Central Asian jihadists in it prompted consternation in the region. In Syria, radical Islamic militants from Central Asia established terrorist organisations of their own. These terrorists have Salafi-Wahhabi inclinations and are among the backers of al-Qaeda, al-Nusra Front, and Daesh groups. In his the Diplomat analysis (20 September 2016), Uran Botobekov, documented videos and extrajudicial killing in Iraq and Syria:

"Recently, Central Asians saw on YouTube a terrible video of a teenager, Babur Israilov from Jalal-Abad in southern Kyrgyzstan, on his way to becoming a suicide bomber. In the video, Babur cries before being sent to his death in an armoured car laden with explosives in Fua, Syria. One of the fighters gathered around encourages him, saying in Uzbek that Satan intervenes at crucial moments to confuse a Muslim's mind, so he should think only of Allah. Further in the video sentimental Arabic music plays, the armoured personnel carrier moves, and, at the fatal moment, the bomb explodes. According to Radio Free Europe/Radio Liberty, Babur Israilov was a member of an extremist group of Uzbeks–Imam Bukhari Jamaat–which fights alongside Jabhat al-Nusra in Syria. Just like the father of the British boy JoJo, resident of Suzak district in the Jalal-Abad region of Kyrgyzstan Tahir Rahitov saw his son Babur via video. According to Tahir, his wife died in 1995 and the boy was raised by his grandmother. In November 2013 Babur left for Russia in search of work. In March 2014, he arrived in Syria via Turkey to join Imam Bukhari Jamaat, and fought alongside Jabhat al-Nusra against the government of Bashar al-Assad".[7]

Pakistan's former Interior Minister, Senator Dr. Rehman Malik (The Nation, 24 September 2020) has written several articles, in which he highlighted terrorist activities of Islamic State (ISIS) in Pakistan and Afghanistan, and warned that the group has been trying to establish a strong terrorist network in Punjab. He noted more than eighty thousand (80,000) Pakistanis, mostly from Southern Punjab of Pakistan have joined the ISIS group in Afghanistan. A women brigade of the ISIS group is already operating in Sialkot District:

"Although the US is emphasising that the Taliban would defeat ISIS, should the US leave the territory but some analysts caution that the US clearly knows about ISIS real motives as the leaders of IS-Khorasan, like their counterparts in Iraq and Syria, seem to be less focused on holding territory, instead of looking to lay the groundwork for a larger resurgence after US forces leave Afghanistan and the USA will inverse the funding for ISIS and ISIS will be used against Pakistan and China and partly against Russia. US intelligence indicates that despite having lost territory in Nangarhar and Kunar provinces, IS-Khorasan still has strongholds in Herat province and parts of Kabul, while maintaining smaller cells in Helmand, Kapisa, and Baghlan provinces. The group's ability to strike alliances with militant organizations like Lashkar-e-Jhangvi and an Islamic Movement of Uzbekistan splinter group is continuously expanding its longevity and resilience, and becoming a threat not only to Afghanistan and Pakistan but also other regional countries, Central Asian republics, Russia, and China. Amid its blame games, India is facing the same threat. The President of Tajikistan and its interior minister told me how Daesh is expanding in his country and most of them have trained in Afghanistan".[8]

Security agencies of Central Asian States have adopted several law-and-order measures to effectively fight against radicalization, but some states failed to intercept the infiltration of the ISIS militants from Afghanistan into the region. Russian intelligence also failed to intercept infiltration of the ISIS terrorist groups fighters into Russia by different means. The power structures, social institutions and local authorities of Central Asian states are unable to work with radical Islamic groups. Analyst Uran Botobekov has also warned that the presence of Central Asian minors in Daesh ranks might possibly cause huge fatalities when they translate their ideologies into violent actions: "According to the special services of Kyrgyzstan, about 140 minors have been taken from Kyrgyzstan to training camps in Iraq and Syria. The vast majority of children are under the age of 14, with an estimated 85 children under the age of 10. Authorities have not reported how many children have come to the Islamic State from Kazakhstan, Tajikistan, Turkmenistan, and Uzbekistan. According to human rights organizations, more than 600 children from Central Asia are in ISIS-controlled areas of Iraq and Syria. Most children were brought into the conflict zone by their parents. According to various estimates, there are 4,000 Central Asians fighting with various groups in Iraq and Syria. Estimates of the number of children from the former republics of the Soviet Union vary, and no one can pinpoint the exact number".[9]

Aside from an Islamic State-linked attack on foreign cyclists, Tajikistan had largely been spared from significant attacks by both international terrorist organizations and radicalized individuals. The ISIS recruitment of Tajikistanis relied heavily on the glorification of celebrity jihadist commanders. Despite this, ISIS recruitment in Tajikistan is perhaps the least organized of all the Central Asian states as they are fighting for ISIS. Tajikistan government restricted religious freedom to an exceptional degree. All but 500 to 1,000 ethnic Uzbekistanis were also fighting in Syria during 2015, with a majority of them believed to be from Southern Kyrgyzstan. However, more than 400 to 500 Islamist fighters with ties to Uzbekistan participated in the battlefields of Syria and Iraq.

Chechen extremist groups have also consistently expressed the desire to obtain, build, and utilize unconventional devices against selected targets, and have innovated by incorporating hazardous materials into their ordnance. The war in Syria and Iraq has significantly altered modern terrorism, with radical Islamic militants from Central Asia being no exception. The terrorists' method for recruiting forces is almost the same in most countries in Central Asia. The majority of ISIS recruits originate in the Middle East, the Maghreb, and Western Europe. Central Asia is the third-largest source of foreign fighters in Syria. More than 4,000 Central Asian fighters were believed to have joined armed groups fighting in Syria, with an estimated 2,500 arriving there in 2014 and early 2015 alone. Russian President Vladimir Putin once stated that as many as 7,000 fighters from Russia and Central Asia have joined the ranks of the Islamic State. There is evidence that terrorist groups tried to acquire the material needed to construct a crude nuclear explosive device, or a dirty bomb. Terrorists use biological agents because they are often difficult to detect. In 2016, after the two ISIS brothers involved in the Brussels bombings, Khalid and Ibrahim el-Bakraoui, were killed and captured, authorities discovered they had been secretly watching a Belgian nuclear scientist who worked at the Tihange Nuclear Power Station.

Nuclear terrorism remains a constant threat to global peace. Access of terrorist organizations to nuclear material is a bigger threat to civilian population. Terrorist groups can gain access to highly enriched uranium or plutonium because they have the potential to create and detonate an improvised nuclear device. Since ISIS has already retrieved nuclear materials from Mosul city of Iraq, we can assert that terrorist groups like ISIS and Katibat Imam Bukhari, and Chechen extremist groups can make access to biological and nuclear weapons with the help of local experts. Nuclear facilities also often store large amounts of radioactive material, spent fuel, and other nuclear waste products that terrorists could use in a dirty bomb. Without access to such fissile materials, extremist and radicalized groups can turn their attention toward building a simple radiological device.

The most difficult part of making a nuclear bomb is acquiring the nuclear material, but some Muslim and non-Muslim states might facilitate the ISIS, Lashkar-e-Toiba, Chechen extremist groups and Afghanistan and Pakistan based groups to attack nuclear installations in Russia and Central Asia. Experts and analysts, Professor of Science and International Security at King's College London, Christopher Hobbs, Director of the Stimson Centre Nuclear Security Program Nickolas Roth and, Fellow at the Centre for Science and Security Studies (CSSS) at King's College London, Daniel Salisbury in their research paper (Security under Strain? Protecting Nuclear Materials during the Coronavirus Pandemic, the RUSI Journal, Volume 166, Issue 213, April, 2021) have highlighted vulnerability of nuclear weapons, nuclear installation, and concern of states and nuclear organizations:

"The pandemic's rapid onset and global impact unsurprisingly generated an initial sense of trepidation within the nuclear industry, raising concerns about the ability of organisations to deliver key services in a safe and secure manner while also ensuring the health and welfare of their staff. For example, in May 2020, Alexey Likhachev, chief executive of Rosatom, one of the world's largest nuclear companies, emphasised 'the direct threat' the pandemic posed to Russia's nuclear towns. While Faradally A. Ollite, Director General of Radiation Safety and Nuclear Security Authority in Mauritius, noted 'the COVID-19 situation is an unprecedented situation, for which the [national] regulatory body was not fully prepared'. Similar concerns were echoed by many others regarding the potential for diminished operator capacity, delay of key services, financial uncertainty, reduced regulatory oversight and supply chain shortages. The diversity of activities involving nuclear and radiological materials, as well as different national and organisational strategies for responding to the pandemic, makes it difficult to draw broad conclusions on its impact......Most nuclear organisations have not made public detailed Covid-19 infection numbers of their workforces, although those that have demonstrate how even relatively small numbers of cases can have a significant impact on operations. For example, in May 2020, over 200 infections were reported at the Fermi-2 nuclear power reactor in Michigan during the midst of a planned refuelling and maintenance outage. This resulted in the outage being temporarily paused while additional measures were put in place in an effort to protect the health of workers".

In 2013, chemical attacks in the outskirts of Damascus posed a direct threat to all Arab states, and forced the UN Security Council to adopt a resolution on chemical weapons in Syria. The international operation of transporting components of these weapons out of Syria was completed in the first half of 2014.[10] In 2015, ISIS tried to gain access to these weapons and used chlorine bombs for terrorist activities in Iraq and Syria. On 06 January 2015, cases of ISIS using chemical weapons in Iraq and Syria emerged. These chemical attacks illustrated that ISIS and the Syrian opposition chased to use chemical weapons preferentially in Iraq and Syria. In Russia and Central Asia, ISIS is seeking these weapons to use against the armed forces of the region. In one of its issues, the magazine (Dabiq), claimed that Islamic State sought to buy nuclear weapons from Pakistan but experts viewed this claim as baseless. Since the beginning of 2017, a string of jihadist terrorist attacks involved Central Asian citizens, mainly of Uzbek and Kirgiz origin. Russia's Federal Security Service (FSB) detained near Moscow Abrar Azimov from former Soviet Central Asia, born in 1990. He was accused as one of the organizers of the attack, and the one who had trained Jalilov.[11] However, Azimov refused to admit his guilt in court during the hearing. By the end of April, the FSB arrested 12 people of Central Asian descent in the Kaliningrad region suspected of involvement with the Jihad-Jamaat Mujahedin extremist group. The alleged leader of the cell was placed by Uzbekistan on a wanted list for extremist crimes.

However, as mentioned earlier, thousands of women from Pakistan, Afghanistan, and possibly from Central Asia have joined the ISIS Sialkot camp for jihad-bil-Nkah. Mr. Uran Botobekov (The Central Asian Women on the Frontline of Jihad: While ISIS draws in men to fight, it draws women to serve, marry, and remarry. The Diplomat, January 10, 2017) has also reported the presence of Central Asian women in Syria and Iraq: "Based on 2014 and 2015 data, there were around 1,000 women from Central Asia in Iraq and Syria's combat zones. According to Indira Dzholdubaeva, prosecutor-general of the Kyrgyz Republic, there are over 120 Kyrgyz women in Syria and Iraq. Chairman of the National Security Committee (KNB) of Kazakhstan, Nurtay Abykaev, has said there were 150 Kazakh women in ISIS ranks in Syria. The authorities of Uzbekistan, meanwhile, have said that up to 500 Uzbek women are in Syria, Iraq, and Afghanistan with various groups. The Ministry of the Interior of Tajikistan claims that over 200 Tajik women have gone to the war zones in Syria together with their husbands."[12] Moreover, analyst and expert of current affairs, Nick Mucerino (The threat to Russia from Islamic State returnees. Global Risk Insights, 05 November 2018) has noted the threat to Russia from Islamic State returnees from Syria, Iraq, Pakistan and Afghanistan:

"The threat posed by Russian speaking fighters who travelled to fight under the Islamic State in Syria presents a complicated problem for both Russia and its allies to address. Just like its Western counterparts, Russia is worried that these returnees will mount deadly attacks on the country's soil. The danger presented by Russian speaking foreign fighters loyal to the Islamic State is not lost on the Kremlin. Since its emergence during Syria's civil war in 2013, Russians and Russian speaking nationals from the former Soviet Union have been a prominent presence among the terror group's fighters. In February 2017, President Vladimir Putin, citing security service figures, stated that approximately 4,000 Russian citizens and 5,000 from Central Asia followed ISIS' appeals for aid. Many took part in helping to establish its 'caliphate', or the proto-state it carved out of the lands ISIS seized from Iraq and Syria. This figure is the largest in Europe and even outnumbers the citizens from Arab states including Saudi Arabia and Tunisia, who travelled to join the Group. The large presence of Russian speakers is further reflected in the fact that it is the second most common language among ISIS fighters and several of its top commanders belong to the former USSR. Independent security experts have estimated that about 400 of those fighters have already returned to Russia after fighting in Syria".[13]

Biological agents are used by terrorists to attain their social or political goals and are used for killing or injuring people, plants and animals. Response of Europe to the threat of future bioterrorism seems limited due to the political and economic reservations of some member states. The approach to searching for biological agents at airports and shipping container entry points, and promoting bio-hazard awareness raised several important questions. Biological terrorism can be loosely categorized based on the agent used. The virus threat includes smallpox, influenza, dengue fever, yellow fever, Rift Valley fever, and haemorrhagic fevers like Lassa, Ebola, and Marburg. Smallpox spreads directly from person to person. The third category of bio-threat is 'bacteria', which includes anthrax, plague, and cholera. There are numerous reports on the genetic development of viruses by some states to use it and achieve their political and economic goal.

One of these reports on insect war is the investigative report of Bulgarian investigative journalist and Middle East correspondent, Dilyana Gaytandzhieva (12 September 2018), who published a series of reports. Her current work focuses on war crimes and illicit arms exports to war zones around the world. Dilyana Gaytandzhieva is an investigative journalist who has published a series of papers and articles in various journals and newspapers. She views the US army as master of deadly viruses, bacteria and toxins in direct violation of the UN Convention on the prohibition of Biological Weapons. The Alternative World Website and Zodlike Productions, a news forum, has published her fresh analysis of future insect war. She has painted a consternating picture of US insect war in her investigative report, and warns that the prospect of biological terrorism is consternating:

"Pentagon's scientists have been deployed in 25 countries and given diplomatic immunity to research deadly viruses, bacteria and toxins at US military offshore bio laboratories under a $2.1 billion DOD program.

Afghanistan is one of 25 countries across the world with Pentagon bio-laboratories on their territory. The project in Afghanistan is part of the US bio-defense program – Cooperative Biological Engagement Program (CBEP), which is funded by the Defense Threat Reduction Agency (DTRA). The DTRA contractors, working at The Lugar Centre in Georgia, CH2M Hill and Battelle have also been contracted for the program in Afghanistan. CH2M Hill has been awarded a $10.4 million contract (2013-2017). The Pentagon contractors in Afghanistan and Georgia are the same, and so are the diseases which are spreading among the local population in both countries. The US Embassy to Tbilisi transports frozen human blood and pathogens as diplomatic cargo for a secret US military program. Internal documents, implicating US diplomats in the transportation of and experimenting on pathogens under diplomatic cover were leaked to me by Georgian insiders".[14]

According to these documents, Pentagon scientists have been deployed to the Republic of Georgia and have been given diplomatic immunity to research deadly diseases and biting insects at the Lugar Center–the Pentagon bio-laboratory in Georgia's capital Tbilisi. In 2014, the Lugar Center was equipped with an insect facility and launched a project on Sand Flies in Georgia and the Caucasus. In 2014-2015 sand fly species were collected under another project "Surveillance Work on Acute Febrile Illness" and all (female) sand flies were tested to determine their infectivity rate. A third project, also including sand flies collection, studied the characteristics of their salivary glands. Sand flies carry dangerous parasites in their saliva which they can transmit to humans through a bite. As a result, Tbilisi has been infested with biting flies since 2015."[15]

Chapter 4

The United States Proxies and Prospect of Nuclear War

The threat of nuclear weapons theft and bioterrorism in South Asia once again came under discussion in the international press. Terrorist organisations in both Pakistan and India want to retrieve biotechnology, or nuclear weapons to use them against civilians and security forces. Recent border skirmishes between Pakistan and India, cloud of civil war in Afghanistan, and the emergence of Islamic State of Iraq and Syria (ISIS), presence of terrorist organisations in the Arab world, further justified the possibilities of complex threat of chemical and biological terrorism. As Pakistan and Afghanistan have been victims of war on terrorism and Talibanisation during the last three decades, establishment of ISIS networks in South Asia may possibly change the traditional concept of terrorism and insurgency in the region. On 05 May 2021, Indian police recovered 7.1 kilograms of uranium from two smugglers. On 03 June 2021, police also arrested seven smugglers and seized 6.4 kilograms of uranium, which caused consternation in South Asia. The increasing incidents of nuclear trafficking in India have rung alarm bells across South Asia. Pakistan called on the world community to take notice of nuclear trafficking in India.

In 2003, Indian army arrested some members of a jihadist group, Jamaat-ul-Mujahideen in connection of uranium theft. In 2009, an employee of an Indian nuclear reactor poisoned dozens of his colleagues with a radioactive isotope. In 2018, a uranium smuggling group was arrested in Kolkata, they were trying to sell uranium worth about $440,000.[1] Recent warning of the Putin administration against the US low-yield is understandable from the fact the US army will intentionally use nuclear weapons against Russia and China in near future. On 29 April 2020; VOA reported reaction of Russian Foreign Ministry to the State Department paper's assertion that the low-yield weapons "reduce the risk of nuclear war by reinforcing extended deterrence and assurance".[2] Moreover, Federation of American Scientists warned (January 2020) that the U.S. Navy had deployed for the first time a submarine armed with a low-yield Trident Nuclear Warhead. However, on 16 April 2020, Associated Press reported Chinese Foreign Ministry response to the allegations of U.S. State Department report about the country's secret nuclear test: "China has always performed its international obligations and commitments in a responsible manner, firmly upheld multilateralism, and actively carried out international cooperation," Foreign Minister Spokeswoman said.[3]

The Trump administration has been in deep trouble since the test of Russia's anti-satellite missiles and its defeat in Afghanistan. NATO and the United States issued warning of the Russian hybrid war in Europe, but they continued to destabilise the Middle East and Central Asia, and used nuclear and biological weapons in Iraq and Afghanistan. However, the EU member states are well aware of their security and friendship with Russia by extending their hand of cooperation due to the hegemonic attitude of the former Trump administration. In this big strategic game, Russians and Americans have the same reason for modernizing their nuclear forces. In the past, President Vladimir Putin developed modern weapons and restored Russia's real place in the international community. Since Russia seized Crimea in 2014, Russians have begun to build basing sites for their advanced systems, including the Iskanders, but nuclear experts warned that if Russia deploys nuclear weapons there, it will spark complex problems. Analyst Scott Ritter (RT News, 28 April 2020) highlighted the START and complication of US and Russia's inventions of modern technologies and weapons, which will exacerbate the process of nuclear war preparations:

> "Both the US and Russia are engaged in the early stages of developing new strategic nuclear weapons to replace older systems. These weapons, which will cost trillions of dollars to develop and deploy, are with few exceptions still many years away from entering into service. A five-year extension of New START would provide both nations time to reach an agreement which responsibly addresses the need for strategic nuclear force modernization while continuing the past practice of seeking additional cuts in their respective nuclear arsenals........China's intransigence runs counter to the official US position, most recently articulated in a State Department report sent to Congress regarding Russian compliance with the New START Treaty. While the report finds that Russia is complying with its treaty obligations, the treaty does not cover enough Russian strategic systems, including several that have been previously announced by

President Putin, and leaves China to operate with no restrictions in terms of the size and scope of its strategic nuclear arsenal".[4]

Perhaps, China is also preparing to build new missile technology, expand anti-satellite capabilities and increase nuclear material production. The question is how China can use nuclear weapons as the country maintains a policy of peaceful coexistence? In 2019, its Defence White Paper noted the country stuck to the policy of no first use of nuclear weapons at any time and under any circumstances, but recent hostile nuclear environment has forced the country to deploy a nuclear triad of strategic land, sea, and air-launched nuclear systems to defend its territorial integrity and national security. Despite the progress made by international conventions, biological and chemical weapons are still a precarious threat in Europe and Central Asia. In his Asia Times article, Richard Javad Heydarian (25 May 2020) has noted the US and China confrontations, quoted Pentagon report about the attitude of the Chinese government:

"In a recent report to the US Congress entitled "United States Strategic Approach to the People's Republic of China", Trump's White House argues that "Beijing contradicts its rhetoric and flouts its commitments to its neighbours by engaging in provocative and coercive military and paramilitary activities in the Yellow Sea, the East and South China Seas, the Taiwan Strait, and Sino-Indian border areas." Submitted in compliance with the National Defence Authorization Act 2019, which mandates a comprehensive approach to dealing with China's perceived threat, the report warned that China has shown "the willingness and capacity...to employ intimidation and coercion in its attempts to eliminate perceived threats to its interests and advance its strategic objectives globally." Portraying Beijing as an expansionist power, the report also argues that China's recent behaviour in the South China Sea and other contested waters "belie Chinese leaders' proclamations that they oppose the threat or use of force, do not intervene in other countries' internal affairs, or are committed to resolving disputes through peaceful dialogue." As part of a broader containment strategy, the US is also seeking the support of other regional powers including India to ring-fence China's naval ambitions in the South China Sea and beyond."[6]

In Europe, there is a general perception that ISIS has already used some dangerous gases in Iraq. Therefore, it can use biological weapons against civilian populations in Pakistan. If control over these weapons is weak, or if their components are available in the open market, there would be huge destruction in the region. In July 2014, the government of Iraq notified that nuclear material had been seized by the ISIS army from Mosul University. ISIS had a 19-page document in Arabic on how to develop biological weapons, and a 26-page religious fatwa that allows the use of weapons of mass destruction. "If Muslims cannot defeat the kafir (non-believers) in a different way, it is permissible to use weapons of mass destruction," warns the fatwa. The effects of chemical weapons are worse as they cause death or incapacitation, while biological weapons cause death or disease in humans. Notwithstanding all these preventive measures, the threat of chemical or biological warfare persists. Pakistan noted in its statement to the Meeting of States Parties in December 2013: "Pakistan ratified the Biological and Toxic Weapons Convention (BTWC) in 1974 as a non-possessor state and remains fully committed to implementing all provisions of the convention."

Nuclear experts warned that terrorists and extremist organisations operating in South Asia must be prevented from gaining access to weapons of mass destruction and from perpetrating atrocious acts of nuclear terrorism. India and Pakistan have applied professional measures to protect their nuclear weapons sites but nuclear proliferation still poses a grave threat to the national security of all South Asian states. Military experts and policymakers have also expressed deep concerns that if the two nuclear-capable states purvey explosives to their favourite terror groups, it might cause huge destruction and casualties for the civilian populations and military installations. Recent events in Pakistan and India have raised the prospect of extremist and jihadist groups using biological, radiological and chemical attacks against military installations and critical national infrastructure in both states. The two states are vulnerable to such attacks by the Taliban and Islamic State (ISIS).

On 09 June 2014, when terrorists attacked Karachi airport and killed two military officers of the Pakistan army, the government stepped up security around nuclear installations across the country — what I had warned in my article published in *Daily Times* on 03 October 2013, became a reality. This was a fresh warning from terrorists and radicalised elements and those whose relatives have been killed or tortured in the military operations in Balochistan, FATA and Waziristan during the last ten years. The terrorist attack on Karachi airport showed that Pakistan's intelligence had badly failed to provide true information about terrorist networks in Karachi. This attack also highlighted the military capability of the Taliban and exposed the gap in the country's security apparatus. After this attack, Pakistanis were apprehensive about possible daring attacks against the country's nuclear installations. The terrorists yet again exposed the failure of the security agencies. This is a clear challenge for the SPD of the armed forces, which has deployed 25,000 nuclear forces around nuclear facilities.[7]

In yesteryears, terrorists attacked Pakistan's nuclear installations. In 2007, terrorists attacked two air force facilities in Sargodha, associated with nuclear installations. On August 21, 2008, terrorists attacked the Ordnance factories in Wah. In July 2009, a suicide bomber struck a bus that might have been carrying A Q Khan Research Laboratory scientists. Moreover, two attacks by Baloch militants on suspected Atomic Energy Commission facilities in Dera Ghazi Khan have also drawn international attention to the security of the country's nuclear installations. On October 10, 2009, nine terrorists, dressed in army uniform, attacked the GHQ. In June 2014, two suicide bombers killed high ranking military officers linked to Pakistan's nuclear programme in Fateh Jang.[8]

The fatalities of dengue and Ebola viruses in Pakistan and West Africa are the worst forms of bioterrorism. In 2011, Pakistan Medical Association called on the ISI to investigate fears of the deliberate spread of the deadly disease in Punjab. There were speculations that, in future, measles, dengue, polio and the Ebola viruses can be used as weapons of bioterrorism in Pakistan. Some states might use drones for the purposes of bio-war against their rival states. In 2013, writing in the Global Policy Journal, Amanda M. Teckman warned that ISIS might possibly use Ebola as a weapon against civilian population: "It remains to be seen if a terrorist group like IS, which has demonstrated a willingness to engage in large scale mass murder, including the uninhibited murder of civilians, has the capability to produce a weaponised version of Ebola." The University of Birmingham Policy Commission Report warned that terrorists could also turn remotely piloted aircraft into flying bombs by hooking them up to improvised explosive devices. Sir David, a former British intelligence researcher, warned that drones had gained a reputation as unaccountable killing machines because of their widespread use in the US's controversial anti-terrorist campaigns in Pakistan, Yemen and Somalia.[6]

According to Russia's new military doctrine, the possibility of limited uses of nuclear weapons at the tactical and operational levels and of chemical and biological weapons is possible. As the United States and NATO have established biological weapons laboratories in Central Asia and Afghanistan and used these weapons against civilian populations, Russian military leadership has taken these developments seriously. New CBRN defines vehicles and equipment that can be used in the fight against coronavirus. Its forces have also undertaken more CBRN training to the future war effectively. The danger from these weapons is so consternating, and the dirty bomb material and its fatalities diverted the attention of terrorist groups to biological weapons. Smuggling of nuclear weapons is a serious challenge in Europe and Central Asia, while smuggling of these weapons in Africa and Europe has threatened the security of the region.

The terror attacks in Brussels also punctuated the issue of nuclear security, when Belgian authorities discovered ISIS was conducting surveillance of a local nuclear scientist and his family. The fear of Pakistani nuclear weapons falling into terrorists' hands has existed since the 1990s. In an article in New York Times in April 2017, Rahmatullah Nabil, the former head of Afghan intelligence, claimed that Pakistan's internal classified documents had expressed concerns regarding terrorists' threats to the country's nuclear assets.[9] However, on 18 May 2020, TASS News reported Russian Deputy Foreign Minister Sergey Ryabkov that the deployment of US land-based intermediate-and shorter-range missiles in Europe after their deployment in the Asia-Pacific region was possible:

"However, in their reply, they let us know that they did not intend to follow our example and would not introduce a moratorium on the deployment of their new missiles. By all indications, their corresponding test programs will be activated in the short term and subsequently, such systems may begin to be deployed on the ground," Ryabkov said. On August 2, 2019, the Intermediate-Range Nuclear Forces (INF) Treaty was officially terminated at the US initiative.[11] The US claimed that its actions were provoked by Russia's refusal to comply with the American ultimatum-like demand to eliminate the new 9M729 cruise missiles, which, as Washington and its NATO allies believe, violate the INF Treaty.[10] Moreover, on 18 May 2020, RT News reported an escalation of US-China hostility. However, TAAS news agency reported deployment of a batch of six Project 22800 missile corvettes, armed with the Kalibr cruise missiles in the Baltic Fleet:

"Soon, the surface part of the Baltic Fleet will be reinforced with a batch of six Project 22800 missile corvettes. Four of them will carry a naval version of the Pantsir system. Odintsovo will become the first one, the Pantsir system will undergo testing on this ship," the Commander's congratulatory telegram to the sailors, dedicated to the Fleet's 317th anniversary, says, according to the Fleet press service. The Project 22800 corvettes are equipped with Kalibr cruise missiles, modern control, radio, navigation, electronic warfare systems, counter-diversion armaments, man-portable air-defense systems. The ships are designed to act either as part of naval groups or on their own.[11]

South Asian states are facing the threat of terrorism and violent extremism. The unending civil war in Afghanistan and Pakistan has destabilised the whole region. Terrorism in Afghanistan affects Pakistan and Iran, its heat touches the Iranian border while the flames are clearly seen in China and Russia as well. As South Asian states have been embroiled in protracted conflicts for decades, the lack of proper strategies to counter the TTP, ISIS and Indian extremism, and the clash of interests, have further aggravated the problem. The debate about bioterrorism is not entirely new in the region because both Pakistan and India have developed these weapons to use them in a future war. The Indian government has recognised the threat from bioweapons as real and imminent. Both the Ministry of Defence and the Ministry of Home affairs placed a high priority on this issue. India understands that Pakistan-based terrorist groups may possibly use these weapons in Kashmir in the near future. Pakistan too, has expressed deep concern about the use of these weapons against its security forces either by the Taliban or Baloch insurgents. The emergence of recent polio and bird flu cases in Pakistan is the primary warning of danger. The nucleation of my debate on nuclear terrorism is that, once the TTP or other terrorist group steals biological and nuclear weapons, they will use them against military and nuclear installations. National security experts in the UK and US believe that the most likely terrorists to obtain a nuclear bomb will not be to steal or purchase a fully operational device but to buy fissile material and construct their own.

Chapter 5

Pakistan's Nuclear Technology and Non-Nuclear States in South Asia, Middle East and South-East Asia

Over the past decades, longstanding concerns over nuclear proliferation have become increasingly acute in light of a number of worrisome developments, including the status of India and Pakistan as an overt nuclear-weapon state."[1] The continued nuclear weapons build-up in India and Pakistan, and their unnecessary confrontation on Kashmir is a threat to the peace and stability of South Asia. Recent threats of using nuclear weapons against each other has prompted deep anxiety in the neighbouring states that the use of nuclear bombs would also affect their social, economic and health sectors. In the contemporary geopolitical landscape, the greatest threat of nuclear exchange between the two states has created a climate of fear as they possess significant nuclear arsenals consisting of short and intermediate range ballistic missiles as well as nuclear-capable aircraft. Mahmudul Huque (01 February 2020) highlighted confrontation between the two states:

> "Their eventual nuclearization gave them the status of nuclear states which constituted a significant erosion of the non-proliferation norms as stipulated by both these treaties aimed at nuclear disarmament. Pakistan's position in this regard was quite straightforward, offering to sign the treaties if India did the same. New Delhi, however, looked upon the NPT regime as discriminatory as it formalized two categories of states in the world: the legitimate nuclear weapons states (NWS) and the non-nuclear weapons states (NNWS). India considers the NPT regime as a "thinly disguised form of 'nuclear apartheid,' intended to ensure the dominance of the few over the many in the international system." India also considered Pakistan's offer to sign the NPT a bluff. But, according to the Asia Society Study Group Report, "it is a bluff

New Delhi has been unwilling to call." The perennial India-Pakistan hostility over Kashmir is one of the major reasons for India-Pakistan arms race—whether conventional or nuclear. India's enmity with China, especially after its defeat in the 1962 Sino-India War, is also a great security concern for New Delhi."[2]

In June 2015, Indian security forces carried out military operations against insurgents in Myanmar, which caused tension between India and Pakistan when Indian leaders warned that it could happen in Pakistan as well. Prime Minister Nawaz Sharif and Defence Minister Khwaja Asif responded with strong words. Asif warned India that Pakistan was a nuclear state and the country does not maintain a nuclear bomb just to use it as a firecracker. "If forced into war by India, Pakistan will respond in a befitting manner; our arms are not meant for decoration," he said. Former President General Musharraf also responded aggressively in turn, saying that Pakistan would adopt a tit-for-tat approach and would react immediately: "Don't attack us, don't challenge our territorial integrity because we are not a small power, we are a major nuclear power."[3]

The issue of nuclear terrorism in South Asia has become very complicated as both India and Pakistan threaten each other with an attack by nuclear weapons. On 28 February 2015, the US government warned about the possibility of an Indian nuclear attack on Pakistan if terrorists attacked India. Recently, in the US Senate, government officials and researchers warned that in case of an Indian attack, Pakistan would use nuclear weapons against the country. "South Asia is the most likely place nuclear weapons could be detonated in the foreseeable future. This risk derives from the unusual dynamic of the India-Pakistan competition," Carnegie researcher Perkovich said.

However, General Khalid Kidwai, a former Director-General of the Strategic Planning Division of Pakistan remarked that Pakistan had enough nuclear weapons to ensure that a war in the subcontinent was no longer an option. His remarks appeared to suggest that the nuclear deterrence debate in this region has been settled. General Kidwai implicitly acknowledged that Pakistan used extremist groups as foreign policy instruments. He blamed the crisis in Kashmir and Afghanistan to justify Pakistan's actions. Deterrence is not a condition achieved from simply possessing nuclear weapons; it is based on the perception of military power in general. Nuclear weapons drastically enhance a state's strength by creating the capacity to cause catastrophic amounts of damage in a very short period of time, with strikes that are largely indefensible. Mahmudul Huque (01 February 2021.)

noted the weaknesses of both states to end the crisis. However, he views this unending confrontation as an evolving threat of nuclear war:

"In South Asia, Pakistan is the revisionist power and would start the conflict to upset the status quo." This analyst points out a very potent flaw in Pakistan's drawing the red-line at which India should stop or otherwise be prepared for Pakistan's nuclear reprisal. As he mentions, "India does not know really where this mythical line called the nuclear threshold is situated and would disbelieve any 'early' attempt by Pakistan to declare that the threshold has been reached. This is exactly what happened during the Kargil crisis when junior ministers in Pakistan were obviously primed to say that the threshold had been reached." Flaws of Deterrence Therefore, based on the experiences of the India-Pakistan conflicts that occurred after the two countries became nuclear capable one cannot rule out the possibility of a nuclear exchange between the two countries. Their doctrinal preferences, engendering mutual miscalculations, reinforce this danger. Moreover, deterrence is far from fool-proof in South Asia. Particularly, Pakistan's reliance on preventing Indian conventional attack with nuclear deterrence may prove dangerous. If India crosses the Pakistani thresholds, even unintentionally, and Pakistan uses nuclear weapons, the latter is certain to retaliate in kind and inflict unacceptable damage on Pakistan. Indian doctrine emphasizes a retaliatory strike against any nuclear attack. Such a situation will jeopardize Pakistan's physical existence given its size and lack of strategic depth. Precisely what was the message the then Indian Defence Minister George Fernandes conveyed at the onset of the 2001-2 crisis? Warning Pakistan not to consider the use of nuclear weapons, he said: "We could take a strike, survive, and then hit back.... Pakistan would be finished."[4]

Construction of new nuclear power plants in Pakistan raised some questions that by expanding its nuclear installations network, Pakistan does not comply with the principles of the International Atomic Energy Agency (IAEA) non-proliferation policy. Having ignored international concerns on nuclear power plants, the Environmental Protection Agency of Sindh province approved the twin nuclear project and allowed its construction. Now, as both the states are nuclear powers, Pakistan recognises that terrorist attacks from its territory against India are not in its interest. In fact, the access of terrorist groups to fissile materials in both states is evident from the fact that the safety and security of nuclear sites in India is not satisfactory. The same question arises in Pakistan, where party politics in the Atomic Energy Commission and a lack of civilian oversight has received deep criticism from world's media.

The threat of chemical, biological and nuclear terrorism in South Asia also causes deep frustration and anxiety, as the region hosts many militant organisations. These groups have already learnt techniques of making nuclear explosive devices and the illegal transactions of poorly protected materials remain a threat. The Subcontinent is the most volatile region because India and Pakistan are engaged in a dangerous nuclear arms race. India is enjoying conventional superiority. The addition of a nuclear dimension to this conflict is a matter of great concern. India's National Security Advisor admitted in one of his recent speeches that a fourth-generation war is being fought against Pakistan with different tactics and dimensions. Strategically speaking, India and Pakistan have their own threat perceptions, which are quite similar. India wants to be a strong nuclear state because of its fear of Chinese aggression, while Pakistan also needs nuclear weapons because of its fear of Indian aggression. China helps Pakistan in upgrading its nuclear weapons and provides sophisticated weapons to the country's army, while the US helps India.

The misinterpretation of each other's motives has also caused misunderstandings. First, they threaten each other with nuclear bombs and then assess the consequences and fatalities. This issue has also been highlighted in a recently published book by Nathan E Busch: "Due to continual mistrust between the two countries, each would be likely to misinterpret military movements, missiles tests, or accidental detonations as an impending attack by the other side. The risks of misinterpreting each other's motives are compounded by the vulnerabilities of their nuclear forces and the short flight times of the forces to key targets."[5] The jihadist organisations in South Asia, and even the Islamic State (ISIS) and Taliban, have already demonstrated their interest in retrieving chemical and nuclear weapons, but at present, there is no evidence of their attempts to get access to these weapons. ISIS recently claimed that it was engaged with Pakistan for nuclear weapons delivery, but this cannot be confirmed through any research papers or news reports. There are confirmed reports that ISIS retrieved chemical weapons from Iraq, while jihadist groups in South Asia are struggling to obtain chemical weapons capability.

Pakistani Prime Minister Imran Khan who handed his government to militablishment wants a nuclear war between India and Pakistan. In his General Assembly speech, he warned the UN of potential nuclear war in Kashmir. Imran Khan warned that the move was driven by the Hindu nationalist ideology of the Indian Prime Minister Narendra Modi, whom he called a "fascist". The Muslim-majority territory is currently under heightened security, while mobile and internet services have been cut, but Prime Minister Khan predicted a popular backlash once such measures are lifted. "They'll come out on the streets. What happens then?" Khan told journalists at the UN general assembly. He pointed to the presence of a 900,000-strong Indian force there currently enforcing security. "I fear there will be a massacre and things will start to go out of control," the Pakistani leader said. "My main reason for coming here was to meet world leaders at the UN and speak about this. We are heading for a potential disaster of proportions that no one here realises," Khan said. "It is the only time since the Cuban crisis that two nuclear-armed countries are coming face to face.[6]

Meanwhile, Mr. Khan said he had been asked by both the US and Saudi Arabia to act as a mediator with Iran. "President Trump asked me and also Prince Mohammed bin Salman asked me to speak to the Iranians, and we are trying our best that this should not develop into a conflict," Khan said. "The good thing about President Trump is that I feel he's not a pro-war person, although I can see that there are others who are egging him on. But his instinct, quite rightly, is not for war ... I think that's very admirable. Dawn reported"[7]

In January 2015, Islamic State (ISIS) announced the formation of another terrorist group named Islamic State of Khorasan (ISKP), which represents a Salafi school of thought and allegedly receives financial assistance from secret channels across the Durand Line. The membership of this newly established terrorist group in Afghanistan and Pakistan is more than 80,000 at present, but keeping in view its sphere of influence and operations, experts fear that the group's fast growing cadre can spread across South Asia in a relatively short space of time. The Islamic State of Khorasan has recently approached extremist sectarian groups of Pakistan for support, and distributed leaflets and other propaganda material in Pashtu, Urdu, and Persian languages to invite young people from different communities. This group also threatened India and Russia, and became a consecutive headache for Afghanistan. The group has established its networks in South and North Waziristan, Jalalabad, Kunar, and Nooristan province. Expert and analyst, Siddhartha Roy, (The Diplomat, 05 November 2019) has noted the threat of the emergence of the ISIS Khorasan terrorist group that has challenged authority of India and Pakistan governments, and recruits young fighters from both the states. The ISIS has formed another group for Kashmir as well named Ansar Ghazwat-ul-Hind (AGH) chat room

"Essentially, South Asia is witnessing the emergence of a new brand of terrorism. Unencumbered by the strings of foreign state influence, or the weight of partisan politics and regional status quos, the new jihadists of the Islamic State era are driven by a unifying dream that transcends individual leaders. Rooted as they are in the immediate issues of local politics, building as they may be on the fertile soil of long-festering discontent and systematic persecution, they're actively connecting local issues to global ones and building a platform that goes beyond the old demarcations of territorial fiefdoms followed by older jihadist groups. Both in life as a professional jihadi, and in death as a rebel martyr, Musa played by the rules of this new game: fluid allegiances and stubborn refusal to let any nation-state dictate the agenda of building the grandest state of them all — the global Islamic State — the Caliphate. A "home-grown" Indian Islamist, he was born Zakir Rashid Bhat in Noorpora in South Kashmir. He lived and studied in the state through high school. Then, like innumerable young Indian men from middle-class families, he gained admission to a private engineering college in 2011-12 — the Ram Devi Jindal College in Chandigarh. Academic straitjackets didn't suit him well. Dropping out barely a year from admission, he returned home to Kashmir and "disappeared." Get first-read access to major articles yet to be released, as well as links to thought-provoking commentaries and in-depth articles from our Asia-Pacific correspondents".[8]

High profile defections in the Afghan and Pakistani Taliban increased the strength of the group, and expanded its military blanket to remote areas of Afghanistan. Police and intelligence experts in Pakistan believe the networks of Islamic State (IS) in Balochistan, Khyber Pakhtunkhawa and parts of Punjab can at any time engage with security forces. Punjab is the centre of dozens of sectarian extremist groups operating with impunity. In July 2013, the TTP spokesman told BBC that the group had established its network in Syria with the help of Arab terrorists who fought in Afghan jihad in the 1980s. He also admitted that 12 Pakistani Taliban with expertise in information technology had gone to Syria in 2016. In Afghanistan, close cooperation between Daesh and some disgruntled Taliban groups has added to the pain of the Unity Government. The Khorasan terrorist group, which emerged with strong military power in 2015, is in control of important districts in Jalalabad province. The group's military tactics include beheading, public prosecution, kidnapping, and torture, looting and raping, and also forcing families from their homes. Kunwar Khuldune Shahid, (Islamic State Comes for South Asia: The Islamic State has completed its shift from the Middle East to South Asia. The Diplomat, June

18, 2019) has noted some violent aspects of the ISIS group in Afghanistan and Baluchistan and argued that some ISIS affiliated groups are also active in India:

"The two provinces have been carved out of the erstwhile Islamic State of Khorasan Province (ISKP), which encompassed the Af-Pak border region. ISKP, which was founded in January 2015, months after IS had announced its so called caliphate in the Iraq and Levant, spearheaded all activity in Afghanistan and Pakistan, and was the source of IS-affiliated militant activity in India as well. The two IS provinces in India and Pakistan were announced in the immediate aftermath of the group claiming responsibility for gun attacks on security forces in Shopian district of Indian-administered Kashmir. During the same week, IS claimed a similar gun attack in Mastung district of Pakistan's Baluchistan province. A month before the Islamic State's creation of the Wilayah Pakistan, the group bombed the Hazarjangi market in Baluchistan's capital of Quetta, killing 20 people. April's Quetta bombing targeted the Shia Hazara ethnic group, which, along with the local Christian community, has been regularly targeted by the Islamic State and its affiliates, in line with the ideological goal of purging religious minorities from areas it intends to occupy. Pakistan's Hazara community has been the Islamic State's most frequent targets, thanks to an almost two century-old history of violent persecution in the region owing to their Shia identity, and easily identifiable physical features owing to their Uzbek and Turkic ancestry. The presence of already marginalized religious communities, coupled with Baluchistan's multipronged volatility – owing to a Baloch separatist movement, jihadist turf wars, and a continuum of military operations – makes the province the ideal ground for IS. After having been driven out of the Middle East, it is in Balochistan that the Islamic State saw a pathway into South Asia."[9]

The influx of terrorist groups like Khorasan and Taliban in Jalalabad province has challenged the writ of the local administration. Former Afghan President Ghani had warned that 30 terrorist groups operating across the country posed a serious threat to the national security of Afghanistan. The UN experts also believed that more than 45,000 terrorists are fighting against the Afghan National army and between 20 to 25 percent are foreigners. Propaganda machine of the Islamic State (ISIS) was also causing a great concern for parents as their school going children become victim of the so called jihadist culture. The full body of Islamic State machine is strong as its radio stations, photographic reports, and bulletins are being circulated in different languages. The Internet is also the source of propaganda of the ISKP groups where experts of the group disseminate controversial information through videos and articles. Moreover, the group has challenged the presence of US and NATO forces in Afghanistan. The US and NATO also raised the question of foreign financial support to the terrorist group, and asked the Unity Government to positively respond to the brutalities and atrocities of the ISIS commanders. However, Daesh has also spread its evil tentacles to the North to control provinces bordering Russia and China. The group wants to infiltrate into Chinese Muslim province and parts of Central Asia and challenge the authority of local governments.

The emergence of Islamic State (ISIS) and its successful attacks against the Afghan security forces was considered a sign of the return of civil war to the country. Despite their drive to work together on national issues, President Ashraf Ghani and his partner Dr Abdullah were locked in an unnecessary battle for control of their war-torn country. There was a conflict amongst them regarding the appointments of Defence Minister, attorney general and the governor of Kabul Bank. The failure of the Afghan intelligence (NDS) to provide reliable information about the Taliban and ISIS's military strength raised serious questions about the credibility of the intelligence mechanism of the unity government and its international partners.

One of the important functions of an intelligence agency is to provide timely warnings of hostile military action in the battlefield. Unfortunately, NDS and the army intelligence corps could not provide immediate information about IS's attack on the Afghan national army camp in Badakhshan province. On April 16, 2015, governor of Balkh province accused the NDS of doing nothing to stop ISIS attacks on army posts. In an interview with Tolonews, Atta Muhammad Noor said that the National Directorate of Security (NDS) and the National Security Council (NSC) had received information two months prior to the planned attack on the attorney general's office in Mazar-e-Sharif, in which 19 people were killed, but they failed to take action.

The fate of 31 Hazara men and women kidnapped by ISIS remained uncertain. The NDS failed to determine the whereabouts of these people. President Ghani refused to deal with ISIS authorities regarding the fate of illegally incarcerated Hazaras. The presence of ISIS in Afghanistan's 17 provinces was a challenge for the Afghan army and intelligence agencies. The group operated within a strong intelligence network. It has employed military experts, espionage and geospatial intelligence professionals, and executes its plans and strategies via an efficient professional mechanism. The group uses various types of encryption software in its communications. In January 2015, Afghan army commanders in Ghazni and Paktia provinces warned that terrorists associated with ISIS had entered eastern Afghanistan posing as refugees. They revealed that more than 800 Arab, Pakistani and Chechen fighters had established recruitment camps in Zabul and Ghazni. On April 19, 2015, Tolonews reported that Paktika Governor Abdul Karim Mateen had said that the National Security Council of Bermal district had donated $200,000 to displaced families, which ended up in the pockets of IS fighters.

On April 12, 2015, ISIS forces killed more than 20 Afghan soldiers, beheaded 28 and kidnapped 10 others in Badakhshan province. Local Afghan army officials said that around 250 insurgents, including foreigners, had attacked the outpost. Some members of parliament told Tolonews that they would expose the NDS officials and military generals who had received millions of dollars from IS in Kabul. Sources in Kabul told me that the Badakhshan battalion commander had sold his military post to IS commanders. Thus, ISIS is now in control of 20 military posts in the region. Defence analyst Javed Kohistani said that more than 70 soldiers had been killed, taken captive or beheaded. He said that "the NDS was told about this a few days ago but, unfortunately, they did not pay attention to it".

Former Afghan Army Chief General Karimi blamed the commander of Shaheen Brigade, Azizullah Roufi, for criminal negligence: "Our battalion commander, without informing anyone, was in Kabul when the attack took place and now, he is under investigation." Moreover, the spokesman for the Afghan ministry of defence, Dawlat Waziri, accused local provincial officials for colluding with IS forces in Badakhshan and ultimately contributing to the massacre of Afghan troops. The police chief of Badakhshan also claimed that some local government officials, MPs and members of the provincial council had provided covert support to IS fighters. "One of the Taliban's commanders, known as Mr Abdullah, was wounded in Jurm district and was transported by a person who serves in the government," General Baba Jan told Tolonews. Now the story becomes more interesting and it is obvious from the aforementioned argument that both the Afghan and Pakistani governments and their armies do not have the authority to kill or arrest a single IS fighter within their territories.

On April 19, 2015, a member of the Afghan senate complained that in northern Afghanistan, an Afghan army commander had systematically left his post and weapons to the commanders of ISIS. Since ISIS was now in control of 20 check posts in Badakhshan, there were speculations that the theft of military equipment by ISIS fighters, during their attack on the military headquarters, feared to destabilise the region. The stolen equipment included eight ranger military vehicles, five armoured vehicles and six heavy weapons, including two DSHK heavy machine guns and two mortars. The spokesman of the Afghan Defence Ministry said that the Afghan army would never forgive those who killed its soldiers. On April 18, 2015, ISIS claimed to have carried out a deadly suicide attack in Jalalabad in which 40 people were and 125 injured.[10]

In light of the deteriorating security situation in the country, on April 15, 2015, Afghan lawmakers demanded resignation of President Ashraf Ghani, Chief Executive Dr. Abdullah and Army Chief General Sher Muhammad Karimi. The Interior Minister and intelligence chief were summoned to parliament to explain the facts of these killings. Because the unity government failed to respond to terrorist attacks against civilians and army units across the country, the former Minister of water and power, Mohammad Ismail Khan, warned that if the government does not resolve its own issues, it would face another war—this time with the notorious ISIS terrorist group. Khan said that "if the national unity government does not reach an agreement and does not bring stability and learn to tolerate each other, this will be a critical issue to us. We fear that another war with Daesh is looming but we hope that this will not happen."[11]

A document from Pakistan's Internal Security Policy (2014-2018) categorically stated that the country's security faces would prevent nuclear terrorism. The threat, according to the document's contents, is in addition to the possibility of chemical and biological terrorism. As the fatal war against terrorism has entered a crucial phase, another powerful extremist militant group (ISIS) has emerged with a strong and well-trained army in Afghanistan and parts of Pakistan to establish an Islamic state. The massacre of 100 innocent civilians, including an Afghan national army soldier in the Ajristan district of Ghazni province, Afghanistan by ISIS forces, and the brutal killings of children in the army school in Peshawar by Pakistan army special forces raised serious questions about the future of security and stability in South Asia. The Tehreek-e-Taliban Pakistan (TTP) claimed responsibility and called it a revenge attack for the Pakistan army's Operation Zarb-e-Azb in North Waziristan and FATA regions.

In October 2014, six leaders of the TTP announced their allegiance to ISIS. The ISIS propaganda material has begun to crop up in various parts of Pakistan. Secret networks of IS are in contact with different sectarian and political groups in Khyber Pakhtunkhwa province and receive financial assistance from business communities. The TTP commanders of Orakzai Agency, Kurram Agency, Khyber Agency, Peshawar and Hangu district have announced their allegiance to the IS military command.[12] The problem of nuclear and biological terrorism deserves special attention from the governments of Pakistan and Afghanistan because the army of ISIS can develop a dirty bomb in which explosives can be combined with a radioactive source like those commonly used in hospitals or extractive industries. The use of this weapon might have severe health effects, causing more disruption than destruction. Political and military circles in Pakistan fear that, as IS has already seized chemical weapons in Al Muthanna, in northern Iraq, some disgruntled retired military officers or experts in nuclear explosive devices might help the Pakistan chapter of the group deploy biological and chemical weapons. A letter by the Iraqi government to the UN warned that the militant-captured chemical weapons site contains 2,500 chemical rockets filled with the nerve agent Sarin.

The most recent pattern of intense attacks by Islamic State (ISIS) and its Taliban allies in Afghanistan put the credibility of Afghan unity government and its security forces into question. ISIS has become a potential threat, benefiting from the changing loyalties of ethnic groups in the north and sectarian groups in the south and southwestern parts of the country. The Ghani-Abdullah government was disunited on national counterterrorism strategy and stood at the crossroads. Both the chief executive and the president had different political priorities, which possibly caused their unsystematic approach to the ongoing, unbridled wave of terrorism. The international media carried stories on the presence of ISIS and its recruitment centres in Afghanistan and Pakistan, funded by the Taliban, sectarian groups, drug smugglers and radicalised business firms. This terrorist group also possessed a bigger challenge for the Afghan and Pakistani security forces. In September 2014, more than 800 members of the IS terrorist group stormed the Ajristan district of Ghazni province, killing 100 people, including the Afghan national army soldiers.

The ISIS, later on, established its headquarters in Ander district where it recruited male and female Afghans for the purpose of suicide attacks. The Afghan unity government was in deep crisis and worried that this terrorist group might turn its arms on Afghanistan's weak security forces under the IS's banner. The President had already banned new appointments in the Afghan army and police department, which caused more riddles. The Afghan army was shrinking and increasingly ramshackle by the day, while the police turned to drug trafficking as police personnel have not been paid their salaries for the last six months. A police officer from Helmand told this scribe that his force had refused to defend the country without salary. The police continue to sell their arms to Taliban and criminal militias.

They were in trouble. Their children suffered starvation and were living in rented houses. This inadvisable treatment of the police and Afghan army by the unity government served the interests of IS. Now, after the Ajristan massacre, there were speculations that IS had spread in Afghanistan and Pakistan. On November 18, the Daily Mail reported that a splinter group of Pakistan's Taliban pledged support to IS. The Jundullah group also announced its allegiance to the group. "They (IS) are our brothers, whatever plan they have, we will support them," said Jundullah spokesman Marwat. In Afghanistan's Baghlan province, the police arrested six Jundullah militants.[13]

The Daesh group is also in contact with Lashkar-e-Jhangvi (LeJ) and Lashkar-e-Taiba in Punjab. On December 11, 2014, former Interior Minister of Pakistan Mr Rehman Malik told a local news channel that IS had established recruitment centres in Gujranwala and Bahawalpur districts of Punjab province. The wall-chalking campaign and leaflets prompted fears about the terrorist group making inroads in the country. According to the leaked government circular in Balochistan and Khyber Pakhtunkhwa provinces, IS recruited more than 10,000 to 12,000 fighters for the next sectarian war in Pakistan. In Kabul, on December 8, 2014, Reuters reported that a 25-year-old student from Kabul University had vowed to join the mujahideen of IS. "When hundreds of foreigners, both men and women, leave their comfortable lives and embrace Daish, then why not us?" he asked.[14]

ISIS is trying to make inroads into Afghan educational institutions to retrieve the support of students. However, on the same day, the BBC reported that the Lal Masjid's seminary had announced its allegiance to ISIS. On December 13, 2014, in an interview with a local television channel, the chief of the Red Mosque, Maulana Abdul Aziz, confirmed the video message of his seminary students. In November 2014, Pakistan's National Counter Terrorism Agency (NACTA) warned that IS was spreading like a viral disease across the country while the group's leader, Abu Bakkar al-Baghdadi, appointed Abdul Rahim Muslim Dost as chief of its Khurasan chapter and started gearing up to muster the support of former jihadists. Abdul Rahim Muslim Dost (an Afghan national) was arrested by Pakistani agencies in Peshawar after the 9/11 terrorist attack in the US. After his release, he wrote a book (in Pashto language) against the brutalities and torture tactics of Pakistani agencies against detainees. No sooner had his book been released by a local publisher in Peshawar, the ISI arrested him again and disappeared for a long time. Later on, he was shifted to Guantanamo for three years.[15]

Chapter 6

Pakistan Nuclear Weapons – 2021

Hans M. Kristensen and Matt Korda

Abstract

The Nuclear Notebook is researched and written by Hans M. Kristensen, director of the Nuclear Information Project with the Federation of American Scientists, and Matt Korda, a research associate with the project. The Nuclear Notebook column has been published in the Bulletin of the Atomic Scientists since 1987. This issue's column examines Pakistan's nuclear arsenal, which may include approximately 165 warheads. The authors estimate that the country's stockpile could realistically grow to around 200 by 2025, if the current trend continues.

Keywords: Ballistic missiles, cruise missiles, delivery systems, nuclear weapons, Pakistan, Nuclear Notebook Pakistan continues to expand its nuclear arsenal with more warheads, more delivery systems, and a growing fissile material production industry. Analysis of a large number of commercial satellite images of Pakistani army garrisons and air force bases shows what appear to be newer launchers and facilities that might be related to the nuclear forces.

We estimate that Pakistan now has a nuclear weapons stockpile of approximately 165 warheads (See Table 1). The US Defense Intelligence Agency projected in 1999 that Pakistan would have 60 to 80 warheads by 2020 (US Defense Intelligence Agency 1999, 38), but several new weapon systems have been fielded and developed since then, which leads us to the higher estimate. The director of the U.S. Defense Intelligence Agency in April this year testified before Congress that Pakistan "likely will increase its nuclear stockpile in 2021" (Berrier 2021, 31).Table 1. Pakistani nuclear forces, 2021 (Table view)

Type/NATO designation	Number of launchers	Year deployed	Range[a] (kilometers)	Warhead x yield (kilotons)[b]	Number of warheads[c]
Aircraft[d]					
Mirage III/V	~36	1998	2,100	1 x 5–12 kt bomb (or Ra-ad)	~36
Subtotal:	**~36**				**~36**
Land-based ballistic missiles					
Abdali (Hatf-2)	10	2015	200	1 x 5–12 kt	10
Ghaznavi (Hatf-3)	~16	2004	300	1 x 5–12 kt	~16
Shaheen-1 (Hatf-4)	~16	2003	750	1 x 5–12 kt	~16
Shaheen-1A (Hatf-4)	-	(2022)	900	1 x 5–12 kt	-
Shaheen-2 (Hatf-6)	~16	2014	1,500	1 x 10–40 kt	~16
Shaheen-3 (Hatf-6)	-	(2022)	2,750	1 x 10–40 kt	-
Ghauri (Hatf-5)	~24	2003	1,250	1 x 10–40 kt	~24
NASR (Hatf-9)	~24	2013	60–70	1 x 12 kt	~24[e]
Ababeel (Hatf-?)	-	-	2,200	MIRV/MRV?	-
Subtotal:	**~106**				**~106**
Ground and air-launched cruise missiles					
Babur GLCM (Hatf-7)	~12	2014	350[f]	1 x 5–12 kt	~12
Babur-2/1(B) GLCM (Hatf-?)	-	-[g]	700	1 x 5–12 kt	-
Ra'ad ALCM (Hatf-8)	-	-	350	1 x 5–12 kt	ʼ

Type/NATO designation	Number of launchers	Year deployed	Range^a (kilometers)	Warhead x yield (kilotons)^b	Number of warheads^c
Ra'ad-2 ALCM (Hatf-?)	-	(2022)	>350	1 x 5–12kt	-
Subtotal:		*~12*			*~12*
Sea-based cruise missiles					
Babur-3 SLCM (Hatf-?)	-	_^{h}	450	1 x 5–12 kt	-

a-Range listed is unrefuelled combat range with drop tanks.

b-Yield estimate is based on the range of yields measured in the 1998 nuclear tests. It is possible that Pakistan since has developed warheads with lower and higher yields.

c-There may be more missiles than launchers but since each missile is dual-capable, this table assigns an average of one warhead per launcher unless noted otherwise.

d-There are unconfirmed reports that some of the 40 F-16 aircraft procured from the USA in the 1980s were modified by Pakistan for a nuclear weapon delivery role. However, it is assumed here that the nuclear weapons assigned to aircraft are for use by Mirage aircraft. When the Mirage IIIs and Vs are eventually phased out, it is possible that the JF-17 will take over their nuclear role in the Pakistan Air Force.

e-Each NASR launcher has up to four missile tubes. But since NASR is a dual-capable system and the primary mission probably is conventional, this table counts only one warhead per launcher.

f-The Pakistani government claims the Babur's range is 700 kilometres (435 miles), twice the 350-km (217 miles) range reported by the US intelligence community.

g-The Babur-2/1(B) seems to be an improved version of the original Babur GLCM. It was first tested on December 14, 2016. A failed test in 2020 indicates additional development is needed before it can be fielded.

h-The Babur-3 SLCM was first test launched from an underwater platform in 2017.

I-In addition to the approximately 154 warheads estimated to be assigned to operational forces, a small number of additional warheads (c. 11) are thought to have been produced to arm future Shaheen-III and cruise missiles, for a total estimated inventory of approximately 165 warheads. Pakistan's warhead inventory is expected to continue to increase.

With several new delivery systems in development, four plutonium production reactors, and an expanding uranium enrichment infrastructure, however, Pakistan's stockpile has the potential to increase further over the next 10 years. The size of this projected increase will depend on several factors, including how many nuclear-capable launchers Pakistan plans to deploy, how its nuclear strategy evolves, and how much the Indian nuclear arsenal grows. Speculation that Pakistan may become the world's third-largest nuclear weapon state – with a stockpile of some 350 warheads a decade from now – are, we believe, exaggerated, not least because that would require a build up two to three times faster than the growth rate over the past two decades. We estimate that the country's stockpile could more realistically grow to around 200 warheads by 2025, if the current trend continues. But unless India significantly expands its arsenal or further builds up its conventional forces, it seems reasonable to expect that Pakistan's nuclear arsenal will not continue to grow indefinitely but might begin to level off as its current weapons programs are completed.

Analyzing Pakistan's nuclear forces is fraught with uncertainty, given that the Pakistani government has never publicly disclosed the size of its arsenal and media sources frequently embellish news stories about nuclear weapons. Therefore, the estimates made in the Nuclear Notebook are based on analysis of Pakistan's nuclear posture, observations via commercial satellite imagery, previous statements by Western officials, and private conversations with officials.

Pakistan's Nuclear Posture

Pakistan is pursuing what it calls a "full spectrum deterrence posture," which includes long-range missiles and aircraft for strategic missions, as well as several short-range, lower-yield nuclear-capable weapon systems in order to counter military threats below the strategic level. According to former Pakistani officials, this posture – and its particular emphasis on non-strategic nuclear weapons – is specifically intended as a reaction to India's perceived "Cold Start" doctrine (Kidwai 2020). This alleged doctrine revolves around India maintaining the capability to launch large-scale conventional strikes or incursions against Pakistani territory below the threshold at which Pakistan would retaliate with nuclear weapons.[1]

In 2015, a former member of Pakistan's National Command Authority, Lt. Gen. (Ret.) Khalid Kidwai, said the NASR short-range weapon specifically "was born out of a compulsion of this thing that I mentioned about some people on the other side toying with the idea of finding space for conventional war, despite Pakistan['s] nuclear weapons." He said that Pakistan's understanding of India's "Cold Start" strategy was that Delhi envisioned launching quick strikes into Pakistan within two to four days with eight to nine brigades simultaneously (Kidwai 2015). Such an attack force might involve roughly 32,000 to 36,000 troops. "I strongly believe that by introducing the variety of tactical nuclear weapons in Pakistan's inventory, and in the strategic stability debate, we have blocked the avenues for serious military operations by the other side," Kidwai explained (Kidwai 2015).

After Kidwai's statement, Pakistan's Foreign Secretary Aizaz Chaudhry publicly acknowledged the existence of Pakistan's "low-yield, tactical nuclear weapons," apparently the first time a top government official had done so (*India Today* 2015). At the time, the tactical missiles had not yet been deployed but Pakistani defence minister Khawaja M. Asif further explained their purpose in an interview with *Geo News* in September 2016: "We are always pressurised [sic] time and again that our tactical (nuclear) weapons, in which we have a superiority, that we have more tactical weapons than we need. It is internationally recognized that we have superiority and if there is a threat to our security or if anyone steps on our soil and if someone's designs are a threat to our security, we will not hesitate to use those weapons for our defence" (Scroll 2016). In developing its nonstrategic nuclear strategy, one study has asserted that Pakistan to some extent, has emulated NATO's flexible response strategy without necessarily understanding how it would work (Tasleem and Dalton 2019).

Pakistan's nuclear posture – and particularly its pursuit of tactical nuclear weapons – has created considerable concern in other countries, including the United States, which fears that it increases the risk of escalation and lowers the threshold for nuclear use in a military conflict with India. Over the past decade-and-a-half, the US assessment of nuclear weapons security in Pakistan appears to have changed considerably from confidence to concern, particularly as a result of the introduction of tactical nuclear weapons. In 2007, a US State Department official told Congress that, "we're, I think, fairly confident that they have the proper structures and safeguards in place to maintain the integrity of their nuclear forces and not to allow any compromise" (Boucher 2007). After the emergence of tactical nuclear weapons, the Obama administration changed the tune: "Battlefield nuclear weapons, by their very nature, pose [a] security threat because you're taking battlefield nuclear weapons to the field where, as you know, as a necessity, they cannot be made as secure," as US Undersecretary of State Rose Gottemoeller told Congress in 2016 (*Economic Times* 2016).

The Trump administration echoed this assessment in 2018: "We are particularly concerned by the development of tactical nuclear weapons that are designed for use in the battlefield. We believe that these systems are more susceptible to terrorist theft and increase the likelihood of nuclear exchange in the region" (*Economic Times* 2017). The Trump administration's South Asia strategy in 2017 urged Pakistan to stop sheltering terrorist organizations, and noted the need to "prevent nuclear weapons and materials from coming into the hands of terrorists" (The White House 2017).

In the 2019 Worldwide Threat Assessment, US Director of National Intelligence Daniel R. Coats said, "Pakistan continues to develop new types of nuclear weapons, including short-range tactical weapons, sea-based cruise missiles, air-launched cruise missiles, and longer-range ballistic missiles," noting that "the new types of nuclear weapons will introduce new risks for escalation dynamics and security in the region" (Coats 2019, 10).

Pakistani officials, for their part, reject such concerns. In 2021, Prime Minister Imran Khan stated that he was "not sure whether we're growing [the nuclear arsenal] or not because as far as I know ... the only one purpose [of Pakistan's nuclear weapons] – it's not an offensive thing." He added that "Pakistan's nuclear arsenal is simply as a deterrent, to protect ourselves" (Laskar 2021). Pakistani officials have also challenged the notion that the security of their nuclear weapons is deficient. Samar Mubarik Mund, the former director of the country's National Defense Complex, explained in 2013 that a Pakistani nuclear warhead is "assembled only at the eleventh hour if [it] needs to be launched. It is stored in three to four different parts at three to four different locations. If a nuclear weapon doesn't need to be launched, then it is never available in assembled form" (*World Bulletin* 2013). Additionally, in 2017 the National Command Authority reviewed the "Nuclear Security Regime" of the nuclear arsenal and expressed "full confidence" in both Pakistan's command and control systems and existing security measures meant to "ensure comprehensive stewardship and security of strategic assets and materials." It lauded the nuclear arsenal's "high standards of training and operational readiness" (ISPR 2017d). These statements on security and safety were, in part, a response to international concern that Pakistan's evolving arsenal – particularly its growing inventory of short-range nuclear weapon systems – could lead to problems with warhead management and command and control during a crisis. Satellite images show that security perimeters around many bases and military facilities have been upgraded over the past decade in response to terrorist attacks.

Nuclear policy and operational decision-making in Pakistan are undertaken by the National Command Authority, which is chaired by the prime minister and includes both high-ranking military and civilian officials. The primary nuclear-related body within the National Command Authority is the Strategic Plans Division (SPD), which has been described by the former Director of the SPD's Arms Control and Disarmament Affairs as "a unique organization that is incomparable to any other nuclear-armed state. From operational planning, weapon development, storage, budgets, arms control, diplomacy, and policies related to civilian applications for energy, agriculture, and medicine, etc., all are directed and controlled by SPD." Additionally, SPD "is responsible for nuclear policy, strategy and doctrines. It formulates force development strategy for the tri-services strategic forces, operational planning at the joint services level, and controls movements and deployments of all nuclear forces. SPD implements NCA's employment decisions for nuclear use through its NC3 systems" (Khan 2019).

The National Command Authority was convened after India and Pakistan engaged in open hostilities in February 2019, when Indian fighters dropped bombs near the Pakistani town of Balakot in response to a suicide bombing conducted by a Pakistan-based militant group. In retaliation, Pakistani aircraft shot down and captured an Indian pilot before returning him a week later and convened the National Command Authority. Following the meeting, a senior Pakistani official gave what appeared to be a thinly veiled nuclear threat: "I hope you know what the [National Command Authority] means and what it constitutes. I said that we will surprise you. Wait for that surprise. ... You have chosen a path of war without knowing the consequence for the peace and security of the region" (Abbasi 2019).

The Nuclear Weapons Production Complex

Pakistan has a well-established and diverse fissile material production complex that is expanding. It includes the Kahuta uranium enrichment plant east of Islamabad, which appears to be growing with the near completion of what could be another enrichment plant (Figure 1), as well as the enrichment plant at Gadwal to the north of Islamabad (Albright, Burkhard, and Pabian 2018). Four heavy-water plutonium production reactors appear to have been completed at what is normally referred to as the Khushab Complex some 33 kilometers (20 miles) south of Khushab in Punjab province. Three of the reactors at the complex have been added in the past 10 years. The addition of a publicly confirmed thermal power plant at Khushab provides new information for estimating the power of the four reactors (Albright et al. 2018a). The New Labs Reprocessing Plant at Nilore, east of Islamabad, which reprocesses spent fuel and extracts plutonium, has been expanded. Meanwhile, a second reprocessing plant located at Chashma in the north-western part of Punjab province may have been completed and become operational by 2015 (Albright and Kelleher-Vergantini 2015). A significant expansion to the Chashma complex was under construction between 2018 and 2020, although it remains unclear whether the reprocessing plant continued to operate throughout that period (Hyatt and Burkhard 2020).

Nuclear-capable missiles and their mobile launchers are developed and produced at the National Defence Complex (sometimes called the National Development Complex) located in the Kala Chitta Dahr mountain range west of Islamabad. The complex is divided into two sections. The western section south of Attock appears to be involved in the development, production, and test-launching of missiles and rocket engines. The eastern section north of Fateh Jang is involved in production and assembly of road-mobile transporter erector launchers (TELs), which are designed to transport and fire missiles. Satellite images show the presence of launchers for Shaheen I and Shaheen II ballistic missiles and Babur cruise missiles. The Fateh Jang section has expanded significantly with several new launcher assembly buildings over the past 10 years, and the complex continues to expand. Other launcher and missile-related production and maintenance facilities may be located near Tarnawa and Taxila.

Little is publicly known about warhead production, but experts have suspected for many years that the Pakistan Ordnance Factories near Wah, northwest of Islamabad, serve a role. One of the Wah factories is located near a unique facility with six earth-covered bunkers (igloos) inside a multi-layered safety perimeter with armed guards. The security perimeter was expanded significantly between 2005 and 2010, possibly in response to terrorist attacks against other military facilities.

A frequent oversimplification for estimating the number of Pakistani nuclear weapons is to derive the estimate directly from the amount of weapon-grade fissile material produced. As of the beginning of 2020, the International Panel on Fissile Materials estimated that Pakistan had an inventory of approximately 3,900 kilograms (kg) of weapon-grade (90 percent enriched) highly enriched uranium (HEU), and about 410 kg of weapon-grade plutonium (International Panel on Fissile Materials 2021). This material is theoretically enough to produce between 285 and 342 warheads, assuming that each first-generation implosion-type warhead's solid core uses either 15 to 18 kg of weapon-grade HEU or 5 to 6 kg of plutonium.

However, calculating stockpile size based solely on fissile material inventory is an incomplete methodology that tends to produce inflated numbers. Instead, warhead estimates must take several factors into account: the amount of weapon-grade fissile material produced, warhead design choice and proficiency, warhead production rates, numbers of operational nuclear-capable launchers, how many of those launchers are dual-capable, nuclear strategy, and statements by government officials.

Estimates must assume that not all of Pakistan's fissile material has ended up in warheads. Like other nuclear weapon states, Pakistan probably maintains a reserve. Moreover, Pakistan simply lacks enough nuclear-capable launchers to accommodate 285 to 342 warheads; furthermore, all of Pakistan's launchers are thought to be dual-capable, which means that some of them, especially the shorter-range systems, presumably are assigned non-nuclear missions as well – perhaps even primarily. Finally, official statements often refer to "warheads" and "weapons" interchangeably, without making it clear whether it is the number of launchers or the warheads assigned to them that are being discussed.

The amount of fissile material in warheads – and the size of the warhead – can be reduced, and their yield increased, by using tritium to "boost" the fission process. But Pakistan's tritium production capability is poorly understood. A German company allegedly provided Pakistan with a small amount of tritium and some tritium-processing technology in the late 1980s (Kalinowski and Colschen 1995; Gordon 1989), and China allegedly shipped some tritium directly to Pakistan (Kalinowski and Colschen 1995, 147, 181). The Khushab complex for years has been rumored to produce tritium, and the PINSTECH complex near Nilore may do so as well (FAS 2000a).[2] However, one rumoured tritium extraction plant at Khushab turned out to be a coal-fired power plant (Burkhard, Lach, and Pabian 2017). Pakistan claimed that all its nuclear tests in 1998 were tritium-boosted HEU designs, but the yields detected by seismic signals were not sufficient to substantiate such a capability. Nonetheless, Thomas Reed and Danny Stillman conclude in *The Nuclear Express* that the tests included two designs, the first of which was an HEU device that used boosting. The second test involved a plutonium device (Reed and Stillman 2009, 257–258).

One study in early 2021 estimated that Pakistan could have produced 690 grams of tritium by the end of 2020, sufficient to boost over 100 weapons. The study assessed that warheads produced for delivery by the Babur and Ra-ad cruise missiles and the NASR and Abdali missiles almost certainly would require a small, lightweight tritium-boosted fission weapon (Jones 2021). If Pakistan has produced tritium and uses it in second-generation single-stage boosted warhead designs, then the estimated 3,900 kg HEU and 410 kg weapon-grade plutonium would potentially allow it to build between 407 and 428 warheads, assuming that each weapon used either 12 kg of HEU or 4 to 5 kg of plutonium.

Despite these uncertainties, Pakistan is clearly engaged in a significant buildup of its nuclear forces and has been for some time. In 2008, Peter Lavoy, then a US intelligence officer for South Asia, told NATO that Pakistan was producing nuclear weapons at a faster rate than any other country in the world (US NATO Mission 2008). Six years later, in 2014, Lavoy described the purpose of the "expansion of Pakistan's nuclear weapons program to include efforts to significantly increase fissile material production to *design and fabricate multiple nuclear warheads with varying sizes and yields*, [and] to develop, test and ultimately deploy a wide variety of delivery systems with a wide range to include battlefield range ballistic delivery systems for tactical nuclear weapons" (Emphasis added) (Gul 2014).[3]

Kidwai acknowledged in March 2015 that Pakistan "possesses a variety of nuclear weapons, in different categories. At the strategic level, at the operational level, and the tactical level" (Carnegie Endowment for International Peace 2015, 6). In December 2017 he provided more details, saying Pakistan's nuclear strategy required the "full spectrum of nuclear weapons in all three categories – strategic, operational, and tactical, with full range coverage of the large Indian land mass and its outlying territories." He further explained that the stockpile should have "appropriate weapons yield coverage and the numbers to deter the adversary's pronounced policy of massive retaliation." The weapons would give the Pakistani leadership the "liberty of choosing from a full spectrum of targets, notwithstanding the [Indian] Ballistic Missile Defence, to include counter-value, counter-force, and battlefield" targets. He added this implied that "counter-massive retaliation punishment will be as severe if not more" (Dawn 2017).

How far Pakistan plans to go in terms of developing a full-spectrum deterrent posture is unclear. It has provided no public statements about its intent. In 2015, however, Kadwai said that "the program is not open ended. It started with a concept of credible minimum deterrence, and certain numbers [of weapons] were identified, and those numbers, of course, were achieved not too far away in time. Then we translated it, like I said, to the concept of full spectrum deterrence" in response to India's Cold Start doctrine. As a result, he went on, "the numbers were modified. Now those numbers, as of today, and if I can look ahead for at least 10 to 15 more years, I think they are going to be more or less okay." He further noted, "We're almost 90, 95 percent there in terms of the goals that we had set out to achieve" 15 years ago (Carnegie Endowment for International Peace 2015, 6, 12).

We estimate that Pakistan currently is producing sufficient fissile material to build 14 to 27 new warheads per year, although we estimate that the actual warhead increase in the stockpile probably averages around 5 to 10 warheads per year.[4]

Nuclear Capable Aircraft

The aircraft most likely to have a nuclear delivery role are Pakistan's Mirage III and Mirage V fighter squadrons. The Pakistani Air Force's (PAF) Mirage fighter-bombers are focused at two bases. Masroor Air Base outside Karachi houses the 32nd Wing with three Mirage squadrons: 7th Squadron ("Bandits"), 8th Squadron ("Haiders"), and 22nd Squadron ("Ghazis"). A possible nuclear weapons storage site is located five km (three miles) northwest of the base (Kristensen 2009), and since 2004, unique underground facilities have been constructed at Masroor that could potentially be designed to support a nuclear strike mission. This includes a possible alert hangar with underground weapons-handling capability.[5] The other Mirage base is Rafiqui Air base near Shorkot, which is home to the 34th Wing with two Mirage squadrons: the 15th Squadron ("Cobras") and the 27th Squadron ("Zarras").

The Mirage V is believed to have been given a strike role with Pakistan' small arsenal of nuclear gravity bombs, while the Mirage III has been used for test launches of Pakistan's Ra'ad (Hatf-8) air-launched cruise missile (ALCM), as well as the follow-on Ra'ad-II ALCM. The Pakistani Air Force

has added an aerial refuelling capability to the Mirage, a capability that would greatly enhance the nuclear strike mission (AFP 2018).

The air-launched, dual-capable Ra'ad ALCM is believed to have been test-launched at least six times, most recently in February 2016. The Pakistani government states that the Ra'ad "can deliver nuclear and conventional warheads with great accuracy" (ISPR 2011c) to a range of 350 km, and "complement[s] Pakistan's deterrence capability" by achieving "strategic standoff capability on land and at sea" (ISPR 2016a). During a military parade in 2017, Pakistan displayed what was said to be Ra'ad-II ALCM, apparently an enhanced version of the original Ra'ad with a new engine air-intake and tail wing configuration (Khan 2017). The Pakistani government tested the Ra'ad-II in February 2020 and stated that the missile can reportedly reach targets at a distance of 600 km (ISPR 2020a). All test launches involving either Ra'ad system have been conducted from Mirage III aircraft, indicating its likely delivery system upon deployment.

There is no available evidence to suggest that either Ra'ad system had been deployed as of July 2021; however, one potential deployment site could eventually be Masroor Air Base outside Karachi, which is home to several Mirage squadrons and includes unique underground facilities that might be associated with nuclear weapons storage and handling.

The PAF's Mirage aircraft are aging, and Pakistan intends to acquire 186 JF-17 aircraft – which are co-produced with China – to replace them (Warnes 2020; Quwa 2021; Gady 2020). According to the Pakistani Senate Defense Committee on National Defence, the pursuit of the JF-17 program was partially triggered by US military export sanctions in response to Pakistan's nuclear program, including the withholding of F-16 aircraft. "With spares for its top-of-the-line F16s in question and additional F-16s removed as an option, Pakistan sought help from its Chinese ally" for the JC-17/FC-1 jet (Senate Committee on National Defense 2016). Initial reports from 2016 suggested that Pakistan intended to incorporate the dual-capable Ra'ad ALCM onto the JF-17 in order to allow the newer aircraft to eventually take over the nuclear strike role from the Mirage III/Vs; however, more recent reporting has not confirmed this (Ansari 2013; Fisher 2016).

The nuclear capability of the PAF's F-16 aircraft is uncertain. Pakistan's F-16A/Bs were supplied by the United States between 1983 and 1987. After 40 aircraft had been delivered, the US State Department told Congress in 1989: "None of the F-16s Pakistan already owns or is about to purchase is configured for nuclear delivery," and Pakistan "will be obligated by contract

not to modify" additional F-16s "without the approval of the United States" (Schaffer 1989). Yet there were multiple credible reports at the time that Pakistan was already modifying US-supplied F-16s for nuclear weapons, including West German intelligence officials reportedly telling *Der Spiegel* that Pakistan had already developed sophisticated computer and electronic technology to outfit the US F-16s with nuclear weapons" (Associated Press 1989). Delivery of additional F-16s, including the more modern F-16 C/D version, was delayed by concern over Pakistan's emerging nuclear weapons program. The United States withheld delivery in the 1990s. But the policy was changed by the George W. Bush administration, which supplied Pakistan with the more modern F-16s.

The F-16A/Bs are based with the 38th Wing at Mushaf (formerly Sargodha) Air Base, 160 kilometres (100 miles) northwest of Lahore. Organized into the 9th and 11th Squadrons ("Griffins" and "Arrows" respectively), these aircraft have a range of 1,600 km (extendable when equipped with drop tanks) and most likely are equipped to each carry a single nuclear bomb on the centreline pylon. Security perimeters at the base have been upgraded since 2014. If the F-16s have a nuclear strike mission, the nuclear gravity bombs would likely not be stored at the base itself but could potentially be kept at the Sargodha Weapons Storage Complex 10 km to the south. In a crisis, the bombs could quickly be transferred to the base, or the F-16s could disperse to bases near underground storage facilities and receive the weapons there. Pakistan appears to be reinforcing the munitions bunkers and installing extra security perimeters at the Sargodha complex.

The newer F-16 C/Ds are based with the 39th Wing at Shahbaz Air Base outside Jacobabad. The wing upgraded to F-16 C/Ds from Mirages in 2011 and so far has one squadron: the 5th Squadron (known as the "Falcons"). The base has been under significant expansion, with numerous weapons bunkers added since 2004. If the base has a nuclear mission, we suspect that the weapons are stored elsewhere in special storage facilities. There are also F-16s visible at Minhas (Kamra) Air Base northwest of Islamabad, although that might be related to aircraft industry at the base.

In light of uncertainties regarding Pakistan's nuclear-capable aircraft, the PAF's F-16s and JF-17s are not identified in this Nuclear Notebook as having a dedicated nuclear weapon delivery system and are omitted from Table 1.

Land-based ballistic missiles

Pakistan appears to have six currently operational nuclear-capable land-based ballistic missiles: the short-range Abdali (Hatf-2), Ghaznavi (Hatf-3), Shaheen-I (Hatf-4), and NASR (Hatf-9), and the medium-range Ghauri (Hatf-5) and Shaheen-II (Hatf-6). Three other nuclear-capable ballistic missiles are under development: the medium-range Shaheen-IA, Shaheen-III, and the MIRVed Ababeel. All of Pakistan's nuclear-capable missiles – with the exception of the Abdali, Ghauri, Shaheen-II, and Ababeel – were showcased at the Pakistan Day Parade in March 2021 (ISPR 2021a).

The Pakistani road-mobile ballistic missile force has undergone significant development and expansion over the past decade-and-a-half. This includes possibly eight or nine missile garrisons, including four or five along the Indian border for short-range systems (Babur, Ghaznavi, Shaheen-I, NASR) and three or four other garrisons further inland for medium-range systems (Shaheen-II and Ghauri).[6]

The short-range, solid-fuel, single-stage Abdali (Hatf-2) has been in development for a long time. The Pentagon reported in 1997 that the Abdali appeared to have been discontinued, but flight-testing resumed in 2002, and it was last reported test-launched in 2013. The 200-km (124-mile) missile has been displayed at parades several times on a four-axle road-mobile transporter erector launcher (TEL). The gap in flight-testing indicates the Abdali program may have encountered technical difficulties. After the 2013 test, Inter Services Public Relations stated that Abdali "carries nuclear as well as conventional warheads" and "provides an operational-level capability to Pakistan's Strategic Forces." It said the test launch "consolidates Pakistan's deterrence capability both at the operational and strategic levels" (ISPR 2013).

The short-range, solid-fuel, single-stage Ghaznavi (Hatf-3) was test launched in 2019, 2020, and 2021 – its first reported test launches since 2014. In an important milestone for testing the readiness of Pakistan's nuclear forces, the 2019 Ghaznavi launch was conducted at night. After each test, the Pakistani military stated that the Ghaznavi is "capable of delivering multiple types of warheads up to a range of 290 kilometers" (180 miles) (ISPR 2019a, ISPR 2020b, ISPR 2021b). Its short range means that the Ghaznavi cannot strike Delhi from Pakistani territory, and Army units equipped with the missile are probably based relatively near the Indian border (Kristensen 2016)

The Shaheen-I (Hatf-4) is a single-stage, solid-fuel, dual-capable, short-range ballistic missile with a maximum range of 650 km that has been in service since 2003. The Shaheen-I is carried on a four-axle, road-mobile TEL similar to the one used for the Ghaznavi. Since 2012, many Shaheen-I test launches have involved an extended-range version widely referred to as Shaheen-IA. The Pakistani government, which has declared the range of the Shaheen-IA to be 900 km (560 miles), has used both designations. Pakistan most recently test launched the Shaheen-I in November 2019 and the Shaheen-IA in March 2021 (ISPR 2019b, ISPR 2021c). Potential Shaheen-1 deployment locations include Gujranwala, Okara, and Pano Aqil.[7]

One of the most controversial new nuclear-capable missiles in the Pakistani arsenal is the NASR (Hatf-9), a short-range, solid-fuel missile originally with a range of only 60 km (37 miles) that has recently been extended to 70 km (43 miles) (ISPR 2017a). With a range too short to attack strategic targets inside India, NASR appears intended solely for battlefield use against invading Indian troops.[8] According to the Pakistani government, the NASR "carries nuclear warheads of appropriate yield with high accuracy, shoot and scoot attributes" and was developed as a "quick response system" to "add deterrence value" to Pakistan's strategic weapons development program "at shorter ranges" in order "to deter evolving threats," including evidently India's so-called Cold Start doctrine (ISPR 2011b, 2017a). More recent tests of the NASR system – including two tests in the same week in January 2019 – tested the system's salvo-launch capability, as well as the missiles' in-flight manoeuvrability (ISPR 2019c, ISPR 2019d).

The NASR's four-axle, road-mobile TEL appears to use a snap-on system that can carry two or more launch-tube boxes, and the system has been tested in the past using a road-mobile quadruple box launcher. The US intelligence community has listed the NASR as a deployed system since 2013 (National Air and Space Intelligence Center 2013), and with a total of 15 tests reported so far, the weapon system appears to be well-developed. Potential deployment locations include Gujranwala, Okara, and Pano Aqil.[9]

The medium-range, two-stage, solid-fuel Shaheen-II (Hatf-6) appears to be operational after many years of development. Pakistan's National Defense Complex has assembled Shaheen-II launchers since at least 2004 or 2005 (Kristensen 2007), and a 2020 US intelligence community report states that there are "fewer than 50" Shaheen-II launchers deployed (National Air and Space Intelligence Center. 2020). After the most recent Shaheen-II test launch in May 2019, the Pakistani government reported the range as only 1,500 km (932 miles), but the US National Air and Space Intelligence Center (NASIC) continues to set the Shaheen-II's range at 2,000 km (ISPR 2019e; National Air and Space Intelligence Center. 2020). The Shaheen-II is carried on a six-axle, road-mobile TEL and can carry a single conventional or nuclear warhead.

Pakistan's newer Shaheen-III medium-range, two-stage, solid-field Shaheen-III was displayed publicly for the first time at the 2015 Pakistan Day Parade. Following its first two test launches in 2015 and its latest launch in January 2021, the Pakistani government said the missile was capable of delivering either a single nuclear or conventional warhead to a range of 2,750 km (ISPR 2021d). The Shaheen-III is carried on an eight-axle TEL reportedly supplied by China (Panda 2016). The system will likely still require several more test launches before it becomes operational. The Pakistani army test-launched a Shaheen-III medium-range ballistic missile in January 2021 (archive image from 2015 via Pakistani military)

The range of the Shaheen-III is sufficient to target all of mainland India from launch positions in most of Pakistan south of Islamabad. But the missile was apparently developed to do more than that. According to Gen. Kidwai, the range of 2,750 km was determined by a need to be able to target the Nicobar and Andaman Islands in the eastern part of the Indian Ocean that are "developed as strategic bases" where "India might think of putting its weapons" (Carnegie Endowment for International Peace 2015, 10). But for a 2,750-km range Shaheen-III to reach the Andaman and Nicobar Islands, it would need to be launched from positions in the very Eastern parts of Pakistan, close to the Indian border. If deployed in the Western parts of Balochistan province, however, the range of the Shaheen-III would for the first time bring Israel within range of Pakistani nuclear missiles.

Pakistan's oldest nuclear-capable medium-range ballistic missile, the road-mobile, single-stage, liquid-fuel Ghauri (Hatf-5), was most recently test-launched in October 2018. (ISPR 2018c). The Pakistani government states that the Ghauri can carry a single conventional or nuclear warhead to a range of 1,300 km (807 miles), although NASIC lists the range as 1,250 km (776 miles) (National Air and Space Intelligence Center. 2020). NASIC also suggests that "fewer than 50" Ghauri launchers have been deployed (National Air and Space Intelligence Center. 2020). The extra time needed to fuel the missile before launch makes the Ghauri more vulnerable to attack than Pakistan's newer solid-fuel missiles, so it is possible that the longer range versions of the Shaheen may eventually replace the Ghauri [10]

93

Potential deployment areas for the Ghauri include the Sargodha Central Ammunition Depot area.[11]

On January 24, 2017, Pakistan test-launched a new medium-range ballistic missile – Ababeel – that the government says is "capable of carrying multiple warheads, using multiple independent reentry vehicle (MIRV) technology" (ISPR 2017b).[12] The three-stage, solid-fuel, nuclear-capable missile, which is currently under development at the National Defense Complex, appears to be derived from the Shaheen-III airframe and solid-fuel motor and has a range of 2,200 km (1,367 miles). (ISPR 2017b; National Air and Space Intelligence Center. 2020). After the test-launch, the Pakistani government declared that the test was intended to validate the missile's "various design and technical parameters," and that Ababeel is "aimed at ensuring survivability of Pakistan's ballistic missiles in the growing regional Ballistic Missile Defence (BMD) environment," "further reinforce[ing] deterrence" (ISPR 2017b). Development of multiple-warhead capability appears to be intended as a countermeasure against India's planned ballistic missile defence system (Tasleem 2017).

Ground- and sea-launched cruise missiles

Pakistan's family of ground- and sea-launched cruise missiles is undergoing significant development with work on several types and modifications. The Babur (Hatf-7) is a subsonic, dual-capable cruise missile with a similar appearance to the US Tomahawk sea-launched cruise missile, the Chinese DH-10 ground-launched cruise missile, and the Russian air-launched AS-15. The Pakistani government describes the Babur as having "stealth capabilities" and "pinpoint accuracy" and "a low-altitude, terrain-hugging missile with high manoeuvrability" (ISPR 2011a, 2016b, 2018a). The Babur is much slimmer than Pakistan's ballistic missiles, suggesting some success with warhead miniaturization based on a boosted fission design.

The original Babur-1 ground-launched cruise missiles (GLCM) has been test-launched nearly a dozen times and is likely to be operational with the armed forces. Its road-mobile launcher appears to be a unique five-axle TEL with a three-tube box launcher that is different than the quadruple box launcher used for static display. At different times, the Pakistani government has reported the range to be 600 km (372 miles) and 700 km (435 miles) (ISPR 2011a, 2012a, 2012b), but the US intelligence community sets the range much lower, at 350 km (217 miles) (National Air and Space Intelligence Center. 2020).

Pakistan appears to be upgrading the original Babur-1 missiles into Babur-1A missiles by upgrading their avionics and navigation systems to enable target engagement both on land and at sea. Following the system's most recent test in February 2021, the Pakistani military stated that the Babur-1A's range was 450 km (ISPR 2021e).

Pakistan is also developing an enhanced version of the Babur known as the Babur-2 or Babur-1B GLCM.[13] The weapon has been test-launched at least two times: in December 2016 and April 2018 (ISPR 2016b, 2018a). In March 2020, Indian news media reported that the Babur-2/Babur-1B had failed two other tests, in April 2018 and March 2020; however, this was not confirmed by Pakistan (Gupta 2020). With a physical appearance and capabilities similar to those of the Babur, the Babur-2/Babur-1B apparently has an extended range of 700 km (435 miles), and "is capable of carrying various types of warheads" (ISPR 2016b, 2018a). The fact that both the Babur-1 and the "enhanced" Babur-2/Babur-1B have been noted as possessing a range of 700 km indicates that the range of the initial Babur-1 system was likely shorter. NASIC has not released information on an enhanced system. After the first test in 2016, the Pakistani government noted that the system is "an important force multiplier for Pakistan's strategic defence" (ISPR 2016b). The Pakistani military test-launched the Babur-1 in March 2020. The test was a failure (image via Pakistani military).

Babur TELs have been fitting out at the National Development Complex for several years and have recently been seen at the Akro garrison northeast of Karachi. The garrison includes a large enclosure with six garages that have room for 12 TELs and a unique underground facility that is probably used to store the missiles.[14]

Pakistan is also developing a sea-launched version of the Babur known as Babur-3. The weapon is still in development and has been test-launched twice: On January 9, 2017, from "an underwater, mobile platform" in the Indian Ocean (ISPR 2017c); and on March 29, 2018 from "an underwater dynamic platform" (ISPR 2018b). The Babur-3 is said to be a sea-based variant of the Babur-2 GLCM, and to have a range of 450 km (279 miles) (ISPR 2017c).

The Pakistani government says the Babur-3 is "capable of delivering various types of payloads … [that] … will provide Pakistan with a Credible Second Strike Capability, augmenting deterrence," and described it as "a step towards reinforcing [the] policy of credible minimum deterrence" (ISPR 2017c). The Babur-3 will most likely be deployed on the diesel-electric Agosta class submarines (Khan 2015). In April 2015, the Pakistani government approved the purchase of right air-independent propulsion-powered submarines from China, the first four of which are due in 2022–2023 (Khan 2019). It is possible that these new submarines, which will be called the Hangor-class, could eventually be assigned a nuclear role with the Babur-3 submarine-launched cruise missile.

Once it becomes operational, the Babur-3 will provide Pakistan with a triad of nuclear strike platforms from ground, air, and sea. The Pakistani government said the Babur-3 was motivated by a need to match India's nuclear triad and the "nuclearization of [the] Indian Ocean Region" (ISPR 2018b). The Pakistani government also noted that Babur-3's stealth technologies would be useful in the "emerging regional Ballistic Missile Defense (BMD) environment" (ISPR 2017c).

The future submarine-based nuclear capability is managed by Headquarters Naval Strategic Forces Command (NSFC), which the government said in 2012 would be the "custodian of the nation's 2nd strike capability" to "strengthen Pakistan's policy of Credible Minimum Deterrence and ensure regional stability" (ISPR 2012c). Kidwai in 2015 publicly acknowledged the need for a sea-based second-strike capability and said it "will come into play in the next few years" (Carnegie Endowment for International Peace 2015, 16).

Pakistan also appears to be developing a variant of the Babur cruise missile, known as the Harbah that can be carried by surface vessels. Pakistan describes the system as "a surface-to-surface anti-ship missile with land attack capability" (ISPR 2018d). Although Pakistan did not state the system's range after either of its 2018 or 2019 tests, official photos of the system in-flight bear a strong resemblance to the Babur (ISPR 2018d; Rahmat 2019). It is unknown at this time if the Harbah will be dual-capable.

For analysis of possible Pakistani missile brigade locations, see Kristensen (2016).

Disclosure statement

No potential conflict of interest was reported by the author(s).

Funding

This research was carried out with grants from the John D. and Katherine T. MacArthur Foundation, the New Land Foundation, the Ploughshares Fund, and the Prospect Hill Foundation.

Notes on contributors

Hans M. Kristensen is the director of the Nuclear Information Project with the Federation of American Scientists in Washington, DC. His work focuses on researching and writing about the status of nuclear weapons and the policies that direct them. Kristensen is a coauthor of the world nuclear forces overview in the SIPRI Yearbook (Oxford University Press) and a frequent adviser to the news media on nuclear weapons policy and operations. He has coauthored Nuclear Notebook since 2001. Inquiries should be directed to FAS, 1112 16th Street NW, Suite 400, Washington, DC, 20036 USA; +1 (202) 546–3300.

Matt Korda is a research associate for the Nuclear Information Project at the Federation of American Scientists, where he coauthors the Nuclear Notebook with Hans Kristensen. Previously, he worked for the Arms Control, Disarmament, and WMD Non-Proliferation Centre at NATO headquarters in Brussels. He received his MA in International Peace and Security from the Department of War Studies at King's College London, where he subsequently worked as a Research Assistant on nuclear deterrence and strategic stability. Matt's research interests and recent publications focus on nuclear deterrence and disarmament, progressive foreign policy, and the nexus between nuclear weapons, climate change, and injustice. *Pakistani nuclear weapons, 2021. Hans M. Kristensen &Matt Korda. Pages 265-278 | Published online: 07 Sep 2021 The Bulletin of the Atomic Scientists engages science leaders, policy makers, and the interested public on topics of nuclear weapons and disarmament, climate change, growing energy demands, and disruptive technologies. It has been published continuously since 1945, when it was founded by former Manhattan Project physicists after the atomic bombings of Hiroshima and Nagasaki as the Bulletin of the Atomic Scientists of Chicago. One of the driving forces behind the creation of the Bulletin was the amount of public interest surrounding atomic energy at the dawn of the atomic age. To convey the particular peril posed by nuclear weapons, the Bulletin devised the Doomsday Clock in 1947. The Doomsday Clock appeared on the Bulletin's first cover when it transitioned from a newsletter to a magazine. Its original setting was seven minutes to midnight. The Clock, now set at two minutes to midnight, is recognized as a universal symbol of threats to humanity from a variety of sources: nuclear and other weapons of mass destruction, climate change, and disruptive technologies. In 2007 the Bulletin of the Atomic Scientists won the National Magazine Award for General Excellence, the magazine industry equivalent of an Oscar for Best Picture. The Bulletin also was named one of four 2009 finalists for the Lumity Technology Leadership Award, presented by Accenture to a non-profit organization that is effectively applying innovative technologies. Today, the Bulletin supplements its cutting-edge journalism with interactive infographics and videos and amplifies its messages through social media platforms. It can be found in over 15,000 leading institutions across the globe. All submitted manuscripts are subject to initial appraisal by the Editor. Although the Bulletin does not undertake a formal peer review process, unsolicited articles that are found suitable for further consideration are sent to members of our expert network for their assessment. Journal information: Print ISSN: 0096-3402 Online ISSN: 1938-3282, 6 issues per year. Bulletin of the Atomic Scientists and our publisher Taylor & Francis make every effort to ensure the accuracy of all the information (the "Content") contained in our publications. However, Bulletin of the Atomic Scientists and our publisher Taylor & Francis, our agents (including the editor, any member of the editorial team or editorial board, and any guest editors), and our licensors make no representations or warranties whatsoever as to the accuracy, completeness, or suitability for any purpose of the Content. Any opinions and views expressed in this publication are the opinions and views of the authors, and are not the views of or endorsed by Bulletin of the Atomic Scientists and our publisher Taylor & Francis. The accuracy of the Content should not be relied upon and should be independently verified with primary sources of information. Bulletin of the Atomic Scientists and our publisher Taylor & Francis shall not be liable for any losses, actions, claims, proceedings, demands, costs, expenses, damages, and other liabilities whatsoever or howsoever caused arising directly or indirectly in connection with, in relation to, or arising out of the use of the Content. Terms & Conditions of access and use can be found at http://www. tandfonline.com/page/terms-and-conditions. Hans M. Kristensen & Matt Korda (2021) Pakistani nuclear weapons, 2021, Bulletin of the Atomic Scientists, 77:5, 265-278, DOI: 10.1080/00963402.2021.1964258.*

Chapter 7

India-China Friction and the South China Sea

On 05 August 2019, Government of India revoked special status and curtailed sovereignty of Kashmir under Article 370 of the Indian Constitution after Pakistan army and government allowed Prime Minister Modi to proceed. It tormented the lives of eight million people. The lockdown of nine months and 18 days was a telling proof not only of Kashmiris but also of human rights violations. After this kind of brutal operation, many attempts were made by the international human rights organizations to reach Kashmiries but they were not allowed to report violations of human rights. Media workers were barred from working on October 3, 2019. The Internet and all other services were cut off so that they could report their situation. Analyst and researcher Richard Purcell (28 January 2020-Global Security Review) has assessed and analysed damage of nuclear conflict between great powers:

"Nuclear damage limitation involves reducing the U.S.'s vulnerability to an adversary's nuclear weapons. It is a warfighting capability intended to enable the United States to prevail in a nuclear conflict, should one arise. There are a number of ways to achieve damage limitation, but most discussions of this topic focus on two in particular: neutralizing an adversary's nuclear missiles before they can be fired, generally known as counterforce, and intercepting incoming missiles after they have been launched but before they reach their targets. Current American policy states that damage limiting capabilities are an important component of the nation's overall strategic posture. The most recent U.S. Nuclear Posture Review, released in February 2018, asserts that if U.S. strategic forces fail to deter an enemy attack, the U.S. "will strive to end any conflict at the lowest level of damage possible and on the best achievable terms for the United States, allies, and partners. U.S. nuclear policy for decades has consistently included this objective of limiting damage if deterrence fails." It adds that "U.S. missile defence and offensive options provide the basis for significant damage limitation" in the event of a nuclear conflict. The Pentagon's Missile Defence Review, issued in January 2019, echoes this approach. It affirms that in the event of a conflict, the United States would seek "to prevent and defeat adversary missile attacks through a combination of deterrence, active and passive missile defences, and attack operations to destroy offensive missiles prior to launch."[1]

In 2018 and 2020, President Trump and his NATO allies repeatedly criticized China for flooding global markets with cheap steel and aluminium, but China repudiated their statement. In June 2019, he raised tariffs from 10 to 25% percent on $200 billion of imports from China that were previously targeted, but some states in Asia and Europe criticized the US action. In 2018, China also blocked Singapore-based Broadcom Limited from purchasing the US chipmaker Qualcomm. The rise of China threatens to undermine the US-led security order in Asia. Chinese military modernization, particularly in the maritime sphere, has begun to shift regional balance of power. Analyst Marianne Schneider-Petsinger (Behind the US–China Trade War: The Race for Global Technological Leadership) has highlighted aspects of trade war and technological competition between China and the United States:

"Moreover, President Trump signed the Foreign Investment Risk Review Modernization Act of 2018 (FIRRMA) into law, which expands the jurisdiction of CFIUS. Although this recent legislation did not mention China directly as a target of the measures, it was driven by concerns over the risks to US technological leadership stemming from foreign investment by primarily Chinese firms in American high-tech companies. One of FIRRMA's objectives is to allow for greater scrutiny of 'transactions that involve a country of special concern that has a demonstrated or declared strategic goal of acquiring a type of critical technology or critical infrastructure that would affect United States leadership in areas related to national security'. Without express reference, this nonetheless signals China is a focus of concern. In May 2018, President Trump intervened to overturn a ban imposed by the US Department of Commerce that barred the Chinese telecommunications giant ZTE from buying American technology for seven years. This came after ZTE was found not to abide by the rules of a previous settlement agreement over violations of US sanctions on Iran and North Korea. In the case of Huawei, another Chinese multinational technology company, the US Department of Justice filed a number of criminal charges against the company and its chief financial officer in January 2019, including for the alleged evasion of sanctions on

Iran and the alleged theft of robotic technology. Moreover, the Trump administration has asked US allies – including Germany, Italy, and Japan – not to use the company's 5G network equipment, citing espionage concerns. In May 2019, President Trump declared a national emergency and signed an Executive Order that prohibits US companies from using any information and communications technology and services from 'foreign adversaries' that are considered to pose 'an unacceptable risk to the national security of the United States.'"[2]

Ballistic and nuclear missile competition among states in South Asia has caused consternation that these missiles can inflict huge fatalities on the human population. India's development of Ballistic Missile Defence (BMD) and number of Pakistan's missiles and warheads are exhibiting threat to each other. During the last 40 years, Pakistan and India doubled the number of their nuclear warheads, making them the fastest-growing nuclear weapons states in the world. However, India deployed a nuclear triad of bombers, missiles and a submarine capable of firing nuclear weapons. Pakistan also developed a network of nuclear weapons factories, plutonium reactors and nuclear missiles. India invested a lot on spy satellites, aircraft, drones and early warning radar, while Pakistan has developed spy and modern warning systems.

At present, both the states hold a massive nuclear stockpile and the size of this stockpile doubled since 1998. Both states have developed cruise missiles and are seeking nuclear submarines. China's tacit support to Pakistan for boosting the country's nuclear weapons has strategic implications for India. All these weapons and strategic developments in both states mean that confidence-building measures remain only on paper with no one wanting to extend the hand of cooperation. The main threat to Pakistan's nuclear installations might also come from a virus or worm activated within the computer. On 09 June, 2014, when terrorists attacked Karachi airport and killed two military officers of the Pakistan army, the government stepped up security around nuclear installations across the country. The terrorist attack on Karachi airport showed that Pakistan's intelligence had badly failed to provide true information about terrorist networks in Karachi. This attack also highlighted the military capability of the Taliban that exposed the gap in the country's security apparatus. After this attack, Pakistanis were apprehensive about possible daring attacks against the country's nuclear installations. Terrorists yet again exposed the failure of security agencies. This was a clear challenge for the SPD of the armed forces, which had deployed 25,000 nuclear forces around nuclear facilities. Ravi Agrawal in his recent paper has highlighted military confrontations between China and India in the Ladakh region:

"In the best of times, both India and China restrict journalists from entering border areas, and the pandemic has made it more difficult to get accurate information. Let's start with what we know. This month, Foreign Policy highlighted two clashes between Indian and Chinese soldiers, on May 5 and May 9, at separate border areas in India's east and north. While no one was killed in those hand-to-hand combat skirmishes, more than 100 soldiers were injured. The Indian press, aided by trickles of information from defence officials, has since reported that Chinese army brigades comprising thousands of soldiers have crossed into Indian Territory to set up tents and trenches at key points near the Himalayas. In response, India's army has deployed reinforcements, sparking fears of a larger conflict. The Economist reports that on Wednesday, New Delhi and Beijing activated a high-level diplomatic channel to diffuse tensions. And China's ambassador to India, Sun Weidong, struck a calming tone, telling reporters, "We should never let differences overshadow our relations."[3]

India and Pakistan have applied professional measures to protect their nuclear weapons sites but nuclear proliferation still poses a grave threat to the national security of all South Asian states. Military experts and policymakers have also expressed deep concerns that if the two nuclear capable states purvey explosives to their favourite terror groups, it might cause huge destruction and casualties for the civilian populations and military installations. Recent events in Pakistan and India have raised the prospect of extremist and jihadist groups using biological, radiological and chemical weapons against military installations and critical national infrastructure in both states. The two states are vulnerable to such attacks by the Taliban and Islamic State (ISIS). Pakistani politicians are confident that the country's army is capable of preventing nuclear weapons from falling into the hands of the Taliban and IS. The fear that India and Pakistan could use nuclear weapons against each other in case of a major terror attack has not ebbed. Pakistan says it will not use nuclear weapons against its neighbours without any reason but if India were to do so, the country has the right to respond to an Indian attack.

The greatest threat to the national security of Pakistan and India stems from nuclear smuggling and terror groups operating in Punjab, Balochistan, Assam and Kashmir. Increasingly sophisticated chemical and biological weapons are accessible to organisations like ISIS, Mujahedeen-e-Hind (MH), and the Taliban and their allies, which is a matter of great concern.

These groups can use more sophisticated conventional weapons as well as chemical and biological agents in India and Pakistan in the near future, as they have already experimented in Iraq and Syria. They can disperse chemical, biological and radiological material as well as industrial agents via water or land to target schools, colleges, civilian and military personnel. On June 6, 2015, Pajhwok News reported that dozens of schoolgirls were targeted by unknown terrorists using biological agents in Panj Aab district of Bamyan province. This could also happen in Punjab, Balochistan, Sindh and Khyber Pakhtunkhwa or Delhi and Mumbai unless the export control regime is tightened.[4] Mir Sajad in his article (Modern diplomacy 29 May 2020), noted some important aspects of India-China confrontations in Ladakh. He believes that the Indian government treats people of Kashmir like slaves, and basic democratic right of exercising the political freedom too has been robbed off as more than half of political leaders are under the house arrest:

"After scrapping Article 370 in August previous year China has emboldened its stand on raising the Kashmir issue twice in the United Nations joining many international countries in the unprecedented criticism of India's action in Kashmir. Before August, the last time that Kashmir Issue got resonated at the UNSC forum was in 1971 and has been flagged twice since then within a span of five months. China was the main actor in highlighting the 'disputed' nature of Kashmir's historical and political entanglements. A new dimension of China's Kashmir policy has been the issuance of loose-leaf/stapled visas to Kashmiris considering the entire J&K as disputed (Jayadeva Ranade, "The Age of Region: China seems to Review its Asia Strategy", The Times of India, New Delhi, 13 January 2010) Furthermore, in July 2010, China denied a visa to Indian Army General BS Jasawal (Indian Army General) on the grounds of his posting in a territory that was "head of the sensitive Northern Command based in J&K. Clarifying the denial, Beijing stated that it would not be possible to give Jasawal a visa because of his posting in the territory that was "difficult" ("Now Three Chinese Army Officers refused Visas", The Hindustan Times, New Delhi, 28 August 2010). There seems an intersection of interests in China-Pakistan relations with China investing heavily in Pakistan and seemingly 'all-weather' friendship bond between the two with Kashmir hyphenating perfectly on this mutual regional integration. In the Rambo-styled film 'Wolf Warrior 2' in 2017, China exhorted the geo-strategic message through this film by flashing the Han dynasty saying, "Whoever offends China will be punished, no matter how far they are". Chinese have been enhuming the ghosts of 'silk route' by announcing to the world the 'new silk route' (The Return of Marco Polo's

World; War, Strategy and American Interests in the Twenty-First Century by Robert D. Kaplan, 2018) and Kashmir remain the core of that grand project".[5]

The international task force on prevention of nuclear terrorism has warned that "possibility of nuclear terrorism was increasing" because of a number of factors, including "the conventional forms of terrorism" and the vulnerability of nuclear power and research reactors to sabotage and of weapons-usable nuclear materials to theft. Terrorists may possibly retrieve nuclear materials from India or Pakistan and use them against civilian and military installations. Another development that has also worried nuclear scientists is cyber-attacks during nuclear crisis management. Cyber warfare has the potential to attack or disrupt successful nuclear crisis management. India and Pakistan have developed strong networks of cyber armies and have often attacked each other's sensitive computers in the past. Analyst Haris Bilal Malik (Modern Diplomacy 28 May 2020) highlights the 22 years of nuclearization of Pakistan and India, the danger of nuclear war and the evolving nuclear posture of India:

"May 2020 marks the 22nd anniversary of the overt nuclearization of South Asia. The evolved nuclear doctrinal postures of both India and Pakistan have been a key component of their defence and security policies. During this period; India has undergone gradual shifts in its nuclear doctrinal posture. The Indian posture as set out in the 1999 'Draft Nuclear Doctrine' (DND) was based on an assertion that India would pursue the 'No First Use' (NFU) policy. The first amendment to this posture, which came out in January 2003, was based on a review by the Indian Cabinet Committee on Security (CCS) of the nuclear doctrine. It stated that if India's armed forces or its people were attacked with chemical and biological weapons, India reserves the right to respond with nuclear weapons. This review could, therefore, be considered a contradiction to India's declared NFU policy at the doctrinal level. On the basis of this notion, it could be assumed that India has had an aspiration to drift away from its NFU policy since 2003. Subsequently, the notion of a pre-emptive 'splendid first strike 'has been a key part of the discourse surrounding the Indian and international strategic community since the years 2016-2017. According to India's assessment, Pakistan was found to be deploying nuclear weapons, in a contingency, India would resort to such a splendid first strike. With such a doctrinal posture, India's quest for pre-emption against Pakistan seems to be an attempt to neutralize the deterrent value of Pakistan's nuclear capabilities. In this regard, India has been constantly advancing its nuclear weapons capabilities based on enhanced missile programs and the development of its land, sea, and air-based nuclear triad thus negating its own NFU policy"[6]

As international media focuses on the looming threat of chemical and biological terrorism in Asia and Europe, the ISIS is seeking nuclear weapons but retrieving these weapons is not an easy task. Pakistan has established a strong nuclear force to safeguard all nuclear sites 24 hours a day with modern military technology. The crisis is going to get worse as the exponential network of ISIS and its popularity in Afghanistan creates deep security challenges for Pakistan and its Taliban allies. This group could use chemical and biological weapons once it gains footing in Afghanistan. For this reason, Pakistan is trying to push the Afghan Taliban towards a political settlement in Afghanistan to prevent IS from gaining control of the country. The IS and the Taliban are not the only security challenges for Pakistan; the country is also facing many social and economic problems, including electricity shortages. Pakistan is seeking civilian nuclear technology to meet its electricity needs. For this reason, the country entered its seventh round of strategic dialogue with the US, which ended without any result. The US turned down Pakistan's demand of access to civilian nuclear technology and argued for focus on its non-proliferation credentials because the country always suffers from a negative image due to its tenuous nuclear non-proliferation regime.

India's policymakers are facing a strategic conundrum about how to undermine or respond to the terrorist threat emanating from Pakistan and Afghanistan. In 2002 and 2008, both Atal Bihari Vajpayee and Manmohan Singh's governments faced an unstable situation in India. The issue of Cold Start doctrine and the possibility of an Indian abrupt nuclear attack in Pakistan has been elucidated in a recently published research paper (George PerKovich and Toby Dalton, 2015): "Today, Indian military analysts also increasingly recognise the risk of even limited ground operation, notwithstanding initial excitement over the more finely calibrated plans proffered by proponents of the so called 'Cold Start' doctrine, similar to the ground option, with Indian forces limiting the depth of their thrust so as not to cross Pakistan's nuclear red lines. Yet, even a limited response that puts Indian boots on Pakistani soil could quickly escalate to major operations that would result in more casualties than would have been suffered in the initial terrorist attack. And, the more Indian forces were succeeding on Pakistani territory, the greater the incentive Pakistan leaders would feel to use nuclear weapons to repulse them."[7]

However, experts say that India does not have the capability to carry out a special operation inside Pakistan with precision air support. Pakistan has a strong air force and has adorned its submarines with nuclear weapons. In February 2012, the country announced that it had started work on the construction of nuclear submarines to better meet the Indian navy's nuclear threat. The current threat of nuclear, biological and chemical weapons proliferation signals trouble, particularly in the Middle East and South Asia, which will not be redressed without resolving regional conflicts, which may, in turn, require internal political changes. India and Pakistan need to implement nuclear risk reduction measures. Terrorists want to buy or steal nuclear material to fabricate a crude bomb or to make or detonate radiological weapons. Bilal Malik (Modern Diplomacy 28 May 2020) highlights the latest versions of ballistic and cruise missiles, indigenous ballistic missile defence (BMD) systems in addition to Russian made S-400, nuclear submarines, and enhanced capabilities for space weaponization:

"India's rapid augmentation of its offensive doctrinal posture vis-à-vis Pakistan is based on enhancing its strategic nuclear capabilities. Under its massive military up-gradation program, India has developed the latest versions of ballistic and cruise missiles, indigenous ballistic missile defence (BMD) systems in addition to Russian made S-400, nuclear submarines, and enhanced capabilities for space weaponization. In the same vein, India's aspiration for supersonic and hypersonic weapons is also evidence of its offensive doctrinal posture. Furthermore, India has been carrying out an extensive cruise missile development program having incredible supersonic speed along with its prospective enhanced air defence shield. Through considerable technological advancements, India has shifted its approach from a counter-value to a counter-force doctrinal posture, as it demonstrates its ambitions of achieving escalation-dominance throughout the region. These technological advancements are clear indicators that India's doctrinal posture is aimed at destabilizing the existing nuclear deterrence equilibrium in South Asia".[8]

Pakistan's tactical range 'Nasr' missile is widely regarded as a 'weapon of deterrence' aimed at denying space for a limited war imposed by India. The induction of 'multiple independent reentry vehicle' (MIRV), the development of land, air and sea-launched cruise missiles and the provision of a naval-based second-strike capability have all played a significant role in the preservation of minimum credible deterrence and the assurance of full-spectrum deterrence at the strategic, operational and tactical levels. Contrary to India's declared NFU policy, Pakistan has never made such an assertion and has deliberately maintained a policy of ambiguity concerning a nuclear first strike against India. This has been carried out to assure its security and to preserve its sovereignty by deterring India with the employment of Full Spectrum Deterrence (FSD) within the ambit of Credible Minimum Deterrence.

This posture asserts that since Pakistan's nuclear weapons are for defensive purposes in principle, they are aimed at deterring India from any and all kinds of aggression. This has been evident from recent crisis situations as well during which Pakistan's deterrent posture has prevented further escalation. Therefore, even now Pakistan is likely to keep its options open and still leave room for the possibility of carrying out a 'first strike' as a viable potential deterrent against India if any of its stated red lines are crossed. Hence, the security dynamics of the South Asian region have changed significantly since its nuclearization in 1998. The impact of this has been substantial and irreversible on regional and extra-regional politics, the security architecture of South Asia, and the international nuclear order. As has been long evident India has held long term inspiration to become a great power.

There have been continuous insinuations about India's nuclear doctrinal posture transforming from 'No First Use' to counterforce offensive posture. The current security architecture of South Asia revolves around this Indian behaviour as a nuclear state. In contrast, Pakistan's nuclear doctrine is based solely on assuring its security, preserving its sovereignty, and deterring India by maintaining a credible deterrence posture. Based on the undeniable threats from India to its existence, Pakistan needs to further expand its doctrinal posture vis-à-vis India. This would preserve the pre-existing nuclear deterrence equilibrium and the 'balance of power' in the South Asian region.[9]

This day-to-day militarisation of potential conflict, the withdrawal of NATO and US forces from Afghanistan, and civil wars in the Middle East have all intensified the war of interests between the two states. In the presence of all these weapons, the danger of nuclear terrorism, the potential spread of nuclear materials in the black market and the recent threatened control of nuclear materials by Sunni terrorist groups (ISIS) in Iraq has raised serious questions about the safety and security of nuclear weapons in South Asia. Pakistan faces a series of threats to its national security. These threats come from the Taliban and the likely potential use of chemical, biological, radiological and nuclear (CBRN) devices by domestic terrorists and extremist groups.

The international task force on the prevention of nuclear terrorism has also warned that the "possibility of nuclear terrorism is increasing" because of a number of factors including "the conventional forms of terrorism" and the vulnerability of nuclear power and research reactors to sabotage and of weapons-usable nuclear materials to theft. Terrorists may possibly retrieve nuclear materials from India or Pakistan and use them against civilian and military installations. Another development that has also worried nuclear scientists is cyber-attacks during nuclear crisis management. Cyber warfare has the potential to attack or disrupt successful nuclear crisis management. India and Pakistan have developed strong networks of cyber armies and have often attacked each other's sensitive computers in the past. In the subcontinent, India's nuclear programme originated not out of a regional rivalry, but from the argument that non-proliferation should be global. Either no one should have weapons of mass destruction or everyone should have the right to own them.[10]

Chapter 8

The US–China Rivalry in the Emerging Bipolar World: Hostility, Alignment, and Power Balance

Suisheng Zhao

Abstract

This article argues that although the US–China rivalry has not presented with some essential elements of the US–Soviet Cold War, the emerging bipolarity has led to misplaced ideological hostility and repeated failing attempts of building alliance systems. Delicate power balance between the two countries has further complicated the rivalry by giving each side the false conviction to prevail.

Introduction

As China has significantly narrowed power gap with the US and widened power gaps with the rest, the Post-Cold War unipolar moment and multi-polarity have given way to an emerging bipolar world in which the US–China rivalry has affected virtually every aspect of international politics and caused significant power realignment.[1] Distinguishing it from the classical vision of a colliding set of roughly equivalent great powers, the emerging bipolarity is imbedded in the multipolar world. As one Chinese scholar stated, 'the world structure has changed from one superpower, many great powers (一超多强), to two superpowers, many great powers (两超多强).[2] In other words, the US and China have competed for dominance but European Union, Russia, India, and some other countries remain independent and can upset the balance of power.

Bipolarity does not necessarily lead to a cold war or violent conflict. But some scholars have declared the arrival of the Sino-US Cold War with its geographic centre of gravity in the Indo-Pacific. The risk of limited war is higher in the Cold War concentrated on maritime East Asia than the Cold War concentrated on continental Europe.[3] In fact, structural realists have long predicted that China's rise would bring it into conflict with the US because the US will not tolerate China as a peer competitor.[4] The so-called Thucydides Trap that an irresistible rising China is on course to collide with an immovable America has reinforced the prediction.[5] Warning about the US–China power showdown, power transition theory confirms that the distinct absence of cultural and ideological affinity between China and the US could make the transition violent.[6]

But other scholars have cautiously rejected the Cold War analogy and argued that the US– China rivalry has not presented with some essential elements of the cold war such as global ideological struggle, opposing alliance systems for spheres of politico-military influence, starkly separated economic blocs, and military power parity. Pointing out the areas of disagreement between the US and China, these scholars believe that there are too many structural barriers and too much prosperity at stake for political leaders in Washington and Beijing to risk a cold war.[7]

Moving beyond the debate, this article argues that although structural realist prediction of the inevitable conflict is a fallacy and the Cold War analogy is a distortion for US–China relations today, the emerging bipolarity has helped intensify the US–China rivalry, leading to misplaced hostility and the attempts to force their allies and partners to take a side. Viewing each other as trying to subvert its political system and fighting to preserve its exclusive way of life, each is determined to maximize its position to gain an advantage and deter the other from threatening its security and prosperity. Neither can get what it wants without depriving the other. The delicate power balance has further complicated the rivalry. Although China is rising quickly, it is yet to match the US across the full spectrum of power assets and capabilities. But China does not have to perfectly equal US power to become a cross-board rival. This complicity has generated misperceptions that one side can prevail over the other. Although no single power can create a cold war on its own, as the rivalry intensifies, there is a real possibility that missteps by either side may lead to escalation to cold war or even hot war.

Misplaced Ideological Hostility

Facilitated by the US engagement to assist China's economic development with the expectation that political liberalization and democracy would follow, an infinitely richer and powerful China has maintained its authoritarianism and challenged the US global primacy. Calling engagement failure and redefining China as a powerful authoritarian rival, the Trump administration declared great power competition as the focus of the US national security strategy and launched a trade war. Using the language in the cold war, his Secretary of State Pompeo even incited the Chinese people to topple the CCP regime.[8]

Although the Biden administration has not used Cold War terms, it has continued many of Trump's get-tough policies, increased public criticism of China's human rights violations in Xinjiang and Hong Kong, and countered Chinese adventures in the Taiwan Straits and the South China Sea. Casting the rivalry as a battle between democracies and autocracies, the Biden administration has placed a strong emphasis on democratic values and reengaged like-minded allies to impose costs for China when it challenges the US values and interests. Demonstrating intentions to further develop the Quadrilateral Security Dialogue (Quad) revived by the Trump administration among four democracies of the US, Australia, India, and Japan as a mini-NATO, President Biden's first multilateral meeting was to host the Quad summit as a 'critical part of the architecture of the Indo-Pacific.[9] One of the primary objectives of his first overseas trip to Europe was to rally allies to constrain China's influence, including boosting infrastructure projects to counter China's Belt and Road Initiative (BRI) and pushing back against China's nonmarket policies and human rights abuses.

The Chinese government has criticized the US for adopting the Cold War mentality based on zero-sum mindset and ideological prejudice.[10] President Xi warned just days after President Biden's inauguration that 'To build small circles or start a new Cold War . . . will only push the world into division and even confrontation.'[11] Rejecting the Cold War, China, however, has taken tit-for-tat actions to confront the US in almost every realm and everywhere in the world, including expelling American journalists, banning them even reporting from Hong Kong and Macao, sanctions on high-level American officials, advancing suppression in Xinjiang, tightening control of Hong Kong, sanctioning the American officials and punishing US allies and partners that challenged China's core interests.

Criticizing the performance of Western democracies, President Xi has highlighted the China model of authoritarianist modernization. China's success in containing the outbreak of COVID-19 by strict confinement measures provided an opportunity to prove the China model. The outbreak

111

was initially predicted as China's Chernobyl moment, a mishandled disaster for the Chinese leadership to perhaps lose legitimacy. Although the government discouraged the early and transparent recognition of the threat, the state went into crisis mode once realizing the scale of the threat and took zealous and heavy-handed actions and quickly controlled the outbreak. After the herculean fight, China orchestrated a propaganda campaign to turn the pandemic into a celebration of the strong capacity of the Chinese state in contrast to the incapacity of Western democracies in the crisis.

Appearing confident in its model of development, China, however, has no messianic ideology to export. Its appeal derives from its economic and political performance, not its ideas. Without 'satellites,' 'allies,' or entente partners, Beijing has no ideological soul mates, committed followers, or dedicated sycophants abroad.[12] China has not defined itself as the vanguard to transplant its authoritarianism throughout the world or undermine democracies to the same degree as the Soviet Union promoted communism and the US promoted liberal democracy. While the longevity of China's one-party rule has constituted an important source of US–China rivalry, Beijing has not built its relations with other countries based on an ideological litmus test. China's version of repressive authoritarianism and high-tech surveillance state has not offered a morally compelling alternative to liberal democracy for most countries in the world. Rejecting Western liberal values, the Chinese leadership has not articulated a universally accepted vision to substitute the norms and values underpinning the current world order.[13]

Beijing is, therefore, more afraid of America's advocacy of expanding democracy and civil liberties into China and overthrow of its one-party rule than the US is afraid of China's authoritarianism into the US. Instead of engaging in a determined effort to undermine democracy and spread autocracy, Beijing has constructed an information firewall and tightened ideological control domestically. Insisting that every country has the right to choose its own political system without foreign pressures, Beijing's influence operation in the US and other Western countries has focused on changing their attitudes and policies toward CCP rule and Beijing's position in Xinjiang, Hong Kong, and Taiwan. Rejecting human rights, freedom, and democracy as universal values, China has sought primarily to legitimize its development model and make the world more accommodating to its political system.[14]

While the Western countries have criticized the Chinese brand of state capitalism, China is the biggest trading partner of three-fourths of the world's other economies and an active participant in global capitalism. Guided by industrial policy, not central planning, Beijing has not coerced other countries to reject US-style capitalism for an alternative command economic model because Chinese economy is highly intertwined and entangled with the global economy, including the American and other market economies. A showcase of capitalism with second only to the US in number of billionaires in China, Beijing has become home to more billionaires than New York City and is the new billionaire capital of the world in 2021.[15]

But the emerging bipolarity has exaggerated China's ideological hostility. Many American politicians have portrayed China as an existential threat to liberal democracy and vowed to forge an alliance of democracies against the world's autocracies because China's success under authoritarian rule has challenged the western belief that liberal democracy always works best for every country at every level of development. Though comfortingly simple, the description of the world as 'dividing into distinct if not purely ideological camps, with both China and the United States hoping to lure supporters' won't help grasp the topsy-turvy world reality and has reinforced the cold war thinking to see stark ideological antagonism.[16] Reflecting this simple divide, a poll published in March 2021 revealed that nine of 10 Americans viewed China as a competitor or enemy and nearly half believed the U.S. should seek to limit China's power.[17]

The Enemy of My Enemy Is My Friend

From the Chinese perspective, the US hostility indicates the intention to deny China's rightful place in the sun and change its regime, a core national interest that Beijing cannot compromise. Managing the rivalry with the US, Beijing has constructed and enhanced strategic partnerships with Russia and Iran featured the shared sentiments against the US, a fearsome enemy. Zbigniew Brzezinski warned in 1998 about the scenario of an 'ant hegemonic' coalition united not by ideology but by complementary grievances.[18] Although the axis of anti-American powers has taken shape, these relationships are transactional rather than sentimental. Following the principle of making partners but not alliance China has not created anything even close to the Warsaw Pact. Russia has become China's most significant strategic partner for its diplomatic clout and remaining military might. President Xi made the point by choosing Moscow as the destination of his first Presidential trip in 2013. Although Russians initially had reservation, the Western sanction to its annexing Crimea and supporting rebel movements in Ukraine in 2014 pushed Moscow toward Beijing to dip into China's deep pockets and align China as a strategic counterweight.

Sharing a list of geopolitical distastes for the US operation in their backyards, China has backed Russian military exercises to intimidate countries in Europe and the Middle East and held the joint Sino-Russian naval operations in the Baltic amid the heightened tension between Russia and NATO in 2017. In reciprocity, Russia took part in joint naval exercises in the South China Sea in 2016 and started joint air patrol over the Pacific in 2019. Russia invited the Chinese to its largest military exercises since the fall of the Soviet Union, Vostok-2018, the first-time Beijing participated in Moscow's simulated war games as opposed to drills under the rubric of counterterrorist cooperation, a ground-breaking sign of heightened trust.

Believing that the West has orchestrated subversion of authoritarian regimes and therefore their own legitimacy by promotion of human rights and democracy, Moscow has been troubled by the Georgian and Ukrainian revolutions while Beijing by separatist agitation in Xinjiang and democratic protest in Hong Kong. In a phone call, Putin supported China's Hong Kong National Security Law and Xi supported Russia's revised constitution.[19] Sharing a strong desire to impose tight controls over their own societies, President Xi has bolstered the party's role, akin to Putin's effort to tame Russian oligarchs and crush political opposition. While Russian officials expressed admiration for China's comprehensive internet censorship and 'social credit' system to rank citizens based on their loyalty and behaviour, China was inspired by Russia's legislation cracking down on nongovernmental organizations.[20] Both Xi and Putin have amended the constitutions to stay in power for life.

The US rolling back the power aspirations of China and Russia has contributed to their collusion. Acting in accordance with the geostrategic calculation that the enemy of my enemy is my friend, their strategic partnership has advanced with mutual empathy and understanding at the top political level. Holding summits twice annually and developing a strong personal rapport, President Xi claimed that 'Russia is the country that I have visited the most times, and President Putin is my best friend and colleague.' State media of both countries featured the two leaders making blinis together, topping them with caviar and downing shots of vodka.[21] Immediately after the rocky Anchorage meeting with his counterparts in the Biden administration in March 2021, Chinese Foreign Minister Wang Yi welcomed Russian Foreign Minister Sergey Lavrov to China. Highlighting the significance of the meeting, Chinese media warned that 'It would be disastrous for any country to confront China and Russia through forging an alliance with the US.'[22]

For many years, Washington held that the burgeoning China–Russia ties were a shallow partnership of convenience and bound to be undermined by diverging national interests and distrust. There is ample evidence to support this view. Both Russia and China see themselves as deserving to be great powers and highly value the independence of their respective decision-making. Chinese leaders were never comfortable with the junior brother position and pecked order from the big brother in the 1950s. Forging a new bond, the power relationship has shifted in favour of China. But Russia is far from being a subordinate. Acting as a junior partner belies Putin's dream of resurrecting Russia as an imperial power. Moscow has viewed itself as a quintessential Eurasia power and regarded much of Central Asia, the main stage for BRI, as its own backyard. China's incursions into Central Asia have caused a deep-seated fear in Russia. In the meantime, China is not happy that Russia has maintained close military ties with and sold advanced weapons to India and Vietnam, both are locked in territorial disputes with China. More importantly, China cannot forget that Russia took the territories in northeast China more than 100 years ago. On 2 July 2020, the Russian embassy in Beijing posted a video of a party celebrating the 160th anniversary of the founding of Vladivostok, which means 'ruler of the east' in Russian and was annexed from China by the Tsarist Empire in 1860. The video reminded the Chinese emotions over historic wounds and prompted an online backlash with the posts such as 'Today we can only endure, but the Chinese people will remember! 'This ancestral land will return home in the future!'[23] Because Russia is hardly amenable to accepting a junior role and Beijing cannot forget the unhappy history, a full-blown alliance is not in sight. Great powers do not mate for life. The US policy toward them largely determines their position toward each other. China cannot afford an unexpected rapprochement between Washington and Moscow, and vice versa. As such, the China–Russia relationship is still more anchored in shared grievances than in common visions.

Ironically, as an increased awareness and rising concern about Sino-Russian cooperation undermining U.S. interests, the sceptical view has given way to an emerging American consensus that the Beijing–Moscow axis is built on real commonalities has a strong foundation and a positive future.[24] The Worldwide Threat Assessment by the U.S. intelligence community in 2017 grouped Russia and China together as America's top threat and explicitly pointed out that they were 'more aligned than at any point since the mid-1950s'.[25]China and Russia were also listed together as the top threats in the 2017 US National Security Strategy. The Biden administration has exhibited continued efforts to confront both China and Russia. The US Interim National Security Guidance published in March 2021 labelled both as rivals. While the US–China relationship has come to a historical low point, the Biden administration has imposed tough sanctions against Russia for its interference in the US elections and other malign activities. The US and Russia have grown antagonistic in theatres from the Middle East to Eastern Europe. Publicly and simultaneously piling pressure on both China and Russia, the US has compelled them to advance their strategic partnership.

China has enlisted Iran in the Axis of the anti-hegemonic coalition because it is the only major Middle East power not allied with the US. The US-led sanctions have scared away badly needed foreign trade and investment, including the access to the international banking system and provided Beijing with a unique, multi-layered monopoly over the Iranian economy. China bought Iranian oil and the money deposited in Chinese banks. Chinese businesses offered services and products to Iran that their American and European counterparts could not. Benefiting from working with the Chinese, Iran quickly jumped on board as Eurasian hub for China's BRI. The China–Central West Asia Economic Corridor, the 10,399 km long 'Silk Railway' to link the Iranian capital to Yiwu in China's Zhejiang province, has carried goods and passengers travelling only in 14 days, as opposed to the month-and-a-half the same shipment would take by sea. President Xi visited Iran and signed the Comprehensive Strategic Partnership with his counterpart Hassan Rouhani in 2016. Both countries are authoritarian and reject Western intervention in their domestic affairs. The partnership was enhanced after the Trump administration's unilateral withdrawal from the Iran nuclear deal in 2018.

China vocally opposed U.S. sanctions and rebuffed the proposed extension of the UN Security Council arms embargo on Iran. Amid COVID-19, while the US refused to lift sanctions, the Chinese airlifted supplies and medical personnel to Tehran. Moving from working on ad hoc projects to the commitment for broad and long-term cooperation, China and Iran signed a 25-year comprehensive cooperation agreement in March 2021 to vastly expand Chinese investments. In return, Iran would regularly supply China with oil at a discount. The agreement also deepened military cooperation, including joint training and exercises, joint weapons research and intelligence sharing. For Iran, the expanded partnership offered an escape from the US maximum pressure that was to end its nuclear program, if not the regime itself. For China, it would extend Chinese footprints deeper into the Middle East, a geopolitical win in the rapidly accelerating strategic competition with Washington.[26] At a time when Biden was trying to bring Iran back to the nuclear negotiating table, China demonstrated its newfound influence with this action.

Standing up to China but Not Taking a Side

The emerging bipolarity has compelled the Biden administration to rally like-minded nations in the contest with China. But many US allies and partners have charted their own course and don't want to be squeezed between Washington and Beijing. With different economic and strategic priorities, threat perceptions, and comfort levels from the US to collectively counter China, these countries have deep anxieties about US creditability and capability. Undermining and denigrating liberal values and alienating many US allies, Trump's poor handling of COVID-19 and incitement for the insurrection against the democratic institutions left many people with no illusions about the US as the beacon of democracy. President Biden has faced uphill battles to make the US version of democracy competitive again and demonstrate that the US is reliable after the election in which Trump received more votes than any presidential candidate in history other than his opponent.

No longer loyal to the US on the grounds of shared ideals and the trust on US strength, these countries have weighed the costs and benefits and made their decisions accordingly. They have confronted China because of their sense of the threat for their economic and strategic interests and adjusted these calculations as China's power grows and their economic ties with China tightened. Navigating the complex and ever-changing rivalry between the US and China, many US allies, such as the European Union (EU), Australia, and Japan, have stood up to China but not taken a side.

The EU began to push back unfair Chinese trade and economic practices and promote greater reciprocity in 2016, including the completion of a landmark investment screening legislation and the release of common guidelines for addressing the security risks that Chinese companies posed. Wary of China's economic expansion across the continent, the European Commission (EC) published in 2019 a ground-breaking 'Strategic Outlook' that labelled China for the first time a 'systemic rival'. Although the term vexed Beijing, EC President Ursula von der Leyen reaffirmed China as a systemic rival at the virtual EU-China summit in June 2020.[27] Failing to produce a joint statement, the EU issued its own press statement that expressed 'grave concerns' over the situation in Hong Kong, human rights in Tibet and Xinjiang, and the imprisonment of Canadian and Swedish citizens in China.[28]

But the rivalry has not led to a desire of the EU to squarely align with the US against China because European leaders see Beijing as a systemic rival as well as a partner. Some nations such as Italy and Portugal are enthusiastic backers of BRI. The '17 + 1' group, which includes 12 EU states, set up by China with Central and Eastern European countries (CEEC) has actively promoted cooperation. Although Lithuania pulled out of the group in 2021, Beijing downplayed it as a small country and played an insignificant role in the China-CEEC mechanism. Becoming the first European country to use Chinese COVID-19 vaccines for mass rollout, Serbia's Prime Minister Ana Brnabic personally welcomed the shipment in the airport. Hungary was the first EU member to approve Chinese vaccines. The EU reached Comprehensive Agreement on Investment (CAI) with China weeks before President Biden's inauguration. The agreement was politically symbolic. Tearing between the opportunity to close one of the best investment agreements and the desire to seize the early days of the Biden administration to improve transatlantic relations, the EU sent a message to President Biden that the US must earn European cooperation in a matter as important as relations with China.

Australia has long walked a fine line between its economic and strategic interests. Beijing cultivated and developed a very strong economic relationship with Australia, hoping to weaken the longstanding Australian-US alliance and create a powerful pro-Beijing constituency. President Xi visited Australia in 2014 and delivered a speech to Australian parliament. But the relationship soured after 2016 when Canberra introduced foreign interference laws and pinpointed China as the main threat. In 2017, Australia became the first nation to ban Huawei from its 5 G network. The advent of COVID-19 added more strain to the tension. In April 2020, Foreign Minister Marise Payne called for a global independent inquiry into China's handling of the outbreak and the origins of the coronavirus. Irking by the snowball effect, China launched an increasingly shrill campaign to denounce Australia with a palpable sense of anger and resentment. Urging Canberra to 'grow up and reflect on its wrong deeds',[29] China announced the 212% raise of tariff on Australian wine, imposed high tariffs on the imports of Australia's agriculture, seafood and mineral products, and warned its tourists and students to reconsider Australia as a destination. Punishing Australia as an example to other countries, the Chinese embassy in Australia presented a list of 14 grievances and called for corrections.[30]

But Australia was not deterred. As diplomatic tension worsened, five Australian warships joined the US and Japanese forces in the Philippine Sea to show solidarity and strength in July 2020. Australia joined the US in a declaration filed at the United Nations (UN) rejecting China's claims in the South China Sea as inconsistent with the United Nations Convention for the Law of the Sea (UNCLOS). Foreign and defines ministers travelled to Washington for the annual Australia–US Ministerial Consultation in the risk of the pandemic quarantine after their return home. The joint statement expressed some of the most direct criticism of Beijing to date, highlighting the 'repression of Uyghurs and members of other minority groups in Xinjiang'; national security legislation in Hong Kong that 'imperilled the rule of law'; and maritime claims in the South China Sea that were 'not valid under international law'.[31]

Some observers believed that Canberra's action demonstrated Washington's success in bringing Australia to its side of the tug of war with China.[32] But the Australian position was more nuanced. At the Australia–US consultation, while Australia's defines minister vowed to deepen defines cooperation with the US, she stopped short of committing to more aggressive freedom of navigation exercises closer to disputed islands in the South China Sea. Australia's foreign minister also expressed 'no intention of injuring' its relationship with China, reflecting the delicate balance that Canberra sought to strike as it took a tougher line on China.[33] The US and Australia have overlapping strategic objectives, but their interests and threat perceptions regarding China are by no means symmetrical. Reflecting this delicate position, Prime Minister Scott Morrison called on both the Biden administration and China to show more 'latitude' to smaller nations. Declaring Australia did not want to be forced into a 'binary choice', he asked for 'a bit more room to move'.[34]

This delicate position has tested other US allies in the Pacific. These countries cannot afford to become a contested ground for great-power rivalry because China's attraction of the enormous economic size has made it the largest trading partner of many countries. Beijing has turned economic clout into diplomatic advantage to punish countries that criticize its human rights abuses, question its performance on COVID-19, or resist its regional expansion. Singapore's Premier therefore stated that Asia-Pacific countries wanted to cultivate good relations with both China and the US. If Washington tried to contain China's rise or Beijing sought to build an exclusive sphere of influence in Asia, they would put the long-heralded Asian century in jeopardy.[35] Japan is a case in point. A long-time US ally, Japan's security and prosperity have depended on an open and inclusive order sustained by US leadership and its military presence in the region. Such an environment has enabled Japan to maintain constructive engagement with China. For Japan, it would be a nightmare to wake up one day to find the US and China ganging up to divide the Pacific Ocean or the world.[36] But Japan has become increasingly concerned about the growing Chinese military capabilities and aggressive sovereignty claims. Chinese vessels have sailed continuously into the contiguous zone of the Japanese-administered Senkaku/Diaoyu islands.

Responding positively to the US strategic initiatives, including the revived Quad, and strengthened its efforts for securing the freedom of navigation, Japan, however, has been reluctant to make a choice between its security cooperation with the US and socio-economic ties with China. Facing China's assertiveness, Japan is too economically integrated with China to activate a full-scale confrontation. The US withdrawal from the Trans-Pacific Partnership (TPP) put Japan in an awkward position hedging against Chinese economic dominance of the region. Japanese Prime Minister Yoshihide Suga became the first foreign leader in-person meeting with President Biden in April 2021. Their joint statement encouraged the peaceful resolution of cross-Strait issues for the first time since the meeting of Eisaku Sato and Richard Nixon in 1969. But the US tried unsuccessfully to persuade Suga to state publicly that, if necessary, Japan would stand by America and help defend Taiwan.

The Japanese government also avoided condemning China's repression of human rights in Hong Kong and Xinjiang and resisted imposing sanctions. Clarifying his position after returning to Japan, Suga told the Diet that the reference to Taiwan in the joint statement 'does not presuppose military involvement at all.'[37] Because both China's strategic partners and US allies have maintained their delicate position to manoeuvre between the two superpowers, the emerging bipolar world has not been dominated by two rigid antagonistic alliance systems. The complex structural configuration, however, has not prevented the US from the attempts to form alliances based on liberal values against China based on the logic of bipolarity.

Delicate Balance of Power

Underscoring the US–China rivalry has been the geopolitical incompatibility between the rising and incumbent powers. The dynamics of the rivalry is, therefore, dictated by their balance of power between the two countries. But the power balance has been delicate. On the one side of the equation, as China has indulged itself in a state-managed banquet of positivity, the culture of inflated self-congratulation rapidly becomes corrosive. Declaring the arrival of a new era in which profound changes unseen in a century created the opportunity for China's inevitable rise while the US is in relative decline,[38] President Xi has become increasingly confident that time and momentum are on China's side. Beijing has, therefore, no longer bended to America's pressure and accommodated its demands without conditions.

Reflecting the changing mode, China's top diplomat Yang Jiechi made two fresh points to his counterparts at their meeting in March 2021. First, 'the United States does not have the qualification to say that it wants to speak to China from a position of strength.' Second, the United States must stop advancing its own democracy in the rest of the world" when it was dealing with discontent among its own population. Chinese Foreign Minister Wang Yi added another point that 'It is time for the US to correct the longstanding bad practice (老毛病)' of wilfully interfering in China's internal affairs.[39] Encouraged by the boundless confidence of the Chinese leadership, many Chinese people have believed China could seize islands in the East and South China Seas and take back Taiwan by force even if the U.S. military were to intervene in the conflicts.

Beijing's rhetoric, however, does not match the reality that China is not a superpower of the same scale as the US and the world is only a loose bipolarity. The endogenous hubris and narratives of the inevitable rise of China has tended to cover-up the serious external and internal challenges. Internally, in addition to environmental destruction, corruption, and aging crisis that has increased the costs of caring for the elderly, the level of inequality is alarming. China stopped publicizing its Gini coefficient in 2014. But Premier Li Keqiang admitted in 2020 that over 600 million people still lived on a monthly income of less than 1,000 yuan (US$140).[40] The most acute internal challenge is that, making himself the president for life, Xi Jinping has effectively prevented China from establishing an institutionalized mechanism for power succession, possibly leading to political turmoil if anything happens to him.

Externally, China's expanding access to foreign markets and technology during the decades of catch-up growth have exhausted. Export-led growth has hit the limits. Decimating its own natural endowments and importing more food and energy than any other nation, China needs unfettered access to global markets, resources and technology to reach the critical break-through. China is instead shut out by one country after another in response to its authoritarian turn and diplomatic provocations. A fragile rising power, it is not clear if China could become the first authoritarian regime to avoid the middle-income trap that had kept many emerging economies from entering the club of high- income countries. Although China's nominal GDP has come close to the US, China's per capita GDP is about 15% of the US's. It is true that overall economic size matters more than per capita income for power heft. But when the world's biggest economy has a per capita income well below middle powers, it is not clear how sustainable it could affect the global power balance.

China has spent enormous sums to modernize its military, which has become much stronger but still cannot match the US. China's growing military threat to the US has been primarily limited to the theatres of the Asia-Pacific. Its imperial outposts such as Piraeus harbour in Greece and activities in other parts of the world are vulnerable without the regional assets anchored by Chinese military. Comparing with over 60 US allies and partners, most of which are industrialized countries, China has fewer partners of global weight or credibility. Eschewing formal alliances as such pacts involve trading some autonomy and flexibility for more security and influence, China has not created anything akin to the Warsaw Pact. The balance of power was revealed by the countries who supported and opposed China's imposition of the Hong Kong national security law in the United Nations Human Rights Council (UNHRC) in 2020. The 53 countries in hock to China comprised only 4% of world GDP. The rich democracies coalesced into a united front against China's Hong Kong policy.

Russia is the most important pseudo-ally, but its economy is only about the size of Australia. In addition, their power centres are a continent apart. Russia's centre of gravity has been in Europe with a zone of strategic tension of its own to the west. China's geopolitical sore spots are located largely in the Asia-Pacific, thousands of miles away from Russia. Surrounded by many worrying countries, China has only two allies in the neighbourhood, North Korea and Pakistan, which are more of a liability than an asset. Japan, South Korea, Vietnam, Australia, and India are all on the spectrum from cool to hostile towards China and are allies or friendly with the US.

China's power aspirations in the diverse and crowded neighbourhood are checked by the presence and influence of the US and other regional powers. While it becomes difficult for the US to hold primacy, it is more difficult for China to overtake the US anytime soon. Pushing the US out so that it would no longer worry about its neighbours counting on American military power, China's ambitions have often exceeded its grasp and unintendedly helped the US stay in the neighbourhood. Many of China's neighbours used to ask 'what we could get from the Americans in return for their military personnel and basing rights. The new question is, what will we have to give them to get them to stay? And it's all because of China.'[41] President Trump's failing policy in the region bestowed a gift on China. But China failed to take this opportunity to gain trust. Demonstrating a remarkable ability to press its expanded interests, China picked fights even amid COVID-19. Setting up two new administrative districts, China announced the naming of 80 islands, reefs, seamounts, shoals, and ridges in the South China Sea in April 2020. The last time China named the geographical features there was 1983. Chinese ships repeatedly harassed ships from Japan and Vietnam in areas they consider their exclusive economic zone (EEZ).

Although Beijing's effort at seduction and coercion was successful earlier in shifting the geopolitical orientation of the Philippines under President Duterte away from Washington, including announcing the termination of the 1999 Philippine–US Visiting Forces Agreement (VFA), Manila reversed course to scrap the agreement in June 2020. After Joe Biden was elected President, the Philippines suspended the decision to abrogate the VFA for the second time so 'that the two allies can work on a long-term mutual defence arrangement.'[42] Pressuring the Philippines to make a choice between China and the US, a fleet of about 220 Chinese vessels presented at Whitsun Reef within the Philippines's EEZ in March 2021. The Philippines lodged diplomatic protest over the presence of what it believed was Chinese maritime militia vessels. Although most of the vessels left in late April, Chinese Foreign Ministry spokesman reiterated China's position that the reef was Chinese territory and the Philippines should 'immediately stop wanton hype-up.'[43]

Chinese troops clashed with Indian troops in a series of tense encounters along the disputed Himalayan border in May 2020, resulting in casualties on both sides, the most serious conflict since 1962. Indian Prime Minister Narendra Modi had tried for years to maintain good relations with both the US and China. The border clash erupted with anti-Chinese sentiment, advocating a sharp foreign policy shift for a robust US relationship because enjoying the best of both worlds was no longer possible. In the transition from non-aligned to strategic autonomy, a growing number of Indian strategists, and increasingly the Modi government, have concluded that India's strategic autonomy could be enhanced by a strategic partnership with the United States.[44]

Driving the Philippines, Vietnam and India to lambast China's heavy-handed territorial actions, China allowed a series of disparate incidents to congeal into anti-China sentiment in its neighbourhood. A leading Chinese scholar has advocated for many years to change non-alliance orthodoxy and establish a system of formal alliances.[45] Although this vision seems far-flung, many countries do not seek China's protection because of increased distrust and fear of Chinese power to their own security. China cannot win the rivalry with the US without winning the support of its neighbours and pre-empting their balancing motives. It is true that American hegemony has declined, and the US has yet demonstrated its resilience this time. But people have claimed the decline of the US for decades and have recanted their predictions many times. Although the US has gone through many dramatic moments and crises after World War II, it has boasted a superior continuity and a formidable ability to overcome critical phases because of the benefit to regularly elect new leaders to correct course.

Juggling the array of challenges requires nothing short of adroit diplomatic engagement to ameliorate the tensions between China and other countries. One observer, therefore, suggested that 'Chinese need to reflect deeply and appreciate their own weaknesses and the enemy's extraordinary strengths and ability to recover from catastrophes.' Neither China's undeniable successes nor America's decline is inevitable.[46] Far from the position to dislodge American power even in its own neighbourhood, hegemony is 'unnecessary to secure China's interests and not something to be particularly wished for because pursuing global hegemony would be counterproductive and destabilizing in ways that would not be conducive to China's interests or its security.'[47] It is certainly prudent that Beijing continues to assure at least for now that 'China does not want to replace U.S. dominance in the world.'[48]

China's Competitive Edge

Because the balance of power is still in the US favour, American leaders are determined to win the rivalry and crush China of its imagination. President Trump declared that a trade war with China would be easy to win but 'did little to fully prepare for an American economy geared for the war.'[49]

Vowing to invest heavily to ensure America prevails in the race, President Biden has pledged to prevent China from passing the US to become the most powerful country under his watch. Refusing to accept China as a peer power has driven America's reflexive efforts to undermine China's rise. But it is not clear how the US can stop China's rise or defeat China easily. Going far beyond the tottering command economy that defined the Soviet Union in its final years, China's global economic clout and integration are many multiples of the Soviet Union's and continue to grow. Not a lopsided Soviet-style overriding focusing on the military sector, China has built advanced and broad-based technology and a dynamic economy globally competitive.

Taking advantage of a relatively benign external environment when the US was preoccupied by the wars in Iraq and Afghanistan, the Chinese leadership at the 16th Party Congress in 2002 identified an extended period of strategic opportunity to focus on economic development. The precept was validated by the 17th Party congress in 2007 and the 18th Party Congress in 2012. Facing a more precarious and competitive external environment, President Xi has grasped the narrowed window to catch up quickly. The US trade war and threat of technology decoupling was a wakeup call for the vulnerability of high dependency on the US market and technologies. China adopted a strategy different from the US in the science and technology contest. The US focused on pioneering basic research. China prioritized applications and focused on deploying rather than developing cutting-edge science capabilities because advances in science and technology were easy to access in the globalized world. It is much more expensive and riskier to invest in basic research than to obtain something already developed or close to maturity. This strategy helped China get to the end cheaply but could not let China win the science and technology race.[50]

In response to the US market and technology denials and geopolitical tensions, President Xi announced a domestic and international dual-circulation strategy (DCS). Leveraging 1.4 billion consumers and emphasizing domestic production for home consumption, including domestic supply chains and import substitution for technology, DCS has built an urgent political and national security agenda to lessen China's dependence on the US and pushed hard for indigenous innovation and basic science and technology investment. Recalling the Maoist slogan, self-reliance, President Xi has encouraged Chinese firms to localize key industrial products and systems because 'there is no way that China can ask for or rely on buying the key and core technology from foreign countries.'[51]

The high-tech sector is at the core of the rivalry. China has used all the levers of industrial policy to support indigenous innovation, moved rapidly in developing key technology sectors and sharpened focus on the development of US embargoed and controlled technologies. China spent 2.5% of GDP on research and development (R&D) during the 13th FYP of 2016–2020, the second largest amount globally after the US, and launched the 'Medium and Long-Term Plan for Science and Technology 2021–35' to make China a technological powerhouse. The previous plan for 2005–2020 was the basis for the Made in China 2025 industrial policy, now barely mentioned due to the Western criticism. But the policy has continued apace and advanced in the new plan and worked in concert with China's other industrial policies, including the China Standards 2035 to set global standards for the next generation of technology. Strengthening the relative integrity and autonomy of the domestic industrial chain, particularly in chokepoint areas and strategic links,[52]China has become the only country in the world that owned all the industrial categories listed in the UN Industrial Classification, with 39 industrial categories, 191 intermediate categories and 525 subcategories. The system can independently produce all industrial products from clothing and footwear to aerospace. Some technologies have progressed from 'running to follow' to 'running parallel' and to 'running to lead' [53]

The 2020 Nikkei survey of 74 high-tech products and services indicated that Chinese companies expanded their presence for dominance in global high-technology markets with a boost from robust domestic demand. China topped Japan and chased the US in the number of sectors in which it took top market share.[54] Former Google CEO Eric Schmidt reveals that China is on a trajectory to overtake the US in the rivalry for artificial intelligence (AI) supremacy. China's edge begins with its big population, which affords an unparalleled pool of talent, the largest domestic market in the world, and a massive volume of data collected by companies and government in a political system that always places security before privacy.[55] China has withstood the US attempt at decoupling because the US and China are interdependent in ways that it never was with the Soviet Union. For many American companies and organizations, China is still their largest non-US market. Although the trade war hastened a trend toward diversification in the production chains, 'Made in China' has continued a lucrative option for most investors because of China's enormous market and strong business ecosystem. It is tough for any country to match, at least initially, the high standard set by China as a manufacturing hub, making the exodus from China not just cost-intensive, but also heavily weight competence in comparison with China's manufacturing skillset.[56]

Profiting from the success at getting COVID-19 under control, China had the quickest economic recovery from the pandemic of any major country and was the only major economy to post positive GDP growth of 2.3% in 2020. Despite 3 years of Donald Trump's trade war and COVID disruptions, China's export in the first quarter 2021 jumped nearly 40%, testifying to China's robustness as a manufacturing base, the breadth of goods that it can produce and the skill of its exporters in navigating tough times. Policymakers exploited this strength to tackle structural issues such as financial leverage, internet regulation and their desire to make technology the main driver of investment.[57] Other than economic assets, China has brought the domestic approval to sustain the strategic rivalry. Strengthening the CCP position as a disciplined organization, President Xi has relied on the party masquerading as an elite of more than 90 million members and hundreds of million government and State-owned Enterprise (SOE) employees with vested interests in the Party. Enjoying performance legitimacy for the decades of high economic growth, the CCP has invested more in social policies and absolute poverty eradication when the economy has slowed and the largesse to dispense benefits diminished. China's success in lifting millions of people out of poverty has helped the CCP maintain legitimacy.

The party's firm response to potentially existential challenges such as from pro-democracy protests in Hong Kong, separatist activities in Xinjiang, and the devastating coronavirus has helped solidify the support of the Chinese people. Those who complained about the party's initial coronavirus cover-up reflected more positively on their experience after they saw how much worse it could have been in America and other countries. President Xi has emerged from the crisis stronger than ever. The University of California survey revealed that the average levels of Chinese trust in the government increased from 8.23 in June 2019, to 8.65 in February 2020, and to 8.87 in May 2020. Average scores (1 to 5 Likert scale) on the question whether they prefer living under China's political system as compared to others increased from 3.89 in June 2019 to 4.14 in February 2020, and to 4.28 in May 2020. In contrast, Chinese favourability toward the US on a scale of 1 to 10 dropped from 5.77 in June 2019 to 4.77 in May 2020. Although the reliability of such surveys could be questioned because the Chinese government exercised extensive control over the information available to its citizens, China's relative success in controlling the coronavirus' spread and the dismal performance of the US contributed to these results.[58]

The rising domestic support has given President Xi confidence to announce the 'Five Never Allows', including never allowing any force to 'separate the CPC from the Chinese people or counterpoise the party to the Chinese people; to impose their will on China through bullying, . . . '[59] Taking the lesson that the Soviet Union collapsed because the ruling communist party's ideals and convictions wavered and conceded ground to Western liberal values, President Xi has leveraged China's emergence as the first major economy to return to growth after Covid-19 to strengthen his personal authority, doubled down on core authoritarian values and brushed aside international concern about the country's rising authoritarianism to crack down on basic freedoms from Xinjiang to Hong Kong. Unlike the Soviet Union, China is far from an ideologically disillusioned and exhausted adversary. The US policies of containment or regime change in China have often been counterproductive. If any change were to take place it would be because of the Chinese people. China survived the US-led isolation and containment during the Mao years and muddled through the blowout after the end of Cold War. The CCP celebrated its centenary in July 2021 and its 72 years of untrammelled power in October 2021, far surpassed that of the former Soviet Communist Party.

Although China has overreached in some respects, it has not followed European imperial powers to invest heavily in overseas colonies only to have them rebel or demand their release peacefully or expend heavily on long-term overseas conflicts with few tangible benefits like the US did. With its disciplined hierarchy of national security priorities, China's leadership has picked its battles literally and figuratively and not truncated its rise with ruinous wars.[60] China has come to conflicts with many of its neighbours. But the US has not built an encircling cold war alliance because China is the biggest economic partner for many of the US allies in the region, including Japan, South Korea, Australia, and many Southeast Asian countries.

While China has faced immense challenges, the US has faced no less challenges internally and externally. While the US remains the most powerful nation in the world, its relative declined is clear. The US produced nearly half the world's GDP after the WWII, one-quarter at the end of the Cold War, and only one-seventh today. Once almost-universal admiration for the US has given to the disappointment over repeated displays of racism, political venality, and xenophobia. U.S. foreign policy has become as partisan as domestic policy, often driven by special rather than national interests and is unrealistic, strategically incoherent, divisive, and fickle. The wars in the Islamic world that it can neither win nor end have siphoned off the trillions of dollars needed to keep its human and physical infrastructure at levels competitive with those of China and crippled U.S. statecraft by defunding non-military means to advance or defend American interests.[61]

The deeply rooted internal division hampered America's ability to confront external challenges and fuelled a tendency to scapegoat China for many problems that Americans largely inflicted upon themselves. It was discordant that the US politicians continued pointing to China as the chief threat when President Trump's supporters stormed the U.S. Capitol to halt the constitutional process of affirming the results of the presidential election. The US cannot compete with autocrats to win when its own democracy so hangs in the balance and has resources being diverted from bipartisanships and other efforts that made the US strong in the past. Facing an increasingly malfunctioning and disaggregated US version of democracy, Chinese propaganda has pointed to the relative success of China as an indicator of its institutional advantage and readily portrayed the US as chaotic and weakened. Such propaganda is most effective when reality provided ample ammunition. Freedom House's annual survey in 2021 revealed that less than 20% of the world's population lived in a free country, the smallest proportion since 1995.

Nearly 75% of the world's population lived in a country that faced a deterioration of democratic freedoms. It admitted that 'as a lethal pandemic, economic and physical insecurity, and violent conflict ravaged the world in 2020, democracy's defenders sustained heavy new losses in their struggle against authoritarian foes, shifting the international balance in favour of tyranny'.[62] The democratic backsliding in the US and other countries has made the Chinese system look better by comparison to sustain the rivalry. The US image has tarnished among the Chinese people. One polling of 14 countries found that although America's image abroad improved by an average of 9 points 100 days after President Biden's inauguration, the American image declined 9 points in China. Approximately 74% of Chinese adults held unfavourable views of the US.[63]

Conclusion

The Sino-US rivalry can hardly end with the collapse of one power. Both countries would like to lose if they pursue the path of power dominance.

While Beijing cannot expect the US to accept its authoritarian system or replace the US power dominance in the world, neither can Washington alter Beijing's intrinsic values, change China's regime, and stop China's rise. The two powers incapable of dominating each other have dictated the durability of the bipolarity. A world of multiple systems competition and coexistence is normal in history. But neither the US nor China is willing to accept the reality. Misplacing each other's hostility and attempting the impossible mission of building opposing alliance systems, these two countries have defined their rivalry in terms of survival versus collapse, which has hindered their joint pursuit of shared responsibilities based on their overlapping interests such as climate change, nuclear proliferation, and pandemic prevention.

As the two largest greenhouse emitters, the US and China have contributed to an environment in which neither could survive if they don't work together to constrain emissions. With the rhetoric of needs for cooperation on these shared interests, each has pointed fingers on the other for non-cooperation. The US and China as the two nuclear-armed powers have a genuine and shared interest in keeping the rivalry within boundaries to avoid an unconstrained struggle leading to escalation and mutual destruction. But they have not established strategic rules of the road and effective mechanisms to manage conflicts at the embryonic stage of bipolarity to avoid the risk of accidental military frictions. While a duopoly with China and the US working in tandem is unlikely because of their competitive relationship, a large-scale confrontation and race toward the bottom are extremely costly. The delicate power balance has produced the durability of bipolarity in which cooperation between rivals may be uncomfortable but necessary. The idea that countries could compete ruthlessly and cooperate intensely at the same time may sound like a contradiction. 'It is natural for big powers to compete. But it is their capacity for cooperation that is the true test of statecraft, and it will determine whether humanity makes progress on global problems.'[64]

Journal of Contemporary China.https://doi.org/10.1080/10670564.2021.1945733 The US–China Rivalry in the Emerging Bipolar World: Hostility, Alignment, and Power Balance Suisheng Zhao To cite this article: Suisheng Zhao (2021): The US–China Rivalry in the Emerging Bipolar World: Hostility, Alignment, and Power Balance, Journal of Contemporary China, DOI: 10.1080/10670564.2021.1945733 To link to this article: https://doi.org/10.1080/10670564.2021.1945733. Published online: 13 Jul 2021.Contact Suisheng Zhao szhao@du.edu University of Denver, USA. Journal of Contemporary China is the only English language journal edited in North America that provides exclusive information about contemporary Chinese affairs for scholars, business people and government policy-makers. It publishes articles of theoretical and policy research and research notes, as well as book reviews. The journal's fields of interest include economics, political science, law, culture, literature, business, history, international relations, sociology and other social sciences and humanities. Taylor & Francis make every effort to ensure the accuracy of all the information (the "Content") contained in our publications. However, Taylor & Francis, our agents (including the editor, any member of the editorial team or editorial board, and any guest editors), and our licensors, make no representations or warranties whatsoever as to the accuracy, completeness, or suitability for any purpose of the Content. Any opinions and views expressed in this publication are the opinions and views of the authors, and are not the views of or endorsed by Taylor & Francis. Notes on contributor: Suisheng Zhao is Professor and Director of the Center for China-US Cooperation at Josef Korbel School of International Studies, University of Denver and Editor of the Journal of Contemporary China. Disclosure statement: No potential conflict of interest was reported by the author(s).

Chapter 9

Combating Nuclear Smuggling? Exploring Drivers and Challenges to Detecting Nuclear and Radiological Materials at Maritime Facilities

Robert Downes, Christopher Hobbs, and Daniel Salisbury

Abstract

International concern over nuclear terrorism has grown during the past few decades. This has driven a broad spectrum of efforts to strengthen nuclear security globally, including the widespread adoption of radiation-detection technology for border monitoring. Detection systems are now deployed at strategic locations for the purported purpose of detecting and deterring the smuggling of nuclear and radioactive materials. However, despite considerable investment in this area, few studies have examined how these programs are implemented or the operational challenges they face on a day-to-day basis. This article seeks to address this with a focus on radiation-detection efforts at maritime facilities. Utilizing practitioner interviews and a survey, this article identifies the factors that influence the planning and use of these systems in this fast-moving environment. The results clearly demonstrate that the implementation of these systems varies significantly across different national and organizational contexts, resulting in a fragmented global nuclear-detection architecture, which arguably undermines efforts to detect trafficked nuclear-threat materials. Greater consideration should therefore be given to developing international standards and guidance, designing and adopting tools to support key parts of the alarm assessment process, and broader sharing of good practice.

Keywords: nuclear terrorism nuclear security, radiation detection, maritime supply chain, border monitoring

The theft and accidental loss of nuclear and radioactive materials, resulting in so-called material out of regulatory control (MORC), is a global issue of long-standing concern. A number of sources document this persistent phenomena, most notably the International Atomic Energy Agency (IAEA) Incident Trafficking Data Base (ITDB), established in 1995.[1] The ITDB contains information on several thousand "unauthorized activities" involving a wide range of materials including radiological sources, radioactively contaminated scrap metal, natural and highly enriched uranium, and plutonium,[2] the loss of control over which represents a clear health risk and environmental hazard.[3] The ITDB also contains several hundred incidents that involve the deliberate trafficking or malicious use of certain nuclear and radioactive materials.[4] Studies have illustrated how, if obtained in sufficient quantities by actors such as terrorist groups, these materials could cause significant death, destruction, and disruption.[5]

International efforts to reduce the loss of material control and aid their recovery date back several decades. These include improving physical protection measures at facilities holding nuclear and radiological materials, replacing high-risk materials with safer alternatives, and sting operations designed to flush materials out of black-market circulation.[6] One nuclear-security measure that has garnered extensive investment in recent years is the installation of border-monitoring systems, focused on identifying the characteristic radiation emitted by nuclear and radiological materials. Billions of dollars have been spent on deploying detection technology at national border crossings, key chokepoints, and high-value targets around the world.[7] These systems can reduce nuclear and radiological risks in two interrelated ways. First, direct detection can disrupt attempts to illicitly traffic materials while in motion. Second, raising technical barriers to covertly moving materials serves to dissuade adversaries from engaging in illicit trafficking, a commonly utilized counterterrorism strategy of deterrence-by-denial.[8]

Given the scale of efforts to develop and deploy border-monitoring systems, it is surprising that few studies have sought to explore how these systems are implemented, the challenges encountered in their operation, and the opportunities available to further strengthen the global nuclear-detection architecture. Most research in this area has either examined high-level policy decisions, explored hypothetical scenarios involving the trafficking of materials, or focused on narrow technical issues. Official reports have

133

tended to assess the effectiveness of particular programs by focusing on issues such as the number of systems installed, equipment uptime, and the provision of training.[9]

One explanation for the lack of detailed published studies in this domain is the risk of publicly revealing sensitive operating information, which adversaries could potentially exploit to circumvent detection systems. This is a legitimate concern when studying the implementation of this and indeed any nuclear-security measure. However, it is possible to mitigate this risk by purposefully limiting the specificity of the research conducted and information released. The following article takes this approach, with an anonymous survey used to probe the operation of radiation-detection systems at maritime facilities. Survey responses were contextualized using data from the existing literature and through a number of semi-structured interviews with academics and representatives of international organizations, shipping companies, regulators, and trade associations.[10] Information presented in this article is used to compare and contrast different border-monitoring systems, with care taken to ensure that specific countries and maritime facilities cannot be identified. For more details on the survey that underpins this study, please refer to the Appendix at the end of this article.

There are a range of different locations where radiation-detection systems are deployed, including airports, vehicle border-crossing points, subway systems, and government buildings. This study focuses on their use in the maritime supply chain, specifically with regard to the scanning of shipping containers at maritime facilities as opposed to other types of cargo. This is a key environment in which to combat the illicit trafficking of nuclear and radioactive materials, given the volume of global trade that is shipped by sea, with studies postulating that a "functional nuclear weapon" could be readily "moved about in an ordinary shipping container."[11]

To provide context for this study, this article starts by discussing how threat perceptions have shaped international efforts to detect radiation at maritime borders. This is followed by a general discussion on how these efforts can be deployed at maritime facilities and standard protocols governing their use. Next, the article explores how and why systems have been implemented at different facilities, the drivers behind their operation, and some of the difficulties encountered by those operating such systems, commonly referred to as "front-line officers" (FLOs). The closing discussion articulates a series of policy measures for improving the effectiveness of the global nuclear-detection architecture.

The global nuclear-detection architecture: evolving threat perceptions and response

The smuggling of nuclear materials across borders has been a persistent concern since the start of the atomic age, with efforts to identify and intercept materials evolving in response to the changing international geopolitical environment.

Early state-level concerns: the Cold War

In the United States, concerns were initially framed in terms of a clandestine Soviet attack, where a nuclear weapon might be delivered covertly by a means other than a missile or aircraft. In a closed Senate hearing in 1946, Robert Oppenheimer, director of the Manhattan Project, was asked about the possibility of Soviet operatives smuggling an atomic bomb into New York City. In response, Oppenheimer replied, "of course it could be done, and people could destroy New York."[12] Discussion then turned to how such a device could be detected in transit, Oppenheimer famously exclaiming, "with a screwdriver" necessary to open and inspect every box or container entering the city.

The US Atomic Energy Commission later sanctioned a study into how highly enriched uranium (HEU) or plutonium, which forms the fissile core of a nuclear weapon, might be detected if smuggled into the United States.[13] The output, which became known as the "Screwdriver Report," was published in the 1950s and remains classified. It explored how both passive radiation and induced emissions could potentially be used to detect nuclear materials inside a container.[14] The report concluded that detection would only be successful at a relatively short range, and that passive radiation systems would be vulnerable to shielding.[15] The 1950s also saw the first practical deployment of radiation detectors for the purposes of border monitoring, with systems installed at a number of US air- and seaports.[16]

As other US adversaries developed nuclear weapons, concerns regarding potential clandestine nuclear attacks broadened. The 1970 US National Intelligence Estimate noted that China, lacking conventional means of delivery to attack or deter the United States with nuclear weapons, might "see some advantages in clandestinely introducing and emplacing nuclear weapons into the US."[17] There were also fears that, during heightened tensions between the United States and the Soviet Union, Beijing might smuggle into the United States a "nuclear device constructed as to appear to be of Soviet origin."[18] The report envisioned that such an incident could initiate a crisis between the two superpowers, serving Chinese interests.

135

There were also early concerns regarding the possible theft and smuggling of nuclear materials by non-state actors, more than 100 extortion threats (the majority of which were hoaxes) involving nuclear and radiological materials and weapons being reported from the early 1970s to the early 1990s.[19] In response, the United States established the Nuclear Emergency Search Team in the mid-1970s.[20] This team was tasked with countering nuclear and radiological threats by detecting and recovering nuclear and radiological materials, deactivating weapons, and helping to identify perpetrators.

Emergence of a New Threat: the 1990s

In the 1990s, the perceived threat of nuclear and radiological terrorism increased as a result of several factors. First, some analysts believed that the end of the Cold War weakened political constraints on terrorist actions, ushering in an era of "new terrorism."[21] Attacks such as the 1993 World Trade Center bombing, Aum Shinrikyo's 1995 sarin attack on the Tokyo subway, and the 2000 bombing of the USS Cole in Yemen provided the evidentiary basis for a shift toward increasingly high casualties and, in the Aum Shinrikyo case, unconventional terrorism. Second, the collapse of the Soviet Union increased concerns over the availability of nuclear and radiological materials. Early reports offered lurid accounts of "loose nukes" leaking from the poorly secured arsenals of the former Soviet Union states (FSU).[22] While many allegations were quickly discounted, there remained a body of evidence showcasing disconcertingly common losses of weapon-useable nuclear materials.[23] Simultaneously, nuclear and radiological materials as well as contaminated consumer goods and scrap metal entered Central and Eastern Europe with increasing frequency, smuggled by criminals and other individuals.[24]

Starting in 1990, in response to the cross border flows of radioactive materials, a number of European countries established radiation-detection systems at key border crossings, including seaports.[25] However, trafficking continued. In 1994, there were four notable interdictions in Germany involving the smuggling of HEU and plutonium.[26] In response, Germany sponsored a resolution at the 1994 IAEA General Conference, aimed at tackling the illicit trafficking of nuclear materials and improving the current disjointed efforts of states and international organizations.[27] Specifically, it argued for joint efforts involving the European Union and others actors in supporting the "installation of radiation monitoring equipment for border control purposes."[28]

This resolution arguably heralded the beginning of concerted international efforts to counter the illicit trafficking of radiological and nuclear materials. One specific outcome was the initiation of the Illicit Trafficking Radiation Assessment Program (ITRAP) in 1997.[29]ITRAP assessed the ability of commercially available detection systems to identify commonly smuggled nuclear and radiological materials and radioactively contaminated goods.[30] The results of this work fed into an IAEA-sponsored guidance document that advised member states on the use of radiation detection at national borders.[31] The resolution also served to reorient bilateral support programs to the FSU, from physical protection to illicit trafficking, the United States and other actors increasing efforts to provide radiation equipment and training for customs officers and other border-based agencies.[32]

Nevertheless, despite increased budgets and a higher profile, efforts to institute border-monitoring systems struggled from a lack of coordination. For example, US efforts to counter illicit trafficking through providing radiation-detection systems, training, and other assistance were split between a considerable number of federal agencies.[33]With no single agency in charge of leading US efforts, there was a little alignment of approaches to border-security enhancement, resulting in varying capabilities of the detection equipment installed within different countries and facilities[34] As a result, certain border crossings were "more vulnerable to nuclear smuggling than others."[35]

Toward a Global System: the 2000s

While the perceived threat of nuclear terrorism increased during the 1990s, September 11, 2001 brought about a sea change in thinking. Analysts such as Brian Jenkins from the RAND Corporation saw a dramatic shift from terrorists wanting "a lot of people watching, not a lot of people dead … [to, increasingly,] terrorists want[ing] a lot of people watching and a lot of people dead."[36] Because nuclear materials could facilitate particularly devastating attacks, the international community found a renewed focus on nuclear security, which expanded and reoriented the illicit trafficking agenda. Previously, relatively few programs targeted the international flow of goods or containerized trade specifically, and most nuclear-material interdictions resulted from police investigations. However, post-9/11, the growing internationalization of terrorism and related policy responses resulted in a heightened interest in border security[37]A wider range of states now appeared vulnerable to attacks carried out with nuclear materials smuggled into their homeland. Changing priorities can be seen in budget allocations. In the nine years from 1992 to 2001, the United States spent around $86 million on international counter-nuclear-smuggling efforts, whereas more than $700 million was appropriated in the four years from 2001 to 2005.[38]

Seaports emerged as a distinct focus in two ways. First, states sought to protect their own borders using radiation-detection systems. Both the United States and United Kingdom initiated radiation-detection programs at domestic seaports and other border crossings shortly after 9/11. Under Project Cyclamen, fixed radiation-detection systems were installed to scan incoming goods at three major UK ports and one international airport.[39] This has since evolved into Programme Cyclamen, which now covers most major UK port facilities, major airports, and rail links with mainland Europe.[40] A similar situation developed in the United States under the Department for Homeland Security, albeit on a commensurately larger scale. Second, states deemed at high risk of illicit trafficking often lacked the capacity to develop and deploy radiation-detection systems, and were doubly vulnerable as a result. Although this was recognized in the 1990s, 9/11 reinvigorated existing support programs and led to new initiatives by international organizations and third-party states. For benefactors, overseas detection capabilities acted as a second line of defence in the event that the first line of defence—physical protection at nuclear facilities in beneficiary states—was breached.[41]

New programs dedicated to maritime supply-chain security were initiated at this time, including the National Nuclear Security Administration (NNSA) Megaports Initiative.[42] This focused on enabling the screening of containerized freight for radiological and weapon-useable nuclear materials at non-US ports. Detection systems were installed at facilities in tens of countries. Host-country officials operated and maintained the deployed systems, with US support provided to each Megaports installation for three years. The priority accorded to container scanning at foreign seaports is borne out by the program's $850 million budget from 2003 to 2011, with an additional $1 billion spent in fifty-nine partner countries from 2011 to 2015.[43]

The importance of combating illicit trafficking and strengthening detection systems continues to feature prominently in international fora. For instance, the Nuclear Security Summit (NSS) process addressed border monitoring in several summit communiqués. The 2016 NSS joint statement, endorsed by more than ten states, called for increased national, regional, and international coordination of efforts to detect and remove nuclear and radiological materials from the maritime supply chain.[44]

This was supplemented by a "Best Practice Guide" outlining important practical considerations in establishing and sustaining such programs within the maritime domain.[45] However, international approaches in this area frequently diverge, leading to tension and controversy. In 2007, clearly driven by national-security concerns, the Geoge W. Bush administration developed legislation requiring 100 percent of US-bound containers to be scanned by both radiation detection and nonintrusive imaging equipment in their port of origin.[46] This requirement was to have been implemented by 2012, but the deadline has been extended in two-year increments to the present day.[47] The European Union and others have been "fiercely opposed" to such a measure, arguing that it would disrupt trade, dramatically increase costs, and produce few security improvements.[48]

Detecting nuclear materials within the maritime supply chain: an overview

There are particular challenges to detecting smuggled nuclear and radiological material in the maritime environment. This is largely due to the volume and speed of trade flows; the international shipping industry conducts an estimated 90 percent of global trade.[49] This share has grown considerably over recent decades, driven by a widespread move to containerization in the 1980s to 2000s. Recent estimates put the number of 20- or 40-foot containers in circulation at over 43 million.[50] At a busy international port, such as Rotterdam in the Netherlands, more than ten million 20-foot equivalent units (TEUs) pass through port facilities each year, processing tens of thousands of containers every day.[51] This includes the import and export of containers and their trans-shipment—where containers are offloaded from one ship before being loaded onto another, typically without leaving a designated customs area. Ports will also handle non-containerized cargo and may have specific terminals dedicated to the handling of dry bulk (such as coal or grain), liquid bulk (such as industrial chemical or petroleum), breakbulk (such as pipes or machinery), and liquefied natural gas.[52]

The maritime supply chain, therefore, represents a huge and growing cargo stream within which to identify radioactive and nuclear contraband, a particularly acute challenge considering as little as a few kilograms of certain materials could pose a significant threat.[53] Identification must occur rapidly in order to avoid significant disruption to the flow of legitimate goods. Radioactive and nuclear materials are also not the only contraband passing through the maritime supply chain. Far more commonly shipped items include narcotics, conventional weapons, and explosives.[54] Consequently, striking the balance between monitoring for nuclear and radiological materials and other illegal imports is a perennial difficulty given resource constraints, including, not least, the availability of FLOs.[55] Given the challenges outlined above and the limited time and resources available, risk-management-based approaches are typically used to focus inspection efforts aiming to detect contraband passing through maritime facilities.[56] Often this includes the use of profiling tools to identify high-risk containers, for example, the Automated Targeting System (ATS) deployed by the US Department of Homeland Security.[57] This and other systems utilize a set of risk indicators based on recent intelligence and past incidences. Cargo is evaluated against these indicators drawing on information from the customs manifest, shipments that score above a certain pre-defined threshold selected for further inspection.

However, these types of risk-based approaches may not provide the same level of insight when it comes to nuclear and radiological materials.[58] A relative dearth of incidences makes it difficult to determine trends in nuclear and radiological materials trafficking. Furthermore, studies have suggested that smugglers are likely to take a different approach to smuggling nuclear and radiological materials;[59] for contraband that is frequently shipped, such as narcotics, the interception of a certain percentage may be seen as an acceptable loss. Given the difficulties in using profiling tools to flag suspected shipments of nuclear and radiological materials, the emphasis has been on detection systems that scan a significant fraction of container cargo flows for physical signatures characteristic of nuclear and radiological materials. These typically include passive detectors that measure gamma or neutron emissions resulting from the radioactive decay of threat materials.[60] Active detectors are also employed; for instance, X-ray radiography can create an internal image of containers, identifying potential shielding materials that might be used by smugglers to suppress radioactive emissions. Detectors vary in terms of sensitivity, cost, robustness, portability, and their ability to distinguish between different types of nuclear and radiological material, and therefore are most effective when employed in combination.[61]

To operate efficiently, detection systems must be able to distinguish illicit nuclear and radiological materials from common commodities shipped through the maritime supply chain which can also produce significant radioactive emissions. These include radioactive isotopes with legitimate medical and industrial uses, as well as naturally occurring radioactive material (NORM), including granite, bananas, and cat litter.[62] This is far from a trivial task, given that an adversary may seek to mask the radioactive signature of undeclared nuclear or radioactive material by including it, for example, within a NORM shipment. Systems also have to handle a host of ever-changing local factors, including varying background radiation levels, different container speeds, and cross-talk from other lanes.[63]

Detection Protocols: Scanning, Alarms, and Response

Typically, maritime facilities employ a multistage detection protocol. In the first stage, containers move through a passive detector, usually a fixed radiation portal monitor (RPM).[64] On average, a complete scan of a single container takes under a minute, causing only minor disruption to the flow of cargo.[65] At most maritime facilities, this initial scan involves measuring the gamma (and if available neutron) radiation as the container passes through the RPM.[66] If neutrons are detected or if the total gamma radiation received exceeds a predetermined threshold, it triggers an alarm. For imports and exports, a scan typically occurs when a container passes through a point of entry or exit to the port, while for trans-shipments it will take place between unloading and reloading. If there is no alarm, the container continues on its way. If an alarm is raised, officials investigate further. Here, there are three possibilities: a false alarm, an innocent alarm, or a non-innocent alarm.[67]

A false alarm can occur when no radioactive material is present and may be caused by an equipment malfunction or a temporary fluctuation in local radiation levels. Innocent alarms are triggered by the legitimate shipment of NORM or radioactive sources used for industrial, medical, or other purposes. Non-innocent alarms are caused by radioactive material outside of regulatory control, including orphan sources or trafficked nuclear materials. FLOs assess the alarms by analysing both the total radiation reading and the profile of a container.[68] This is compared against the declared content of the container in the shipment manifest, which should list any hazardous or radioactive materials.[69] FLOs look for anomalies that might indicate the presence of undeclared materials, such as a sharp spike in the radiation profile, which could indicate the presence of an undeclared radioactive source within a shipment of NORM.[70]

If it is not possible to adequately determine the cause of the alarm, a secondary inspection is conducted on the container. Typically, a container is moved out of the traffic flow to a secure area, before a manual external inspection is undertaken using a passive, handheld radioisotope identification device (RIID).[71] RIIDs can distinguish between specific radioisotopes so that a comparison can be made with each commodity listed on the shipment manifest. While the time taken to conduct a secondary inspection will vary, studies estimate that manual container scanning takes one customs officer approximately twenty minutes to complete.[72] X-rays may also be taken of the cargo as part of a secondary inspection. Spectroscopic portal monitors can both detect radiation and identify the radioactive source, which could in theory replace RPMs and eliminate the need for secondary inspections, though these have struggled in field testing and have yet to be widely deployed.[73] In cases where secondary inspections are inconclusive, a further, tertiary inspection may be performed. This would typically be undertaken by certified radiation experts and may involve the unpacking of the container contents to determine the source of the radiation readings. So-called "manual unstuffing" is a far more labour-intensive process; one study estimates the costs of five inspectors manually inspecting one 40-foot container over for three hours.[74]

Radiation Detection in practice: Implementation, Drivers, and Challenges

As outlined previously, this study makes use of survey data and interviews conducted with practitioners involved in the planning, operation, and regulation of radiation-detection systems at maritime facilities around the world.[75] This information is combined with the existing literature and used to explore how and why radiation-detection systems are implemented for border monitoring at maritime facilities. This section begins by examining the deployment and operation of border-monitoring systems of different facilities. This is followed by a discussion of the various national and commercial drivers that influence the setup and operation of such systems. Finally, the section explores some of the practical challenges encountered by FLOs.

Implementation: How is radiation-detection capability deployed and used?

IAEA guidance recommends developing a national strategy for identifying and recovering nuclear and radiological MORC when establishing radiation-detection architecture.[76] This should be implemented within an appropriate legal and regulatory framework, drawing on the support of competent authorities and specialized technical agencies, to help translate high-level political goals into effective operational practice. The majority of this study's survey respondents identified the utility of national guidelines and processes governing the development and use of radiation-detection systems.[77] According to one respondent, "National labs provide guidance on needs. Another government agency...then evaluates[s] and purchases the equipment according to [these] recommendations....The Government Accountability Office ensures purchased equipment is ... used and installed effectively."[78] However, a smaller but nonetheless significant number of respondents indicated either that they did not have access to national-level guidance or processes relating to radiation detection, or were unsure whether these existed.[79]

There was significant variation in the percentage of total cargo that passed through radiation-detection systems. Approximately half of respondents reported over 80 percent of imported cargo underwent some form of radiation scanning, while roughly one-third put this figure at less than 20 percent.[80] The vast majority of maritime facilities that scanned under 20 percent also handled relatively small volumes of cargo—less than 500,000 TEU annually. The apparent inverse correlation between cargo volume and scanning percentage may simply reflect that efforts, including the US Mega ports Initiative, have tended to prioritize the installation of detection systems at the busiest global ports.[81] However, high scanning rates at large ports do not necessarily provide protection against an intelligent adversary looking to smuggle radiological or nuclear material. Such an actor could purposefully choose a shipping route that bypasses large maritime facilities in an effort to minimize the chance of detection. This approach would be similar to criminal groups exercising jurisdictional arbitrage by "exploit[ing] the differences in national laws and regulations" to undertake their activities, i.e., moving operations or routing flows of goods through more favourable environments.[82]

The vast majority of cargo-scanning systems cover both imports and exports,[83] though only half of respondents noted that trans-shipments are also included in their radiation-detection program.[84] Implementing systems for scanning trans-shipments can be more challenging than for imports and exports, since there is less likely to be a "natural bottleneck" where detection equipment can be placed.[85] However, an absence of trans-shipment scanning reduces the opportunities for intercepting undeclared nuclear or radiological materials, particularly if they are shipped between distant locations where a container might be offloaded multiple times during its journey.

Respondents were not asked to comment on the relative frequency of innocent versus non-innocent alarms, but it is clear from interviews and other studies that the vast majority of alarms are triggered by either NORM or legitimate shipments of radioactive materials.[86] A 2006 report by

Lawrence Livermore National Laboratory, drawing on data from the Port Import/Export Reporting Service (PIERS), estimated shipments of NORM or legitimate radioactive materials made up approximately 4 percent of TEU imports into the United States.[87] A 2017 report by Oak Ridge National Laboratory, drawing on data from over thirty countries, calculated average alarming rates for RPMs at seaports at just over 1.5 percent.[88] Clearly NORM and other commercial radioactive materials make up a small but significant proportion of total cargo flows. This can result in a large number of alarms at busy maritime facilities which have to be assessed and investigated by FLOs on a daily basis.

The causes of non-innocent alarms identified by respondents were diverse and included contaminated goods, mislabelled sources, orphan sources, and special nuclear material.[89] The presence of the first three types of material in supply chains has been widely reported and clearly demonstrates the ability of detection systems to identify a broad range of radioactive materials. However, there is minimal information available on the frequency of fissile materials such as HEU or plutonium intercepted through radiation-detection systems employed for border-monitoring purposes[90] Some studies have suggested that deployed systems are unlikely to detect these materials.[91] This makes the identification of special nuclear materials by survey respondents a significant finding. Although it was not possible to obtain further information on these cases, it implies that current systems are at least technically capable of detecting special nuclear materials.[92]

In this study, approximately one-third of respondents reported innocent alarm rates greater than 10 percent, while just under 15 percent put this at less than 1 percent.[93] This order-of-magnitude variation may be partially explained by differences in shipping routes for NORM. However, it likely also results from variation in alarming thresholds for RPMs.[94] At facilities where alarming thresholds are set relatively high, only particularly radioactive shipments will trigger alarms, resulting in low alarming rates. This variation is arguably in part due to an absence of international guidance or standards for setting alarming thresholds, but, as is discussed below, commercial considerations are also a strong influence.

There was even greater variation in the assessment of and response to primary alarms. Approximately 10 percent of respondents stated that secondary inspections were undertaken in 10 to 50 percent of cases; for nearly one-quarter of respondents, this occurred between 1 and 10 percent of the time, just under 20 percent claiming that secondary inspections were conducted less than 1 percent of the time following an initial alarm.[95] This is despite the vast majority of respondents stating that they had access to more than one form of radiation detector, including handheld RIIDs for secondary inspections, with some facilities also employing X-ray systems.[96] The observed variation in secondary and tertiary inspections is surprising and implies that, for a significant number of facilities, NORM determination is made almost exclusively by FLOs assessing RPM radiation readings and profiles against the cargo manifest information.

In cases where the implemented scanning protocol uncovers undeclared radioactive materials, response will typically involve a number of domestic agencies, particularly customs, law enforcement, and nuclear and environmental regulators. Further, dependent upon national response plans, international bodies including the IAEA are often informed, as are transit states and, most often, the country of origin.[97]In terms of coordinating the response to MORC discovery, several respondents and interviewees indicated that these are largely ad hoc, "developed on a case-by-case basis."[98] The representative of an international shipping company emphasized that many states appeared to "reinvent the wheel" each time, underlining the lack of a standard response to detection events.[99]

Procedures at different ports and national authorities for dealing with material removed from the maritime supply chain can vary. Typically, materials are initially stored on site at the port, or at an off-site location, most respondents indicating that they eventually seek to return materials to their country of origin (though this is obviously unlikely in the event that threat materials were discovered). There are a number of challenges to this "return-to-sender" policy, including locating a carrier licensed (and willing) to carry radioactive materials.[100]There have also been cases where, for example, the manufacturer of radioactively contaminated goods has gone bankrupt, creating uncertainty as to where the materials should be returned and who should bear the cost.[101]

Drivers: what dictates the implementation of radiation detection?

At the international level, the perceived threat of nuclear terrorism has driven the installation of nuclear- and radiological-detection systems at borders. A small number of states—most notably the United States—as well as international organizations such as the IAEA have promoted these efforts. Their impact is reflected in the survey results, half of all respondents suggesting that their national radiation detection programs were initiated through some form of international partnership.[102] Although border-monitoring systems may have been established through bilateral or international support programs, their precise implementation—as with any nuclear-security measure—rests with the individual state concerned. As discussed in the previous section, there is significant variation between states in the operation of detection systems in the maritime environment. To some extent, this reflects the different priorities of national detection programs: the majority of survey respondents noted that their systems aimed to detect all types of nuclear and radiological MORC, while one in five respondents revealed that theirs were concentrated primarily on identifying radioactive materials that posed a clear health and safety risk.[103] By contrast, the United Kingdom is known to operate a border-monitoring system based on a narrow counterterrorism rationale.[104]

It is unsurprising that safety concerns drive the operation of radiation-detection systems given the relatively high numbers of incidences involving inappropriately packaged radioactive goods, including those that are incorrectly recorded on the manifest as well as contaminated items. In the latter category, there have been hundreds of recorded cases where radioactive sources such as cobalt 60 were introduced into the smelting process for metals such as stainless steel before being transported to buyers around the world.[105] This contrasts with a limited number of instances involving the deliberate trafficking of nuclear or radiological material by potentially malicious actors. This may explain, for example, the observed lack of secondary inspections at certain facilities, as primary alarm assessment may be sufficient to identify the presence or absence of strongly radioactive cargo that poses a clear health risk. However, an approach that focuses primarily on detecting strongly radioactive materials is likely to be ineffective at identifying less-radioactive materials such as HEU.

Commercial drivers also influence the implementation of radiation-detection systems, both national authorities and system operators recognizing the need to minimize disruption to the flow of goods through the maritime supply chain. The provision of "better customer service," reduced "turnaround time," and increased "flow efficiency" are important factors in the selection of container-terminal selection by commercial entities and, hence, are critical for attracting high traffic volumes.[106] The importance of efficiency continues to increase, making the "competitiveness of ports within logistics chains a much higher priority than it was before."[107] These commercial factors clearly have the potential to create tension in the operation of radiation-detection systems given the time it takes to conduct secondary and, in particular, tertiary inspections. On this matter, just under half of survey respondents identified the need to meet a target alarm rate as their number one concern when determining alarming thresholds for RPMs.[108] Somewhat concerning from a security perspective, only one-third of respondents stated that alarm thresholds were dictated by the radiative properties of the MORC that their systems sought to detect.[109]

Challenges: Operational and Global

As discussed earlier, identifying small quantities of radiological and nuclear material in the rapidly moving maritime environment presents a number of intrinsic challenges for the design and operation of detection systems. Arguably, chief among these is the initial assessment of alarms, particularly given the relative abundance of NORM and legitimate shipments of nuclear and radiological materials.[110] For programs aiming to detect all MORC, including low-gamma-activity materials such as HEU, alarm thresholds for RPMs must be set relatively low, which increases both the number of false and innocent alarms as well as the possibility of time-intensive secondary and tertiary inspections. This challenge is compounded by a relative lack of international guidance in this area, and some reluctance to publish or share thresholds among the practitioner community due to perceived security concerns.[111]

Although a significant proportion of respondents felt they were able to manage innocent alarm rates, the effectiveness of protocols in identifying the deliberate trafficking in certain scenarios is unclear.[112] For example, detecting small quantities of nuclear material purposefully concealed within NORM shipments or deliberately shielded could prove problematic or unlikely, given a relative absence of secondary and tertiary inspections at certain facilities. Related to this, for a small but noteworthy fraction of respondents, the most pressing challenge in implementing detection systems was the ability of FLOs to stop and detain alarming containers so that secondary and tertiary inspections could be performed.[113] Human-resource constraints drive this issue, especially at ports with high alarm rates, as does pressure to avoid significant disruption to cargo flows. A high proportion of survey respondents also highlighted resource issues including equipment, operating, and sustainability costs as key challenges to implementing radiation-detection systems.[114] At some facilities, for example, a lack of operational handheld RIIDs directly limits their use in secondary inspections.[115] FLO training was also found to vary significantly:

most respondents reported undergoing training annually or less, while two respondents noted that they had never been offered training.[116]

Sustaining bilateral and multilateral efforts that promote radiation-detection systems can be challenging. A 2012 US Government Accountability Office report on the Mega ports Initiative noted a myriad of related issues including: the limited use of secondary scanning equipment, counter to training provided by US trainers; a lack of or partial buy-in amongst stakeholders; and criticism of sustainability plans.[117] High-level political developments, such as program funding cuts, and deteriorating diplomatic relations with international partners also present challenges in this area that are difficult to mitigate.[118]

Improving detection: information sharing, promoting best practice, and new tools

Given that radiation-detection systems at maritime facilities worldwide have now been implemented for many years (in many cases, upward of a decade), there exists a mature pool of experts comprising a diverse international community of practitioners. However, lessons learned are not always effectively disseminated throughout the border-monitoring community; the overwhelming majority of survey respondents felt that enhanced information sharing with professionals in other countries could help improve the system operation in their own state. Relatedly, respondents were clear that additional guidance from international organizations would be beneficial.[119]This is surprising, given that there already exist a number of IAEA documents relevant to the operation of radiation-detection systems, including one Implementing Guide and two detailed Technical Guides.[120]

This response may reflect the fact that some of these documents are more than ten years old and, consequently, should be updated to take account of more recent developments. Alternatively, a lack of openness and sharing of best practice within practitioner communities due to security concerns may be an issue. For instance, the IAEA guidance document Technical and Functional Specifications for Border Monitoring Equipment has a restricted distribution and can only be requested by a state's relevant mission to the IAEA or nuclear regulatory body.[121] Over half of respondents also suggested that the operation of detection systems could be improved by publishing information on alarming limits for NORM shipments.[122]

As mentioned above, there is a perennial tension between the release of information on nuclear-security measures to improve detection systems and the risk that adversaries will use that information to identify and exploit weaknesses. This balance has long been biased toward the protectionist end of this spectrum, although there has been a considerable shift in favour of greater disclosure in recent years.[123] On the issue of maritime MORC detection in particular, states could engage one another to a much greater extent than they currently do, sharing information about the challenges encountered and how they have been overcome. There are several international fora within which information exchange can occur, notably the IAEA's Border Monitoring Working Group. Further, project-based opportunities including the IAEA Coordinated Research Project format enable states to work together to advance mutual understanding of these issues.[124] However, involvement in these initiatives is currently limited to a small fraction of states that deploy border-monitoring systems and typically requires the investment of both time and financial resources.[125]

With regard to additional guidance, there is scope to update relevant IAEA documents drawing on practitioner experience gleaned over the past decade. There is also scope for a new publication either focused on radiation detection at maritime facilities in particular or dealing with pressing challenges in the maritime environment.[126] For example, innocent alarms rates tend to be higher at seaports than at airports and land crossings, due to the shipment of significant quantities of mildly radioactive bulk commodities in this environment.[127] As a consequence, tailored guidance on how to manage these high rates in a busy operational environment could be beneficial. In developing new guidance, however, there will be limits to the specificity of publishable information: despite the clear benefits to openly sharing information on how to determine alarm thresholds, persistent state-level security concerns are unlikely to change in the immediate future.

Instead of sharing sensitive operational information to help other states more efficiently identify alarms, states could consider developing and sharing new alarm assessment tools. Efforts are already underway in this area, most notably the development of a new IAEA Tool for Radiation Alarm and Commodity Evaluation (TRACE), which is being made available as a mobile application for use by FLOs.[128] This tool provides information on the specific radioisotopes contained within common commodities.[129] Looking ahead, there are increasing opportunities in the application of data-science techniques to the huge volumes of data generated by RPM operators and their international partners.[130] These applications are already used to support resource planning and to extract broader commercial trends. However, data mining could uncover new means of identifying subtle alarming anomalies that may be difficult for a human operator to assess.[131]

Given the diverse rationales underpinning states' detection systems—ranging from public health and safety to nuclear and radiological counterterrorism—renewed efforts should focus on developing an ongoing international nuclear-security dialogue similar to that generated and sustained through the NSS process. This is a challenging task due to states' varying threat perceptions and sensitivities around certain parts of the detection process, such as alarm thresholds. But real-life case studies and table top exercises are one way to ensure that those operating radiation-detection equipment are aware of the credible threat to nuclear and radiological materials, while facilitating discussion of what this means for detection systems and alarm levels.

Though it is difficult to completely mitigate the impact of political developments on radiation-detection programs, there are a number of ways to sustain their operation. Organizations investing in equipment and human resources for radiation detection at the national level and in support of international partners should incorporate plans to ensure the longer-term sustainability of their investments. The United States and others working to spread these capabilities should also ensure that engagement plans emphasize sustainability aspects, factoring in appropriate time and resources to transition away from international support. Requesting partners to invest in these capabilities alongside US financial assistance can also provide a sense of ownership, which is beneficial in the long term.[132]

Conclusion

It is clearly challenging to effectively deploy radiation-detection systems in maritime border-monitoring efforts. Although many systems are developed through bilateral and international partnerships, their effectiveness diverges significantly in various facilities. At some maritime facilities, security concerns drive a system's operation, while for others, safety and commercial factors take precedence. The result is a diverse set of approaches to crucial aspects of the detection process including the assessment of—and response to—alarms generated by cargo passing through RPMs. Arguably, the fragmented approaches observed throughout the maritime supply chain reduce the effectiveness of the global nuclear-detection architecture in stymying the illicit trafficking of nuclear and radiological materials. In order to bring greater coordination to a system characterized by considerable divergence, states and international organizations promoting border monitoring should make serious efforts to renew the waning international nuclear-security dialogue, with a particular focus on the importance of combating illicit trafficking. This discourse should be supported by developing and publishing new and updated international guidance documents, exchanging operational best practices, and developing new tools in support of FLOs. These steps could mitigate some of the practical challenges encountered in alarm assessment, to better identify threat materials in the ever-expanding maritime supply chain.

Non-proliferation Review: 2019, VOL. 26, NOS. 1–2, 83–104, https://doi.org/10.10 80/10736700.2019.1610256

Combating Nuclear Smuggling? Exploring Drivers and Challenges to Detecting Nuclear and Radiological Materials at Maritime Facilities. Robert Downes, Christopher Hobbs, and Daniel Salisbury The Non-proliferation Review index at the James Martin Centre for Non-proliferation Studies. The Non-proliferation Review is a refereed journal concerned with the causes, consequences, and control of the spread of nuclear, chemical, and biological weapons. The Review features case studies, theoretical analyses, historical studies, reports, viewpoints, and book reviews on such issues as state-run weapons programs, treaties and export controls, safeguards, verification and compliance, disarmament, terrorism, and the economic and environmental effects of weapons proliferation. Authors come from many countries and disciplines and include current and former government officials. For more than 20 years, the Review has been an essential resource for policy makers and scholars worldwide. Journal information, Print ISSN: 1073-6700 Online ISSN: 1746-1766. 6 issues per year. Middlebury Institute of International Studies at Monterey and our publisher Taylor & Francis make every effort to ensure the accuracy of all the information (the "Content") contained in our publications. However, Middlebury Institute of International Studies at Monterey and our publisher Taylor & Francis, our agents (including the editor, any member of the editorial team or editorial board, and any guest editors), and our licensors make no representations or warranties whatsoever as to the accuracy, completeness, or suitability for any purpose of the Content. Any opinions and views expressed in this publication are the opinions and views of the authors, and are not the views of or endorsed by Middlebury Institute of International Studies at Monterey and our publisher Taylor & Francis. The accuracy of the Content should not be relied upon and should be independently verified with primary sources of information. Middlebury Institute of International Studies at Monterey and our publisher Taylor & Francis shall not be liable for any losses, actions, claims, proceedings, demands, costs, expenses, damages, and other liabilities whatsoever or howsoever caused arising directly or indirectly in connection with, in relation to, or arising out of the use of the Content. Terms & Conditions of access and use can be found at http://www.tandfonline.com/page/terms and conditions.

To link to this article: https://doi.org/10.1080/10736700.2019.1610256. © 2019 The Author(s). Published by Informa UK Limited, trading as Taylor & Francis Group, Published online: 03 Jun 2019. CONTACT Christopher Hobbs christopher.hobbs@ kcl.ac.uk.

Chapter 10

Not by NPT Alone: The Future of the Global Nuclear Order

Jeffrey W. Knopf

Abstract

The nuclear Non-Proliferation Treaty (NPT) constitutes just one component of broader arrangements that provide global nuclear governance. In recent decades, the other props in the global nuclear order beyond its nonproliferation elements have been eroding, thereby putting more weight on the contributions of the NPT and other aspects of the nonproliferation regime. Unfortunately, recent progress in building up the NPT-based nonproliferation regime seems also to have halted. This article outlines the elements of the global nuclear order and identifies signs of erosion in that order. It discusses whether a greater commitment to nuclear disarmament might help counter that erosion and highlights the underlying cognitive dimension of efforts to avoid nuclear war.

Keywords: Nuclear weapons, global governance, strategic stability, arms control, non-proliferation, disarmament

The preamble to the Treaty on the Non-Proliferation of Nuclear Weapons (NPT) lists the reasons for concluding the treaty. First on the list is recognition of "the devastation that would be visited upon all mankind by a nuclear war and the consequent need to make every effort to avert the danger of such a war" (UN Office for Disarmament Affairs, n.d.). The NPT's goal of preventing the spread of nuclear arms helps limit the opportunities for such a devastating event. But nonproliferation is not sufficient. For this reason, other arrangements have also evolved to "avert the danger" of nuclear war.

Following the invention of the atom bomb in 1945, a nuclear order gradually emerged that provides elements of global governance over nuclear weapons. This article reviews prior discussions of the international nuclear order and recent trends in global nuclear governance. It identifies troubling signs of erosion across all aspects of the nuclear order. For this reason, it is important to add to the recommendations contained in other articles in this special issue that address only the NPT regime. This article proposes doing more to address the underlying cognitive foundations of nuclear peace. Because recognition of the need to minimize the risk of nuclear war is a motivating factor for every element of the global nuclear order, steps should be taken to promote a healthy fear of nuclear war among key actors.

This article identifies three "strands" in the current nuclear order: strategic stability, the nuclear taboo, and nonproliferation (as supplemented by measures to ensure nuclear security). It uses the term "strands" to avoid potential confusion with the three "pillars" of the NPT or the three "legs" of the nuclear triad. The term "strand" also conveys the possibility that the separate elements of the nuclear order can be woven together into a stronger whole. This term also fits well with other terms like "unravelling" or "fraying" that are sometimes employed to describe weakening of the NPT or broader nuclear order. The three strands can be in tension with one another and do not always co-exist easily. But both individually and collectively they work to counteract forces that could make nuclear weapons use more likely. Recent trends, however, reflect weakening in the core elements of the nuclear order. Since the 1990s, the strength of commitments to strategic stability and the nuclear taboo have both declined. In contrast, until recently, non-proliferation was a dynamic and innovative component of the larger nuclear order that was tending to get stronger, but even in this area there are signs of trouble.

The next section of this article describes the overall purpose of the global nuclear order, summarizes past descriptions of this order, and points out how my interpretation differs from prior interpretations. Subsequent sections take up strategic stability, the taboo, and non-proliferation in turn, analyzing trends within each area. The next portion of the article raises the question of whether the nuclear order requires a fourth strand in the form of a more robust commitment to achieving nuclear disarmament. The concluding section highlights an underlying cognitive element that sustains all the elements of the nuclear order and proposes actions to shore up the cognitive dimension of nuclear peace as a way to help arrest erosion in the global nuclear order.

Purpose of the Nuclear Order

To the extent a nuclear order exists, it is not the result of a conscious plan or formal proposal. Although parts of the nuclear order such as the NPT were negotiated, for the most part global governance in this area developed organically. In the seminal work to date on the notion of an international nuclear order, Walker (2012) defines it as "evolving patterns of thought and activity that serve primary goals of world survival, war avoidance and economic development". (p. 12).

The first two of these—survival and war avoidance—take precedence. The overarching goal of the nuclear order is hence often phrased as being to prevent the use of nuclear weapons. But if one considers nuclear tests or deterrence postures as uses of nuclear arms, a more precise phrasing would be that the goal is to prevent nuclear explosions that will kill people—and especially to avert escalation that would kill many millions. Because the nuclear order as a whole was not formally negotiated, its existence and form are matters of interpretation. Analysts infer the outlines of the order from the history of agreements reached, institutions created, and decisions, actions, and statements of relevant states and their leaders. There is considerable overlap in how those who write about the international nuclear order describe that order, but accounts also differ in subtle ways. This article develops a new version that also differs modestly from prior depictions but more accurately reflects the underlying purpose of avoiding nuclear war.

If the sole goal of the global nuclear order were to avoid nuclear use, the obvious solution would be abolition. An effectively verifiable arrangement for nuclear disarmament would seem a logical way to minimize the chances of any future nuclear explosion. In the view of most observers, however, the present nuclear order is not based on disarmament. The reason is simple: Some states still have a preference for nuclear weapons to exist. The current nuclear-armed states value the security and status that they believe nuclear weapons provide. Some non-nuclear weapon states, especially among U.S. allies, also believe they receive security benefits via extended nuclear deterrence. Because some states still value nuclear weapons, the nuclear order is not cantered on plans to move quickly to abolish nuclear arms. Eventual nuclear disarmament is held out as a long-term aspiration, most notably in NPT Article VI, but efforts to keep nuclear peace in the short term focus on other sources of restraint.

The literature on international nuclear order takes inspiration from the seminal work of William Walker. Walker (2000) describes an order based on two logics that can pull in contrary directions: a logic of deterrence and a logic of abstinence. The abstinence dimension of the nuclear order rests primarily on the NPT, but Walker also discusses arms control and other devices for keeping nuclear weapons in check. Those who have followed Walker generally accept deterrence as one element of nuclear order, but disaggregate the abstinence dimension. Horsburgh (2015) identifies four elements: deterrence, nonproliferation, arms control, and disarmament. She differs from most analysts by listing disarmament as a current and equally important element of the nuclear order. To most other observers, the status of disarmament is more ambiguous and potentially in tension with the other elements. They tend to omit it from the current order in order to discuss how it might fit into future evolution of global nuclear governance.

Other analysts identify three elements of the nuclear order, but in place of arms control they include the tradition of nuclear non-use. Hence, Lawrence Freedman and Nina Tannenwald both depict a nuclear order based on deterrence, nonproliferation, and non-use. Both see the goal of disarmament as being at odds with the existing order, but offer opposed prescriptions. Freedman (2013) recommends stepping back from the push for nuclear abolition in the near term. He sees this as an unrealistic goal whose pursuit could weaken the three components of the existing order. As a supporter of abolition, Tannenwald (2018a) argues instead that commitments to deterrence and nonproliferation have become an excuse for nuclear-armed states to avoid pursuing disarmament.

Kutchesfahani (2019) suggests that the nuclear order is better understood as a blend of order and disorder. Each element of the nuclear order can simultaneously contribute to disorder, as when new weapons for the sake of deterrence promote arms races or when nonproliferation goals become a reason for states to take preventive military action. Finally, some analysts adopt a critical perspective. Ritchie (2019) describes the global nuclear order as "hegemonic" and Egeland (2021) depicts it as an "ideology" in service of preserving the status quo. Several of the articles in this special issue mirror these more critical perspectives as well as Tannenwald's interest in moving more quickly on disarmament; hence, they similarly focus on the NPT as an obstacle to the goal of getting rid of nuclear weapons (Egeland, 2022; Hanson, 2022; Noda, 2022; Pretorius & Sauer, 2022).

The analysis here will fall between the perspective of Freedman and that of Tannenwald and the NPT critics. Like Freedman, I caution against frontal challenges to the current order, which however improvised and shaky has done its part to help keep the world from going over the precipice. But unlike Freedman, I do not believe that serious efforts to make progress on the goal of global zero can be indefinitely postponed. Instead, I propose renewed attention to raising awareness of nuclear dangers as a way to both prop up the existing nuclear order and build support for eventual abolition.

Reflecting the goal of preventing nuclear explosions where people are present while accepting that, due to the interests of certain states, the weapons will continue to exist for the foreseeable future, existing nuclear governance relies on a combination of three approaches: strategic stability, the nuclear taboo, and nonproliferation. In contrast to prior analyses, I propose that strategic stability is preferable to deterrence as a label for the first strand of the nuclear order. Deterrence is a double-edged sword. On the one hand, it encourages restraint by implying that nuclear weapons are a category apart and should not be viewed as ordinary weapons available for routine battlefield use. On the other hand, the pursuit of deterrence can contribute to nuclear risks. There are competing theories of deterrence, and one influential school of thought holds that states need usable nuclear options in order to establish dominance at multiple rungs of a purported ladder of escalation (Khan, 1965). To others, the pursuit of war-fighting options and nuclear superiority are likely to provoke responses that only increase the danger of nuclear war (Blair & Wolfsthal, 2019). From the perspective of averting nuclear dangers, strategic stability is a more accurate description of the underlying goal. Stability is compatible with a role for nuclear deterrence but points to the need for states to temper the pursuit of deterrence in ways that reduce the risks of inadvertent escalation. Deterrence is a strategy that states adopt, but stability better matches the ideal type of the goal of averting nuclear catastrophe.

For similar reasons, I use the term "taboo" rather than norm or tradition of non-use. These refer to the same phenomenon, but "taboo" better reflects the purpose of the nuclear order. As will be discussed, there are doubts about whether the norm of non-use is actually strong enough to merit being described as a taboo. The goal of a taboo is more aspirational or an ideal type, while the issue of how strongly it has been embraced is an empirical question. But the same is true of strategic stability and nonproliferation

All three elements of the nuclear order reflect aspirational goals for which levels of support can vary. Assessing the strength of the three strands is the task of this article.

In short, the global nuclear order as it has evolved encourages neither the unbridled pursuit of strategic superiority nor an immediate move to abolition. Rather, as Walker (2012) observes, it strikes a balance between competing impulses toward deterrence and disarmament that aims "to draw states into … a logic of restraint" (p. 5). In a slight modification of prior discussions, I suggest that the international order is best described as resting on the three strands of strategic stability, the taboo, and nonproliferation.

Moves to establish these three strands began emerging early in the nuclear age and were clearly discernable by the 1970s. In the mid-1970s, stability was the strongest among them and nonproliferation the weakest. By 2015, that ranking had probably reversed. In recent years, though, adverse trends have affected all three components of the nuclear order. The next sections of this article discuss stability, the taboo, and nonproliferation in that order.

Strategic Stability

The objective of strategic stability is to reduce or remove incentives for any nuclear-armed state to launch nuclear weapons (Colby & Gerson, 2013). During the Cold War, concerns about strategic stability focused on the U.S.-Soviet relationship. Though neither side welcomed the situation, both sides came more or less to accept a condition of mutual deterrence and a shared understanding of how to keep it stable. The goal was to avoid situations that would give either side an incentive to launch a first strike. In practice, this meant eschewing capabilities that could put at risk the other side's ability to launch a second strike. As long as both sides recognized that some of their nuclear forces could survive a first strike by the other side and be used in a retaliatory attack, the thinking went, both would be confident that they could deter a nuclear attack by the other side, and the resulting stalemate would be stable (Adler, 1992; Freedman, 2003; Mandelbaum, 1979).

The superpowers used various tools to supplement the force postures and declaratory strategies meant to preserve mutual deterrence. These included summit meetings, arms control agreements, and other confidence-building measures (CBMs). Far from being contradictory to deterrence, arms control was in practice designed to help keep it stable. Nuclear arms control was used to regulate force postures and allow a dialogue about how to reduce the dangers of nuclear war. From a stability perspective, the 1972 Anti-Ballistic Missile (ABM) Treaty was the most significant agreement. By limiting ballistic missile defenses, the agreement ensured that both sides could maintain a survivable second-strike capability.

The two sides also embraced various CBMs, such as the hotline, and developed a tacit understanding about the need to avoid certain behaviors that could risk escalation (Gaddis, 1986). The goal of strategic stability was never fully embraced or perfectly achieved. In particular, after the two sides deployed multiple independently-targetable reentry vehicles (MIRVs) on their land-based missiles, the improved accuracy of these Intercontinental Ballistic Missiles (ICBMs) increased the potential vulnerability of land-based forces. This created a concern that one party could launch just a portion of its long-range missiles, and because these were armed with multiple warheads they could take out all of the other side's land-based missiles while leaving the first side with some of its missiles in reserve. This undermined stability because fear on either side that its land-based missiles were vulnerable to a disarming first strike would add to pressures to launch first in a crisis. Yet, despite fears about a possible "window of vulnerability" created by MIRVs, in practice both sides behaved cautiously and rarely acted like they actually thought they could win a nuclear war (Jervis, 1989).

The winding down of the Cold War mostly improved strategic stability. Most importantly, it lessened the political and ideological contest that could have fueled escalation. Starting with the 1987 Intermediate-Range Nuclear Forces (INF) Treaty, the two sides also entered a period of significant arms reductions. Developments since then, however, have worked against strategic stability. In 1993, after the loss of its former Warsaw Pact allies and in the face of declining conventional capabilities, Russia abandoned a no-first-use pledge previously adopted by the Soviet Union (Schmemann, 1993). About a decade later, the United States withdrew from the ABM Treaty, long considered a cornerstone of the traditional approach to strategic stability.

Other once positive trends have also been reversed. For a time, arms reductions arising from U.S.-Russia arms control treaties created incentives to move away from MIRVed ICBMs. By 2014 the United States had completely de-MIRVed its land-based arsenal (submarine-based missiles remain MIRVed) (SIPRI, 2015, pp. 467–68). After a period of reducing its MIRVed missiles, however, Russia is moving in the other direction. It has developed several new multiple-warhead missiles, including a new "heavy" missile (the RS-28 Sarmat) that is expected to carry ten or more warheads (Kristensen & Korda, 2020). There are reports, moreover, that around 2015 China also started to deploy MIRVed missiles (Wheeler, 2016). Given China's relatively smaller nuclear force that country is still nowhere near even a hypothetical first-strike capability against the United States, but the move to MIRVs raises questions about China's long-term intentions.

More recently, the Trump administration responded to what it viewed as alarming changes in the Russian nuclear posture by developing and deploying a new low-yield nuclear warhead (the W76-2) for use with submarine-based Trident missiles (Burns, 2020). The administration argued that this would bolster the credibility of nuclear deterrence, particularly in a potential regional conflict in Europe, because these warheads would be seen by adversaries as more "useable" than larger-yield U.S. weapons. But the new warhead also adds to the range of circumstances in which another actor might fear a U.S. nuclear first strike (especially because it would not know which warhead is on a missile launched from a submarine), and the lower-yield option could also make it more likely a U.S. president would be willing to use nuclear weapons in a preemptive attack. For these reasons, the new warhead is not necessarily conducive to stability.

The nuclear arms control process between Russia and the United States has also ground to a halt. The Obama administration charged Russia with violating the INF Treaty by deploying a new medium-range cruise missile (Woolf, 2017). This dispute ultimately led the Trump administration to withdraw from the INF Treaty, leading to its collapse. The Trump administration also withdrew from the Open Skies Treaty, an agreement designed to provide greater transparency about each side's military activities. Such transparency enhances stability by reducing fears on each side that the other might be preparing a surprise attack. These developments left the 2010 New START Treaty as the only remaining agreement limiting U.S. and Russian nuclear arsenals. New START was scheduled to expire in February 2021, but following the inauguration of Joe Biden the United States and Russia agreed to extend the treaty for five years (Sonne, 2021).

Although New START will remain in effect for now, there are currently no negotiations on a potential follow-on treaty. Indeed, the two sides remain far apart. The United States wants any future talks to include non-strategic nuclear warheads, while Russia wants to prioritize new limitations on ballistic missile defenses. In addition, at various points both Moscow and Washington have suggested that future arms control should include the other NPT-recognized nuclear weapon states (NWS). The other NWS all reject demands to join U.S.-Russian arms control talks. They take the position that the two leading nuclear powers must reduce their warheads down to numbers closer to the smaller UK, French, and Chinese arsenals before it would make sense for the other members of the P-5 to join the arms control process. Hence, arms control appears all but dead. This could open the door to a new round of arms racing that could put new strains on strategic stability (Dvorkin, 2019).

In an effort to keep a focus on stability during a rough period for arms control, several years ago the United States and Russia initiated bilateral talks on strategic stability. Several largely fruitless rounds of talks took place over the Obama and Trump administrations. Far from producing consensus on what strategic stability entails, the talks served only to clarify the areas of disagreement between the two countries (Baklitskiy et al., 2020). After Joe Biden entered the White House, his first summit meeting with Russian President Vladimir Putin resulted in an agreement to initiate a new round of strategic stability talks. One goal would be to see if the two sides could develop an agenda for future arms control talks. The first round of the new dialogue took place in late July 2021, with another meeting set for September 2021. The latest dialogue appears to be helping lower the temperature in the tense U.S.-Russia relationship, but the first meeting did not produce any agreement on the future of arms control (Nebehay & Landay, 2021).

In addition, concerns about stability can no longer focus solely on the U.S.-Russian relationship. Three other bilateral relationships—India-Pakistan, U.S.-North Korea, and U.S.-China—also involve disturbing trends. Of these, South Asia has experienced the most severe nuclear crises. In 1998, India and Pakistan both conducted nuclear tests and declared themselves nuclear weapon states. Their relationship since has been quite rocky. Reckless Pakistani actions in the Kargil region the following year produced a low-level border war (Lavoy, 2009). Subsequent terrorist attacks in India, traced back to Pakistani actors, have also threatened to embroil the region in war (Yusuf, 2019).

Although the two sides have avoided further escalation, suggesting at least some appreciation for the reality of mutual deterrence, they are still adding to their nuclear arsenals. Perhaps more worrisome, they have embraced incompatible nuclear doctrines. India has threatened rapid conventional incursions into Pakistan as a way to deter Pakistani adventurism. Pakistan, in response, has developed tactical nuclear weapons that it believes will deter Indian conventional action (for an evaluation of the implications for stability, see Ahmed, 2016). India, for its part, threatens massive nuclear retaliation as a way to deter Pakistani use of tactical weapons. This mismatch in doctrinal views is a recipe for a potential disaster (Narang, 2009/10; Shankar & Paul, 2016). And unlike the U.S.-Russia relationship, there is no history of arms control between India and Pakistan. Hence, this option is not available as a potential buffer against instability in the subcontinent.

North Korea's acquisition of a small nuclear arsenal creates additional challenges to stability. Starting in 2017, the interaction between North Korean leader Kim Jong Un and new U.S. President Donald Trump appeared to be heading on a path toward escalation. Each side seemed to be trying to outdo the other in rhetorical bluster and personal putdowns. News reports indicate that President Trump pressed the U.S. military to give him options for a potential preventive attack on North Korea's missiles (Landler & Cooper, 2018). If the United States were to attempt a preventive strike that did not fully knock out all of the DPRK's missile and nuclear capabilities, a North Korean nuclear retaliation would remain possible. Tensions de-escalated when Trump agreed to a summit meeting with Kim. But after an initial summit that ended warmly, subsequent Trump-Kim meetings involved frictions between the two sides and did not result in further progress toward resolving U.S.-DPRK differences (Sanger & Sang-Hun, 2020). After the Biden administration took office, they sought to put North Korea on the back burner. But Kim Jong Un has a history of lashing out if he feels ignored, so U.S. efforts to move slowly and give diplomacy with North Korea a low profile will not necessarily keep matters calm.

The U.S.-China relationship has also become more contentious following a rise in China's power and assertiveness. A strategic balance that still has the United States far ahead makes nuclear miscalculation less likely. But in summer 2021 commercial satellite imagery revealed that China has constructed two new ICBM bases with more than 100 silos each (Broad & Sanger, 2021). The purpose behind these bases remains unclear as China is not believed to have enough warheads to fill all these silos. But the sudden buildup is sure to fuel U.S. perceptions of a China threat. And the two sides lack any history of arms control talks that can be used to clarify each side's capabilities and intentions, hence increasing the chances for misperceptions and misunderstandings that could produce unwanted escalation.

In addition, although one should not exaggerate the risk of nuclear terrorism, there are non-state actors with an interest in acquiring a nuclear device (Bunn et al., 2016). Terrorists are not necessarily beyond the reach of deterrence, but compared to state actors the difficulties of deterring them are much greater (Wenger & Wilner, 2012). The emergence of terrorist groups with transnational reach and ambitions hence also tends to reduce strategic stability.

Similar to the heated rhetoric that flared up between North Korea and the United States in 2017, Russian rhetoric has also been a disruptive factor in relation to strategic stability. Most notably, in an annual speech to the nation in March 2018, Putin boasted about several new weapons being tested in Russia, including a nuclear-powered cruise missile with essentially unlimited range. Videos illustrating the new weapons accompanied the speech, including one that showed a nuclear-armed missile heading toward a location in the state of Florida near President Trump's Mar-a-Lago residence (BBC, 2018). Such crude posturing did nothing to alleviate Western concerns about Russian thinking, which in a tense moment could encourage hasty decisions that further erode stability.

Finally, new weapons and technologies also pose potential risks. Some analysts express concern that hypersonic weapons under development could make a disarming first strike appear more feasible, which could place pressure on countries that fear such a strike to launch their nuclear weapons in the midst of a conventional conflict (Wilkening, 2019; for a more skeptical view, see Broad, 2021). Rapidly evolving capabilities with respect to cyber and artificial intelligence might also be creating new risks that could undermine how confident states are in their ability to launch nuclear retaliatory strikes (Futter & Zala, 2021). And President Trump's tweets in his war of words with North Korea drew attention to various ways in which social media could add to escalatory pressure (Trinkunas et al., 2020; Williams & Drew, 2020). These concerns remain quite speculative, and a recent survey of expert opinion concluded that technological change has contradictory implications: potentially destabilizing deterrence relationships but also opening new opportunities for nuclear disarmament (Onderco & Zutt, 2021). At minimum, however, technological developments are adding new sources of uncertainty to the strategic landscape.

The state of strategic stability is not yet dire. Although political tensions have increased in several key relationships, they are not yet at a point that leaves parties on the brink of a major war. And, despite years of warnings, terrorist groups have not yet come close to obtaining a nuclear bomb. Still, compared to where the world appeared to be heading in the mid-1990s, strategic stability has declined and is not moving in a favorable direction.

The Nuclear Taboo

When talking about a taboo on the use of nuclear weapons, the first question is whether a taboo actually exists. Sagan (2004) and Paul (2009) have argued that inhibitions against nuclear use fall short of a true taboo and are better described as a tradition of non-use. Survey research (Press et al., 2013; Sagan & Valentino, 2017) also suggests the U.S. public feels little sense of a taboo and is willing to endorse the first use of nuclear weapons in certain situations (for further discussion and critiques, see Smetana & Wunderlich, 2021).

For purposes of stability, however, public opinion is less consequential than the attitude of elites who would be in charge of decisions about nuclear use. And with respect to elite decision making, the distinction between a taboo and a tradition is not necessarily diagnostic. The term "taboo" has been embraced in policy discourse to describe a sense of inhibition against using nuclear weapons. This reflects an understanding of nuclear weapons as categorically different from conventional arms. It is the strength of this understanding and the associated reluctance to be the first to use nuclear weapons—whether out of genuine moral belief or a more prudential worry about setting a precedent—that matters for the global nuclear order. Hence, while acknowledging that norms against nuclear use might not fulfill the requirements to be a true taboo, this essay will use the word "taboo" to refer to the sense that a norm against nuclear weapons use exists. In relation to the larger nuclear order, the key question is whether that norm is getting stronger or weaker.

Some sense of inhibition against nuclear use was already emerging by the 1950s, when U.S. President Eisenhower shied away from considering nuclear weapons use in the Korean War or to relieve the French at Dien Bien Phu (Tannenwald, 2007). The taboo received an indirect endorsement when Ronald Reagan and Mikhail Gorbachev issued a joint statement in 1985 agreeing to the proposition that "a nuclear war cannot be won and must never be fought" (Dunn & Potter, 2020). By the 1991 Persian Gulf War, U.S. leaders seemed to perceive a robust taboo, as President George H.W. Bush ruled out any consideration of using nuclear weapons in the conflict (Bush & Scowcroft, 1998, p. 463).

Since then, there have been multiple signs of erosion of the taboo. As noted above, Russia abandoned the earlier Soviet no-first-use policy. Today,

164

China is the only nuclear weapon state that officially proclaims a no-first-use policy, but even its commitment seems less than absolute. A senior Chinese military leader is reported to have used an implicit nuclear threat to warn U.S. officials against intervening in a possible conflict with Taiwan, stating he believed the United States would stay out because U.S. leaders care more about Los Angeles than Taipei (Gellman, 1998).

The U.S. posture has varied with each new president, but no administration has ever been willing to embrace no first use. The Clinton administration adopted a stance of "calculated ambiguity" about whether it would retaliate with nuclear weapons against a chemical or biological attack (for a critique, see Sagan, 2000). The George W. Bush administration expanded on this. It sought funding for new, more usable nuclear weapons, and its Nuclear Posture Review (NPR) identified an even broader range of scenarios in which such weapons might be useful (Bleek, 2002). The Obama administration moved to a narrower view of the circumstances under which nuclear weapons might be relevant but still did not rule out nuclear first use. The Trump administration then went back to and in fact beyond the previous Bush NPR in contemplating a range of circumstances under which the United States might consider using nuclear weapons. These included non-nuclear attacks, such as a massive cyber attack on the United States (Klimas, 2018).

The Biden administration seems likely to adopt a nuclear posture similar to that in place when Obama left office. Of note here is that even the Obama administration rejected language that would declare deterring nuclear attacks as the "sole purpose" of the U.S. nuclear arsenal, thereby leaving the door open for the United States to escalate to the nuclear level in circumstances other than responding to a nuclear attack. The Obama team worried that U.S. allies that depend on U.S. extended deterrence would react negatively to a "sole purpose" or "no first use" declaration, and they also wanted to keep a nuclear response option available in the event of a novel biological attack (Kimball & Thielmann, 2010; Panda & Narang, 2021).

In her seminal work on the taboo, Tannenwald (2007, pp. 51–52) highlighted "taboo talk," or explicit references by leaders to norms against nuclear use, as evidence for the taboo. It is also relevant, however, to consider statements that display a lack of taboo talk. In recent decades, many of the nuclear-armed states have at times openly made nuclear threats. This indicates that their leaders do not feel strong normative constraints against engaging in nuclear saber-rattling. Relevant Chinese and Russian statements have been noted above. Indian and Pakistani officials have also issued public nuclear threats during their various crises (Sasikumar, 2019). Pakistan's move to develop tactical weapons is also connected to an explicit threat to use nuclear weapons first in the event of a conventional invasion by India. In addition, although the evidence is inconclusive, statements by various Indian officials have suggested that India may be moving away from its unofficial embrace of no first use (Pant & Joshi, 2020). Turning to the most recent entrant to the nuclear club, North Korea might prove to be deterred from using nuclear weapons by the threat of retaliation, but it is hard to imagine the Kim Jong Un regime feels any normative inhibitions against using such weapons. Fiery threats are stock in trade for the DPRK. And the regime has already defied taboos in the chemical area by using the nerve agent VX to assassinate a half-brother of the current leader (Broom, 2019).

In addition, some of the language used by President Trump hardly conveyed a sense of awe at the unimaginable devastation that a nuclear war would cause. During escalating tensions with North Korea, the U.S. president bragged on Twitter that his nuclear button was "much bigger and more powerful" than Kim's (Baker & Tackett, 2018). The goal here was to bolster deterrence, not to set the stage for using the bomb. But turning to social media for this kind of public, macho posturing does nothing to reinforce the sense of nuclear weapons use as taboo.

A recent controversy over Russia's nuclear strategy also has troubling implications for the taboo. Some analysts claim that Russia has adopted an "escalate to de-escalate" strategy. Under this approach, Russia would be willing to use nuclear weapons first in the case of a conventional conflict in Europe as a way to persuade NATO forces to back down and end the dispute. If true, this would be another sign of the weakening of inhibitions against using or threatening to use nuclear weapons. Critics claim that Russian doctrine has not embraced the idea of nuclear escalation in a European conventional conflict and would only consider nuclear use when survival of the Russian state is under threat (Ven Bruusgaard, 2017). But even this more restrictive interpretation implies a willingness to use nuclear weapons first. And, as noted above, the alleged shift in Russian strategy motivated the Trump administration to develop a new, relatively low-yield sea-launched weapon. The administration asserted these weapons would be a more credible deterrent against a Russian "escalate to de-escalate" strategy, but if so this credibility derives specifically from the fact that the United States would consider such weapons more useable—and hence a step away from the taboo.

There have been countervailing developments that could reinforce the sense of a nuclear taboo. The humanitarian consequences initiative, which took shape in the years between the 2010 and 2015 NPT Review Conferences, attempted to draw renewed attention to the dangers of nuclear war (Gibbons, 2018; Potter, 2017). Modeled on the earlier campaign to ban landmines, this effort highlighted the terrible impact on civilians that would result from a nuclear war. Its goal was to lend new momentum to the push for nuclear disarmament, rather than to deepen the nuclear taboo, but anything that raises awareness of the consequences of nuclear weapons use should help strengthen the norms against such use.

The actual impact of the humanitarian initiative on the taboo, however, is hard to gauge. The initiative, which was spearheaded by middle-power governments and NGOs, was directed primarily at diplomats. There is little evidence its message reached a more general public audience. And, unfortunately, the nuclear weapon states reacted in a largely dismissive way to the initiative. Their top officials mostly did not participate and so were not present at meetings that outlined the consequences that would result from the use of nuclear weapons.

In another promising development, at their first summit meeting Joe Biden and Vladimir Putin reaffirmed the Reagan-Gorbachev statement that "a nuclear war cannot be won and must never be fought" (Kheel, 2021). However, neither country has backed away from ongoing nuclear modernization efforts. Indeed, the Biden administration's first defence budget proposal not only maintained but added to the nuclear modernization plans inherited from the Trump administration (Seligman et al., 2021). This supports the analysis by Orion Noda elsewhere in this special issue that the current nuclear order has not restrained qualitative improvements in the arsenals of all the nuclear-armed powers.

The potentially beneficial effects of the humanitarian initiative and renewal of the Reagan-Gorbachev pledge notwithstanding, most indicators point to erosion of the nuclear taboo since 1991. Reviewing the trends, the preeminent scholar of the nuclear taboo has declared, "The nuclear taboo is weakening" (Tannenwald, 2018b, p. 24).

Nonproliferation and Nuclear Security

Not everything is rosy in the nonproliferation area either. The NPT Review Conference (RevCon) for 2015 involved acrimonious disagreements among the delegates and ended without reaching consensus on a final document (Berger, 2015). (As of this writing, the postponed 2020 RevCon has not yet taken place.) Yet, overall, trends since 1991 with respect to nonproliferation have been more positive than those regarding strategic stability or the nuclear taboo. More recently, however, signs of erosion have emerged here as well.

The 2015 outcome notwithstanding, the NPT has gotten stronger since 1991. Two of the five NPT-recognized nuclear weapon states, France and China, were not treaty parties in 1991 and finally acceded to the treaty the following year. During the 1990s, several more countries that either had nuclear weapons on their territory or were suspected of having nuclear weapons programs also gave up the nuclear option and joined the treaty as non-nuclear weapon states. Key new members included South Africa, Argentina, Brazil, Ukraine, Kazakhstan, and Belarus. In addition, after the treaty's initial 25-year term expired, the NPT Conference in 1995 agreed to extend the treaty indefinitely, effectively making it permanent. To satisfy the concerns of non-nuclear weapon states, the 1995 decision also endorsed a strengthened review process, efforts to promote a Middle East free of nuclear weapons, and efforts to make greater progress toward nuclear disarmament (Rydell, 2005). In furtherance of the latter objective, in 1996 states reached agreement on a Comprehensive Test Ban Treaty (CTBT). And the 2000 and 2010 NPT Reviews adopted final documents containing language and specific action items that seemed to commit the nuclear weapon states more clearly to moving toward disarmament (Meyer, 2011).

Although the NPT is stronger today than it was in 1991, there have been some notable nonproliferation failures. India and Pakistan conducted nuclear tests in 1998 and declared themselves to be nuclear weapon states. North Korea withdrew from the NPT and in 2006 carried out its first nuclear weapons test. With respect to Iran, the current situation is uncertain but not favorable. The Joint Comprehensive Plan of Action (JCPOA), concluded in July 2015, halted and in some areas rolled back Iranian progress toward a nuclear bomb capability. But the Trump administration pulled the United States out of the deal, and in response Iran resumed some of its nuclear activities. After the Biden administration took office, it sought to bring Iran back into the nuclear deal, but as of this writing the prospects do not appear good (Sanger et al., 2021).

In addition, some of the actions promised at the 1995 NPT RevCon have not been fully achieved. First, there is little chance of progress on a Middle East zone free of nuclear and other weapons of mass destruction (WMD). Second, nuclear weapon states are also perceived to be backsliding on prior commitments to nuclear disarmament. Several key countries, including the United States, have so far failed to ratify the CTBT, and as a result that treaty has never officially entered into force. In addition, as highlighted by several of the articles in this volume, developments such as nuclear modernization programs by the nuclear weapon states and their criticisms of the humanitarian initiative and nuclear ban treaty have convinced many non-nuclear weapon states that the NPT may never become a vehicle for achieving the goal of nuclear disarmament promised by Article VI.

A focus just on the NPT, however, is too narrow. The NPT remains the foundation of the larger nonproliferation regime, but over time the treaty has been supplemented by other cooperative nonproliferation arrangements. Since the 1960s, states have created several regional nuclear-weapon-free-zone (NWFZ) treaties. Such zones now exist in Latin America, Africa, Southeast Asia, the South Pacific, and Central Asia (Arms Control Association, 2017a). In addition, states have created a number of non-treaty arrangements to cooperatively promote nonproliferation. These include multilateral export control regimes such as the Nuclear Suppliers Group (NSG). The NSG has grown from an initial seven members in 1975 to 48 members today, with additional states seeking to join (Arms Control Association, 2017b).

The trend toward adding new nonproliferation arrangements accelerated after 1991. The collapse of the Soviet Union led to the innovation of cooperative threat reduction (CTR) programs. Russia has now ended its participation in CTR programs, but the long-term trend has been toward an expansion of threat reduction activities. Recipients of U.S. assistance have expanded to include countries beyond the post-Soviet republics that were the focus of the original program (DTRA, n.d.). The suppliers of assistance have also been multilateralized through measures such as the G-8 (now G-7) Global Partnership program (NTI, 2018).

The 9/11 attacks and revelations about the A.Q. Khan network spurred additional measures. These broadened the focus from preventing proliferation by states to keeping non-state terrorist groups from acquiring WMD. An important component of this agenda involves what has come to be called "nuclear security"—that is, efforts to secure or eliminate nuclear materials that could be used to make a nuclear explosive if they fell into the wrong hands. The George W. Bush administration sponsored two relevant initiatives. The Proliferation Security Initiative (PSI) sought to improve cooperation to interdict illicit shipments of WMD-related materials, while UN Security Council Resolution 1540 mandated a wide range of domestic measures for UN member states to criminalize WMD proliferation-related activities. Other efforts, such as the Global Initiative to Combat Nuclear Terrorism (GICNT), arose from bilateral cooperation, in this case between Russia and the United States. In 2010, the Obama administration launched a series of nuclear security summits as a way to impart momentum to the foregoing efforts. Despite some initial hesitation, most states have accepted the importance of taking steps to reduce the chances that nuclear materials could fall into the hands of non-state actors (Kutchesfahani et al., 2018).

Nonproliferation has experienced both ups and downs. But until 2015, one could discern a clear trend. The nonproliferation regime centered on the NPT had evolved into a multifaceted regime complex. The overall pattern was one of "building cooperation" in three ways: the addition of new initiatives, the growth in participants in the various nonproliferation instruments, and the development of new working relationships to implement programs (Knopf, 2016). Compared to trends with respect to strategic stability and the nuclear taboo, nonproliferation—as supplemented by the increased emphasis on nuclear security—had become stronger. This trend was consistent with the analysis elsewhere in this issue by Smetana and O'Mahoney (2022). They depict the NPT as an "antifragile" institution that actually grows stronger when it is forced to adapt to new challenges. My analysis suggests that until as recently as 2015 this was true not just of the NPT but the broader nonproliferation regime. But the notion of the NPT as an antifragile arrangement may no longer be accurate, as there is little evidence of new adaptations in response to current challenges.

Indeed, with respect to the NPT the recent news is not encouraging. The collapse of the 2015 NPT Review Conference was a bad omen. Ironically, the coronavirus pandemic may have improved prospects for the 2020 Review Conference by causing it to be postponed until at least 2022. The delay allowed for a change of administration in the United States, where the Biden administration is likely to be more committed than was its predecessor to a successful conference. But the underlying fissures among NPT members remain. Even with good will, which cannot be guaranteed, divergent perspectives on disarmament, the Middle East, and how to handle Iran and North Korea could well produce another failed review. And as Gibbons and Herzog (2022) note in their article in this issue, emerging multipolarity driven by China's rise could further undermine several elements of the NPT's past success.

Several other developments also portend trouble on the horizon. Russia's ending of its participation in CTR programs represents a symbolic blow to one of the most innovative areas of cooperation on nonproliferation.

Momentum for adding new initiatives or expanding participation in other existing initiatives has also largely come to a halt. Most importantly, there is little prospect for adding any new regional NWFZ. With respect to a long-sought Middle East zone, Israel has declined to attend talks, objecting that the proposed talks emerged from an NPT process in which Israel is not a member and hence was never consulted (Bino, 2020). Elsewhere, North Korea in the past decade accelerated its testing of nuclear weapons and ballistic missiles. Its nuclear capabilities are now so advanced that the goal of nuclear reversal by North Korea appears all but impossible. The future of the JCPOA also hangs in the balance. If Iran ends up seeking to complete nuclear weapons development, it could trigger additional proliferation in the region, especially by Saudi Arabia (Gheorghe, 2019).

In sum, although trends from the 1990s mostly resulted in strengthening nonproliferation and nuclear security, this progress has largely halted and may be starting to unravel. When added to adverse trends in relation to strategic stability and the nuclear taboo, this raises the obvious question of whether existing global governance of nuclear weapons will remain adequate for the task of preventing nuclear weapons use.

A Role for Disarmament?

So far, the nuclear order seems to be holding in the very important respect that there does not appear to be any imminent danger of nuclear weapons use. But how much longer can the nuclear order last without a nuclear weapon being detonated in a deliberate attack or unfortunate accident? Even in the nonproliferation realm, which I assess fairly positively, there are danger signs. And trends with respect to stability and the taboo have been less favourable. This points to the need for renewed efforts to shore up all three components of the nuclear order.

Even more might be required, however. A nuclear order based on the three strands discussed so far might not be enough. Nuclear disarmament represents an obvious candidate for a potential fourth strand to supplement the nuclear order. Is a more overt commitment to moving toward eventual nuclear abolition necessary to keep the world from again experiencing the consequences of a nuclear detonation in a populated area?

Although there are risks that will accompany any move to eliminate nuclear arms, on balance this question should be answered in the affirmative. An explicit commitment to global zero would have positive synergies with all three other strands of the nuclear order. In the nonproliferation realm, NPT Article VI commits nuclear weapon states to make a good faith effort to achieve nuclear disarmament. Although greater movement toward disarmament will not have uniform effects on nonproliferation, signs that the nuclear weapon states take this obligation seriously should help strengthen other states' commitments to nonproliferation. It is hard to envision non-nuclear states forever accepting a fundamental inequality in which some states get to keep nuclear weapons while all other states are legally forbidden to acquire them. Meaningful efforts by nuclear weapon states to move toward abolition would help shore up the NPT grand bargain (Knopf, 2012/13; for a contrary view, see Kroenig, 2016).

Efforts to promote global zero and the nuclear taboo are also logically related. The taboo rests on a belief that the consequences of any use of nuclear weapons would be too horrific to be acceptable. This view of the consequences of nuclear weapons use has also been the motivation for protest movements, NGOs, and occasional statesmen to promote a world free of nuclear weapons. The arguments that will be advanced to support abolition—that nuclear weapons are too destructive and indiscriminate to be used—will also serve to strengthen the taboo.

The relationship between disarmament and stability is less obvious. It is possible that nuclear arms reductions could weaken deterrence and make certain pathways to potential attacks more likely. Yet nuclear deterrence rests in part on an understanding about how destructive a nuclear war would be, an understanding that motivates state leaders to avoid actions that could lead to a nuclear exchange. Arguments that enhance the sense of taboo therefore also strengthen the deterrent effects of nuclear weapons, which should enhance stability. To the extent that progress toward disarmament bolsters nonproliferation, a more effective nonproliferation regime reduces the chances that weapons will spread to additional actors, which by restricting the number of nuclear-armed actors interacting with each other should also add to stability. Hence, to the extent that a commitment to disarmament strengthens the taboo or nonproliferation, indirectly it should also have positive effects on stability.

How might nuclear disarmament efforts be made more robust? The obvious candidate at present is the Nuclear Ban Treaty. Reflecting their frustration at the slow progress toward global zero, a number of non-nuclear weapon states concluded a Treaty on the Prohibition of Nuclear Weapons (TPNW) at the UN in July 2017 (Gibbons, 2018; Potter, 2017). The Ban Treaty entered into force in January 2021. To its supporters, the treaty represents an effort to strengthen norms against nuclear weapons in hopes of encouraging eventual movement toward actual elimination of nuclear arms. As a result, the treaty is largely symbolic. It does not set a deadline or outline a process for how to eliminate nuclear armaments. The treaty has also failed so far to attract any support from the states whose accession would matter most. All of the nuclear-armed states, along with most U.S. allies, opposed the treaty and boycotted the talks.

For the NGOs and diplomats that worked on behalf of the treaty, bringing the TPNW into being is a remarkable achievement. Based on the record so far, however, it remains far from clear whether the Ban Treaty can as a practical matter lead to further progress toward nuclear abolition, at least in the near term. If anything, the negotiations seem to have led nuclear-possessing nations to dig their heels in further over the disarmament issue. For this reason, it will be important to supplement the Ban Treaty with continued efforts to restore progress in the traditional approaches to arms control and nonproliferation. It remains important to get states to renew their support for the NPT, as well as to continue efforts to get more states to sign or ratify the CTBT, to begin negotiations on a fissile material cutoff treaty (FMCT), and to push for future U.S.-Russia arms control treaties.

The foregoing suggests that nuclear disarmament remains a worthy objective whose pursuit would strengthen the global nuclear order. Linking disarmament and the current order in this way is not an easy sell, as there are critics on both sides. Skeptics of calls for nuclear disarmament have long reacted with realist cynicism, arguing that nuclear abolition is either infeasible or undesirable, or both (for example, Brown & Deutch, 2007). Yet such a cynical resignation to a world where nuclear weapons will exist in perpetuity also carries costs. It will gradually chip away at the foundations of nonproliferation and the taboo, as it becomes harder to explain why any state that wants them should not have nuclear arms. This will put more of the burden of avoiding nuclear weapons use on the effectiveness of deterrence. And to think that nuclear deterrence will work forever against every type of actor and in every possible circumstance takes an act of tremendous faith. Indeed, to think that nuclear deterrence will always work might be a greater form of idealism than is a belief in the feasibility of one day achieving global zero.

Some supporters of abolition, including several articles in this special issue, take the argument further. They no longer see a synergy between disarmament and the nuclear order. Egeland, Hanson, and Noda all argue instead that the NPT has become incapable of serving as a vehicle for the pursuit of disarmament (as does Harrington de Santana, 2011). Pretorius and Sauer (2022) even assert that it is time for states to consider withdrawing from the NPT as a way to pressure the nuclear weapon states to do more. Such an approach carries risks. In the absence of an effective alternative vehicle standing in the wings to take over, actions that chip away at the existing order could simply accelerate the ongoing erosion of the global nuclear order while leaving nothing to replace it. Disarmament is not an end in itself. The overriding goal is to minimize the chances that nuclear weapons are ever used again. In this, disarmament shares a common goal with stability, the taboo, and nonproliferation, making it possible to promote all four strands in the effort to maintain nuclear peace.

Some critics of the renewed push for disarmament, such as Freedman (2013), have called for putting disarmament efforts on the back burner in order to reinforce the existing order. Others, as noted, have become convinced that the current order has become a roadblock to a necessary push for global zero. Although there are clear tensions between the existing order and the pursuit of disarmament, these need not be seen as largely in opposition. They all share in common the goal of averting the danger of nuclear war. Hence, it is important to find ways to shore up both the existing order and the effort to find a viable path to zero. One way to do this is to remind ourselves of the thinking that makes the nuclear order necessary. There is an underlying cognitive dimension to nuclear peace that has not received enough attention. In the short term, it would be useful to promote actions that would remind people of the dangers of nuclear war.

The Cognitive Dimension of Nuclear Peace

A global nuclear order can be described. It developed organically and has never in its entirety been formalized in any agreement. Its goal is to prevent nuclear weapons from being exploded where people are present, subject to the constraint that some states will continue to possess nuclear arsenals for the foreseeable future. The nuclear order has three main strands: strategic stability, the nuclear taboo, and nonproliferation (as supplemented by nuclear security measures). Since 1991, there are clear signs of erosion of both strategic stability and the taboo. In contrast, nonproliferation had been getting stronger and was a realm of dynamism and innovation. Yet, even nonproliferation is not completely robust and the most recent trends here are worrisome. Hence, it is hard to be confident that the current nuclear order can work forever to prevent nuclear weapons use. For these reasons, the international community needs to confront once again the question of whether there is a workable path to a world free of nuclear weapons. Just making and maintaining a stronger commitment to progress toward abolition, even if the goal is not achieved for many years to come, should help strengthen the other elements of the nuclear order.

In the short term, the feasible options for strengthening the international nuclear order appear limited. The prospects do not appear good for building on existing international institutions that regulate nuclear arms. There is also little sign of the kind of peace movement that might apply pressure on world leaders to do more. Young people who might be the base of a new activist campaign face other pressing issues, ranging from climate change to racial justice.

In the immediate future, therefore, the most practical steps available might be cognitive in nature. People are not born knowing how destructive nuclear weapons can be or believing that the danger of nuclear war requires states to behave cautiously. To encourage the "logic of restraint" highlighted by William Walker, a process of nuclear learning is necessary (Knopf, 2012). For the United States and Russia, it has been a long time since Cold War crises forced their leaders to confront the possibility of nuclear war. It would be helpful to find some way, hopefully not involving a new crisis, to refresh their memories as well as those of other current leaders.

One problem may be diminished attention to nuclear dangers in the news media and popular culture. During the Cold War, books and movies like On the Beach and Dr. Strangelove helped inform publics about the dangers associated with nuclear weapons. Watching the 1983 TV movie "The Day After" reportedly made a deep impression on Ronald Reagan (Gault, 2015). A new round of books, movies, and social media posts that highlight nuclear dangers could make world leaders more aware of the necessity of avoiding scenarios that could lead to nuclear use. Some good examples already exist, such as Lewis (2018), the Cranes for our Future campaign (n.d.), the Hair Trigger game (NTI, n.d.), and the N Square Collaborative (n.d.). Beyond these and other similar efforts, however, it would help to have a breakthrough movie, TV show, or popular song that could reach an even larger audience.

Another useful step might be a return to something like the original version of the humanitarian consequences initiative. This time, however, the audience could be broadened beyond diplomats. A Humanitarian Initiative 2.0 could include educating the public as well as the current generation of world leaders on the basic facts of what a nuclear war would do. Having a practical action item as a goal could also help. One promising possibility is a proposal to multilateralize the Reagan-Gorbachev pledge by campaigning to persuade other nuclear-armed states to endorse it (European Leadership Network, 2019).

All the strands of global nuclear governance—strategic stability, the nuclear taboo, nonproliferation and nuclear security, and potentially a greater commitment to eventual abolition—rest on an underlying cognitive foundation. This foundation involves awareness of the potential consequences of nuclear detonations and a belief this requires states to act with prudence to avoid stumbling into disaster. Anything that strengthens this cognitive dimension of nuclear peace will also help reinforce the existing strands of global nuclear governance while also building up support for efforts to find a workable pathway to nuclear abolition.

This article has proposed a new way to describe international nuclear order, as resting on the three strands of strategic stability, the nuclear taboo, and nonproliferation/nuclear security. Currently, there are signs of erosion in all three strands. To improve the prospects for making the situation better, it is first essential to ensure that it does not keep getting worse. Given the status of global nuclear governance today, efforts to hold the line and defend the existing elements of the nuclear order make sense, even as those concerned about nuclear dangers must also persuade world leaders to maintain a commitment to seek progress toward the elimination of nuclear arms.

Disclosure statement: No potential conflict of interest was reported by the author(s). Additional information. Notes on contributors. Jeffrey W. Knopf. Jeffrey W. Knopf is a professor at the Middlebury Institute of International Studies (MIIS), where he serves as chair of the MA program in Nonproliferation and Terrorism Studies. He is also a research affiliate with the Middlebury Institute's James Martin Center for Nonproliferation Studies and with the Center on International Security and Cooperation at Stanford University. Dr. Knopf has published extensively on topics related to nuclear arms control and nonproliferation. His most recent book is a volume he co-edited on Behavioral Economics and Nuclear Weapons (University of Georgia Press, 2019). One of the oldest peer-reviewed journals in international conflict and security, Contemporary Security Policy promotes theoretically-based research on policy problems of armed conflict, intervention and conflict resolution. Since it first appeared in 1980, CSP has established its unique place as a meeting ground for research at the nexus of theory and policy. Spanning the gap between academic and policy approaches, CSP offers policy analysts a place to pursue fundamental issues, and academic writers a venue for addressing policy. Major Fields of concern include: War and armed conflict, Peacekeeping, Conflict resolution, Arms control and disarmament, Defense policy, Strategic culture, International institutions.

CSP is committed to a broad range of intellectual perspectives. Articles promote new analytical approaches, iconoclastic interpretations and previously overlooked perspectives. Its pages encourage novel contributions and outlooks, not particular methodologies or policy goals. Its geographical scope is worldwide and includes security challenges in Europe, Africa, the Middle-East and Asia. Authors are encouraged to examine established priorities in innovative ways and to apply traditional methods to new problems. Journal information: Print ISSN: 1352-3260 Online ISSN: 1743-8764, 5 issues per year: Taylor & Francis make every effort to ensure the accuracy of all the information (the "Content") contained in our publications. However, Taylor & Francis, our agents (including the editor, any member of the editorial team or editorial board, and any guest editors), and our licensors, make no representations or warranties whatsoever as to the accuracy, completeness, or suitability for any purpose of the Content. Any opinions and views expressed in this publication are the opinions and views of the authors, and are not the views of or endorsed by Taylor & Francis. The accuracy of the Content should not be relied upon and should be independently verified with primary sources of information. Taylor & Francis shall not be liable for any losses, actions, claims, proceedings, demands, costs, expenses, damages, and other liabilities whatsoever or howsoever caused arising directly or indirectly in connection with, in relation to, or arising out of the use of the Content. Terms & Conditions of access and use can be found at :http://www.tandfonline.com/page/terms-and-conditions .contact Jeffrey W. Knopf jknopf@middlebury.edu Middlebury Institute of International Studies, 460 Pierce Street, Monterey, CA 93940, USA. © 2021 Informa UK Limited, trading as Taylor & Francis Group

Notes to Chapters

Introduction

1. Richard D.Wolff in his Asia Times analysis (Why the troubled US Empire could quickly fall apart: For the first time in more than a century, the United States has a real, serious, ascending global competitor-31 October 2021.

2. John E. Mclaughlin, in his paper, (Four Phases of Former President Trump's Relations with the Intelligence Community. International Journal of Intelligence and Counterintelligence, Vol. 34, No. 4, 787-794, 2021.

3. Former CIA analyst and expert, John A. Gentry in his research paper, (Trump-Era Politicization: A Code of Civil–Intelligence behaviour is needed. International Journal of Intelligence and Counterintelligence, 34: 757–786, 2021. Taylor & Francis Group, LLC.

4. 06 October, 2021, Congressional Research Service presented a report (U.S.-China Strategic Competition in South and East China Seas: Background and Issues for Congress

5. Kingston Reif and Shannon Bugos- April 2021

6. Wyn Rees and Azriel Bermant (Why does the UK want more nuclear weapons?-20 May 2021

7. UK. Nuclear Weapons: Beyond the Numbers-06 April 2021, Heather Williams

8. In 15 September 2021, an agreement was signed between Australia, US and UK to supply nuclear-powered submarine and underwater-drone technology to Australia, Independent.

9. Mark Valensia, Asia Times, 07 October, 2021

10. The AUKUS agreement. Mark Valensia-Asia Times, 07 October, 2021

11. Elie Perot, The Aukus agreement, what repercussions for the European Union? August 2021

12. Gregory Kulacki-27 April 2020

13. The AUKUS pact, BBC-16 September 2021

14. The Centre for Strategic and Budgetary Assessments, 02 April, 2010

15. Matthew Bunn Martin B. Malin Nickolas Roth William H. Tobey (Project on Managing the Atom Preventing Nuclear Terrorism Continuous Improvement or Dangerous Decline? Belfer Centre for Science and International Affairs Harvard Kennedy School-2016.

16. 07 May 2021, Dawn

17. Ibid

18. Future World of Illicit Nuclear Trade Mitigating the Threat. David Albright, Andrea Stricker, Houston Wood, July 29, 2013, Institute for Science and International Security.

19. Nuclear Madness, Musa Khan Jalalzai, 2021, India

20. Ibid

21. Strategic Vision Institute (SVI), a non-partisan think-tank based out of Islamabad, Pakistan, Sher Bano, 16 June 2020

22. On 24 October, 2021, the Independent newspaper

23. Arjun Gargeyas, Why India, Taiwan should strengthen ties: Taipei and New Delhi could collaborate in several areas, including the semiconductor supply chain, Asia Times, 19 October 2021

Chapter 1: New Cold War, Military Showdown between China and the United States in Taiwan and South China Sea

1. Akriti Vasudeva (US–China Strategic Competition and Washington's Conception of Quad Plus. The Journal of Indo-Pacific Affairs, VOL. 3 N0. 5 Special Issue, 2020.

2. 26 May 2021, BBC

3. Carla Freeman and Andrew Scobell. What's next for US-China Relations amid Rising Tensions over Taiwan: Chinese provocation in Taiwan Strait prompts U.S. and Chinese officials to discuss fraught state of bilateral affairs. October 9, 2021.

4. Robert R. Bianchi (China-US rivalries after the Afghan war-August 24, 2021

5. M Matheswaran (US-China Strategic Competition in the Asia-Pacific. M Matheswaran, 04 August, 2021.

6. Daniel Williams in his article (Bumbling Biden heads to Rome and Glasgow: US president badly needs a foreign policy win but without clear support for his domestic agenda his international credibility is fading-29 October, 2021.

7. Richard Jawad Hedarian. 28 October, 2021

8. Daniel Sneider (Biden's China trade policy is old wine in an old bottle: Administration's promised 'new approach' to China trade relations leaves in place Trump's ineffective and short-sighted policies-28 October, 2021.

9. Strategic Studies Quarterly (An Air Force–Sponsored Strategic Forum on National and International Security-Fall 2021, VOL.15, NO. 3.

10. 25 October, 2021, RT

11. Ibid

12. 24 October, 2021, RT

13. 24 October, 2021, RT

14. Nuclear Notebook: United States nuclear weapons, 2021. Hans M. Kristensen, Matt Korda, January 12, 2021

15. China Is Building A Second Nuclear Missile Silo Field. Matt Korda and Hans Kristensen • July 26, 2021

16. Bertil Lintner in his recent analysis (US encircling China on multiple new Cold War fronts: US-Australia nuclear submarine deal is part of a wider alliance-based strategy to counter and contain China's rise and ambitions, Asia Times, 20 September, 2021

17. Tarik Cyril Amar has noted (NATO's bullish new plan to fight Russia on the seas, the skies & in space could backfire, igniting a catastrophic nuclear conflict, RT, 25 Oct, 2021.

18. Jonny Tickle in his column (Missiles 'aimed at Moscow': Adviser to Ukraine's Zelensky warns Kremlin that war with Kiev would spell 'end of Russia' & its army-25 Oct, 2021.

19. Professor at the University of South-Eastern Norway and an editor at the Russia in Global Affairs journal, Glenn Diesen in his analysis (Beset by flagging economies, rising debt & defeat in Afghanistan, US-led West is lashing out at Russia and China in desperation-RT New, 25 Oct, 2021.

20. Eugene Rumer, Richard Sokolsky, (Grand Illusions: "The Impact of Misperceptions about Russia on U.S. Policy. The Carnegie Endowment, 30 June 2021

21. 04 October 2021, the National Interest published article of analyst David T. Pyne, in which he documented strength of Russia army and danger to US national security.

22. Ibid

23. March 2021, White House national security guidance

24. State Department calculation and Arms Control assessment, 26 October, 2021

25. Hans M. Kristensen & Matt Korda in their research paper on Russian nuclear weapons (Bulletin of the Atomic Scientists, 2021, VOL. 77, NO. 2, 90–10818 Mar 2021: Russian nuclear weapons, 2021.

26. Clint Reach, Edward Geist, Abby Doll, and Joe Cheravitch in their joint research paper (Competing with Russia Militarily Implications of Conventional and Nuclear Conflicts, RAND Corporation, June 2021.

27. Matthew Bunn. Nickolas Roth. William H. Tobey in their research paper on nuclear security and nuclear terrorism, Revitalizing Nuclear Security in an Era of Uncertainty., Project on Managing the Atom. Belfer Center for Science and International Affairs Harvard Kennedy School-January 2019

Chapter 2: Nuclear Jihad against China, South China Sea, Taiwan and the Underwater Nuclear Drones

1. Pentagon spokesman John Kirby statement on Afghanistan

2. Pentagon report 2020

3. Rajeswari Pillai Rajagopalan, Russia Tests Hypersonic Zircon Missile: Growing geopolitical rivalries will continue to drive the development of hypersonic and other lethal weapons systems. The Diplomat-July 22, 2021

4. Michael Mazza, Three scenarios for China's evolving nuclear strategy: Implications for the Taiwan Strait. Global Taiwan Institute-14 July 2021

5. Doyle Mcmanus, A new military alliance, a summit meeting: The U.S.-China face-off is looking like the Cold War, *Los Angeles Times*, 26 September, 2021

6. Bertil Lintner (US encircling China on multiple new Cold War fronts, Asia Times, 20 September, 2021

7. The Congressional Research Service report (China-India Great Power Competition in the Indian Ocean Region: Issues for Congress, April 20, 2018

8. Elie Perot, The Aukus agreement, what repercussions for the European Union? August 2021

9. Zhang Hui. (Global Times, 18 May, 2021 and BBC-16 September 2021

10. 18 September 2021, Al Jazeera, The Centre for Strategic and Budgetary Assessments, 02 April, 2010

11. Gerald C. Brown, noted in his article, Understanding the Risks and Realities of China's Nuclear Forces, (Arms Control Today, June 2021, Matthew Bunn Martin B. Malin Nickolas Roth William H. Tobey (Project on Managing the Atom Preventing Nuclear Terrorism Continuous Improvement or Dangerous Decline? Belfer Centre for Science and International Affairs Harvard Kennedy School-2016.

12. 11Global Times, US should stop eyeing too much on China's hypersonic missiles and broaden its horizons, Oct 17, 2021

13. Michael Keating, 23 April, 2021

14. Ibid

15. Irishnews, 25 January 2021

16. Arms Control Association, Kingston Reif and Shannon Bugos- April 2021

17. Mark Valensia-Asia Times, 07 October, 2021

18. Pakistan's former Interior Minister, Senator Dr. Rehman Malik (The Nation, 24 September, 2020

19. Nuclear Madness, Musa Khan Jalalzai, 2021

20. Ibid

21. Muhammad Wajeeh, a Research Associate at Department of Development Studies, COMSATS Institute of Information Technology, Abbottabad Pakistan, Nuclear Terrorism: A Potential Threat to World's Peace and Security-JSSA Vol II, No. 2

22. Damon Mehl, Damon Mehl, CTC Sentinel, November 2018, Volume-11, Issue-10

23. 20 September 2016), Uran Botobekov

24. Ibid

25. Afghanistan analyst, 26 June 2016

26. Why States Won't Give Nuclear Weapons to Terrorists, Keir A. Lieber and Daryl G. Press, 2013

27. 25 March 2016, Daily Telegraph

28. Ibid

29. Ibid

Chapter 3: New Cold War, Non-State Actors, and Threat of Biological Terrorism

1. 29 April 2020; Voice of America

2. Ibid

3. 16 April 2020, Associated Press

4. Xinhua News Agency in 28 May, 2020

5. Russia's "Biological" Information Operation against the US and Georgia. Nurlan Aliyev. 27 November, 2018

6. Washington Post, 15 August 2018

7. The Diplomat, 20 September 2016, Uran Botobekov,

8. Pakistan's former Interior Minister, Senator Dr. Rehman Malik ,The Nation, 24 September, 2020

9. The Diplomat, 20 September 2016, Uran Botobekov

10. What You Need to Know About Chemical Weapons Use in Syria. Alicia Sanders-Zakre. September 23, 2018

11. Central Asian Jihadists in the Front Line. Ely Karmon, Volume 11, Issue 4, August 2017, Perspective of Terrorism

12. Mr. Uran Botobekov, the Diplomat, January 10, 2017

13. Nick Mucerino, November 5, 2018

14. Bulgarian investigative journalist and Middle East correspondent Dilyana Gaytandzhieva, 12 September 2018

15. Ibid

Chapter 4: The United States Proxies and Prospect of Nuclear War

1. Daily Times, 2021

2. 29 April 2020; VOA

3. 16 April 2020, Associated Press

4. Scott Ritter (RT News, 28 April 2020

5. Asia Times. Richard Javad Heydarian. 25 May 2020

6. Daily Times. 2013

7. Ibid

8. Ibid

9. New York Times in April 2017 Rahmatullah Nabil

10. 18 May 2020, TASS News

11. 18 May 2020, RT News

Chapter 5: Pakistan's Nuclear Technology and Non-Nuclear States in South Asia, Middle East and South East Asia

1. Nuclear Monkey, pp-46

2. Mahmudul Huque. 01 February 2020

3. Defence Minister Khwaja Asif-2015

4. Mahmudul Huque. 01 February 2020

5. 18 August 2021, Prime Minister Imran Khan's UN statement

6. Ibid

7. Ibid

8. Siddhartha Roy, the Diplomat, 05 November 2019

9. Kunwar Khuldune Shahid, Diplomat, June 10, 2019

10. April 18, 2015, IS claimed to have carried out a deadly suicide attack in Jalalabad

11. April 15, 2015, Afghan lawmakers demanded the resignation of President Ashraf Ghani

12. October 2014, six leaders of the TTP announced their allegiance to ISIS

13. November 18, the Daily Mail

14. December 11, 2014, former Interior Minister of Pakistan Mr Rehman Malik told a local news channel that IS had established recruitment centres in Gujranwala and Bahawalpur districts of Punjab province.

15. December 13, 2014, in an interview with a local television channel, the chief of the Red Mosque, Maulana Abdul Aziz, confirmed the video message of his seminary students.

Chapter 6: Pakistani nuclear weapons, 2021, Hans M. Kristensen and Matt Korda

1. For insightful analysis of Pakistan's nuclear policy, see Siddique and Faisal (2016) and Dalton and Krepon (2015).

2. For references to tritium production at Khushab, see Cirincione, Wolfsthal, and Rajkumar (2005) and FAS (2000b).

3. One year after providing this description of the Pakistani nuclear warhead program, Lavoy was appointed as Special Assistant to the President and Senior Director for South Asia at the National Security Council.

4. These estimates are based on reprocessing and uranium enrichment plant capacities in International Panel on Fissile Materials (2015), Global Fissile Materials Report 2015: Nuclear Weapon and Fissile Material Stockpiles and Production report, Appendices 2 and 3, 48–49, <http://fissilematerials.org/library/gfmr15.pdf>, as well as more recent estimates.

5. For analysis of possible nuclear facilities at Masroor Air Base, see Kristensen (2016).

6. For analysis of possible Pakistani missile facilities, see Kristensen (2016).

7. For analysis of possible Pakistani missile facilities, see Kristensen (2016).

8. For an excellent analysis of this doctrine and Pakistan's potential use of battlefield nuclear weapons, see Nayyar and Mian (2010).

9. For analysis of possible Pakistani missile facilities, see Kristensen (2016).

10. The Ghauri MRBM is based on North Korea's No Dong missile.

11. For analysis of possible Pakistani missile facilities, see Kristensen (2016).

12. Note that the correct expansion of MIRV is multiple independently targetable reentry vehicle.

13. It is possible that the Babur-2 and the Babur-1B are the same missile. Both names are referenced as "enhanced" versions of the Babur.

14. For analysis of possible Pakistani missile brigade locations, see Kristensen (2016).

References

Abbasi, A. 2019. "Hope India Knows What NCA Means?" The News International, February 27. https://www.thenews.com.pk/print/437316-hope-india-knows-what-nca-means>

AFP. 2018. "Thrifty at 50: Pakistan Keeps Ageing Mirages Flying." France 24, April 29. https://www.france24.com/en/20180429-thrifty-50-pakistan-keeps-ageing-mirages-flying>

Albright, D., S. Burkhard, C. Chopin, and F. Pabian. 2018. New Thermal Power Estimates of the Khushab Nuclear Reactors, Institute for Science and International Security, May 23. http://isis-online.org/isis-reports/detail/new-thermal-power-estimates-of-the-khushab-nuclear-reactors/12 [Google Scholar]

Albright, D., S. Burkhard, and F. Pabian. 2018. Pakistan's Growing Uranium Enrichment Program, Institute for Science and International Security, May 30. http://isis-online.org/isis-reports/detail/pakistans-growing-uranium-enrichment-program/12 [Google Scholar]

Albright, D., and S. Kelleher-Vergantini. 2015. Pakistan's Chashma Plutonium Separation Plant: Possibly Operational, Institute for Science and International Security, February 20. http://isis-online.org/uploads/isis-reports/documents/Chashma_February_20_2015_Final.pdf [Google Scholar]

Ansari, U. 2013. "Despite Missile Integration, Nuke Role Unlikely for Pakistan's JF-17." Defense News, February 7. [Google Scholar]

Associated Press. 1989. "Pakistani Jets Said to Be Nuclear-Capable." [Google Scholar]

Berrier, S. 2021. "Statement for the Record: Worldwide Threat Assessment, Armed Services Committee, United States Senate." Director, Defense Intelligence Agency, April 26. https://www.armed-services.senate.gov/imo/media/doc/2021%20DIA%20Annual% 20Threat%20Assessment%20Statement%20for%20the%20Record.pdf

Boucher, R. A. 2007. Assistant Secretary of State for South and Central Asian Affairs, Testimony before Senate Foreign Relations Committee. In U.S. Foreign Assistance to Pakistan, 31. Washington, DC: U.S. Government Printing Office. (December 6, 2007). [Google Scholar]

Burkhard, S., A. Lach, and F. Pabian. 2017. "Khushab Update." Institute for Science and International Security, September 7. http://isis-online.org/uploads/

isis-reports/documents/Khushab_Update_September_2017.pdf   [Google Scholar]

Carnegie Endowment for International Peace. 2015. "A Conversation With Gen. Khalid Kidwai." Carnegie International Nuclear Policy Conference 2015, Washington, DC, 4–5, Transcript, March 23. http://carnegieendowment. org/files/03-230315carnegieKIDWAI.pdf [Google Scholar]

Cirincione, J., J. B. Wolfsthal, and M. Rajkumar. 2005. Deadly Arsenal: Nuclear, Biological, and Chemical Threats. 2nd ed. Washington, D.C.: Carnegie Endowment for International Peace. [Google Scholar].

Coats, D. R. 2019. Worldwide Threat Assessment of the U.S. Intelligence Community, Director of National Intelligence, January 29. <https://www.dni.gov/ files/ODNI/documents/2019-ATA-SFR—SSCI.pdf>

Dalton, T., and M. Krepon. 2015. A Normal Nuclear Pakistan, Carnegie Endowment for International Peace/Stimson Center, August. http://www.stimson. org/sites/default/files/file-attachments/NormalNuclearPakistan.pdf [Google Scholar]

Dawn. 2017. "Rare Light Shone on Full Spectrum Deterrence Policy." December 7. https://www.dawn.com/news/1375079/rare-light-shone-on-full-spectrum-deterrence-policy [Google Scholar]

Economic Times. 2016. "US Expresses Concern over Pakistan's Deployment of Nuclear Weapons." March 19. https://economictimes.indiatimes.com/news/ defence/us-expresses-concerns-over-pakistans-deployment-of-nuclear-weapons/articleshow/51465040.cms [Google Scholar]

Economic Times. 2017. "US Worried Pakistan's Nuclear-weapons Could Land up in Terrorists' Hands: Official." August 25. https://economictimes.indiatimes. com/news/defence/us-worried-pakistans-nuclear-weapons-could-land-up-in-terrorists-hands-official/articleshow/60220358.cms [Google Scholar]

FAS. 2000a. "Rawalpindi/Nilhore, PINSTECH/New Labs." Federation of American Scientists, March 18. https://fas.org/nuke/guide/pakistan/facility/rawal-pindi.htm [Google Scholar]

FAS. 2000b. "Khushab/Khusab." Federation of American Scientists, March 15. https://fas.org/nuke/guide/pakistan/facility/khushab.htm [Google Scholar]

Fisher, R. 2016. "JF-17 Block II Advances with New Refuelling Probe." Jane's Defence Weekly, January 27. <http://www.janes.com/article/57508/jf-17-block-ii-advances-with-new-refuelling-probe>

Gady, Franz-Stefan. 2020. "Pakistan Air Force to Take Delivery of First 12 JF-17B Fighters 'In near Future.'" The Diplomat, February 5. https://thediplo-mat.com/2020/02/pakistan-air-force-to-take-delivery-of-first-12-jf-17b-fighters-in-near-future/

Gordon, M. 1989. "German Concern Said to Aid Pakistan A-Weapons." New York Times, January 29. https://www.nytimes.com/1989/01/29/world/german-concern-said-to-aidpakistan-a-weapons.html [Google Scholar]

Gul, A. 2014. "As Pakistan Expands Nuclear Program, China Seen as Most Reliable Partner." Voice of America, May 12. https://www.voanews.com/a/as-pakistan-expands-nuclear-program-china-seen-as-most-reliable-partner/1912529.html [Google Scholar]

Gupta, S. 2020. "Pakistan's Effort to Launch 750km Range Missile Crashes." Hindustan Times, March 23. <https://www.hindustantimes.com/india-news/pakistan-s-effort-to-launch-750km-range-missile-crashes/story-UT5CbOR3K0uVojmiOYoKjO.html>

Hyatt, N., and S. Burkhard. 2020. "New Extension to the Chashma Plutonium Separation Facility." Institute for Science and International Security, November 30. <https://isis-online.org/uploads/isis-reports/documents/Extension_to_the_Chashma_plutonium_separation_facility_Nov30_2020_FINAL.pdf>

India Today. 2015. "We Have Low-yield N-weapons to Ward off India's War Threat: Pakistan." October 20. http://indiatoday.intoday.in/articlePrint.jsp?aid=503185 [Google Scholar]

International Panel on Fissile Materials. 2015. Global Fissile Material Report 2015. http://fissilematerials.org/library/gfmr15.pdf [Google Scholar]

International Panel on Fissile Materials. 2021. "Pakistan." April 29. <http://fissile-materials.org/countries/pakistan.html>

ISPR. 2011a. Press release No. PR40/2011-ISPR, February 10. https://www.ispr.gov.pk/press-release-detail.php?id=1666 [Google Scholar]

ISPR. 2011b. Press release No. PR94/2011-ISPR, April 19. https://www.ispr.gov.pk/press-release-detail.php?id=1721 [Google Scholar]

ISPR. 2011c. Press release No. PR104/2011-ISPR, April 29. https://www.ispr.gov.pk/press-release-detail.php?id=1732 [Google Scholar]

ISPR. 2012a. Press Release PR143/2012-ISPR, June 5. https://www.ispr.gov.pk/press-release-detail.php?id=2088 [Google Scholar]

ISPR. 2012b. Press release PR204/2012-ISPR, September 17. https://www.ispr.gov.pk/press-release-detail.php?id=2150 [Google Scholar]

ISPR. 2012c. Press release PR122/2012-ISPR, May 19. https://www.ispr.gov.pk/press-release-detail.php?id=2067 [Google Scholar]

ISPR. 2013. Press Release No PR20/2013ISPR, February 15. https://www.ispr.gov.pk/press-release-detail.php?id=2242 [Google Scholar]

ISPR. 2016a. Press release No. PR16/2016-ISPR, January 19. https://www.ispr.gov.pk/press-release-detail.php?id=3163 [Google Scholar]

ISPR. 2016b. Press Release No. PR482/2016-ISPR, December 14. https://www.ispr. gov.pk/press-release-detail.php?id=3632 [Google Scholar]

ISPR. 2017a. Press Release No PR344/2017-ISPR, July 5. https://www.ispr.gov.pk/ press-release-detail.php?id=4097 [Google Scholar]

ISPR. 2017b. Press release No. PR34/2017-ISPR, January 24. https://www.ispr.gov. pk/press-release-detail.php?id=3705 [Google Scholar]

ISPR. 2017c. Press Release No. PR10/2017-ISPR, January 9. https://www.ispr.gov. pk/press-release-detail.php?id=3672 [Google Scholar]

ISPR. 2017d. Press Release No. PR615/2017ISPR, December 21. https://www.ispr. gov.pk/press-release-detail.php?id=4459 [Google Scholar]

ISPR. 2018a. Press Release No PR142/2016ISPR, April 14. https://www.ispr.gov. pk/press-release-detail.php?id=4693 [Google Scholar]

ISPR. 2018b. Press Release No. PR125/2018-ISPR, March 29. https://www.ispr.gov. pk/press-release-detail.php?id=4660 [Google Scholar]

ISPR. 2018c. Press Release No. PR308/2018-ISPR, October 8. <https://www.you-tube.com/watch?v=x_fksZHGFWA&ab_channel=ISPROfficial>

ISPR. 2018d. Press Release No. PR-PN-2/2018-ISPR, January 3. <https://www. ispr.gov.pk/press-release-detail.php?id=4480>

ISPR. 2019d. Press Release No. PR37/2019-ISPR, January 31. <https://www.you-tube.com/watch?v=IH3go8W16yU&ab_channel=ISPROfficial>

ISPR. 2019e. Press Release No. PR102/2019-ISPR, May 23. <https://www.youtube. com/watch?v=iPOcXXQZdyI&ab_channel=ISPROfficial>

ISPR. 2020a. Press Release No. PR27/2020-ISPR, February 18. <https://www.ispr. gov.pk/press-release-detail.php?id=5625>.

ISPR. 2020b. Press Release No. PR8/2020-ISPR, January 23. <https://www.ispr. gov.pk/press-release-detail.php?id=5592>

ISPR. 2021b. Press Release No. PR19/2021-ISPR, February 3. <https://www.ispr. gov.pk/press-release-detail.php?id=6035>

ISPR. 2021c. Press Release No. PR59/2021-ISPR, March 26. <https://www.you-tube.com/watch?v=eA8mZ0w2NlM&ab_channel=ISPROfficial>

ISPR. 2021d. Press Release No. PR12/2021-ISPR, January 20. <https://www.you-tube.com/watch?v=pL26yWXgBPc&ab_channel=ISPROfficial>

ISPR. 2021e. Press Release No. PR24/2021-ISPR, February 11. <https://www.you-tube.com/watch?v=p7kSBvkBMYo&ab_channel=ISPROfficial>

ISPR [@OfficialDGISPR]. 2019a. "Pakistan Successfully Carried Out Night Train-ing Launch of Surface to Surface Ballistic Missile Ghaznavi, Capable of Delivering Multiple Types of Warheads Upto 290 KMs. CJCSC & Services Chiefs Congrat Team. President & PM Conveyed Appreciation to Team &

Congrats to the Nation." Tweet, August 29. <https://twitter.com/OfficialDG-ISPR/status/1166955085924130816>

ISPR [@OfficialDGISPR]. 2019b. "Pakistan Successfully Conducted Training Launch of SSBM Shaheen-1 Capable of Delivering All Types of Warheads Upto Range of 650 KMs. Launch Was Aimed at Testing Operational Readiness of Army Strategic Forces Command (ASFC) Ensuring Pakistan's Credible Minimum Deterrence." Tweet, November 18. <https://twitter.com/OfficialDGISPR/status/1196342816777084929>

ISPR [@OfficialDGISPR]. 2019c. "Pakistan Successfully Conducted Training Launch of Surface to Surface Ballistic Missile "Nasr" to Enhance the Operational Efficiency of Army Strategic Forces Command Besides Re-validating the Desired Technical Parameters." Tweet, January 24. <https://twitter.com/OfficialDGISPR/status/1088403258778009600>.

ISPR [@OfficialDGISPR]. 2021a. "Pakistan Day Parade - March 2021." Tweet, March 24. <https://twitter.com/OfficialDGISPR/status/1374914302960893953>

Jones, G.S. 2021. "Pakistan's Nuclear Material Production for Nuclear Weapons." proliferationmatters.com, February 21. https://nebula.wsimg.com/0aab8d9a81ac6cfa0c0c4a986cadd8f6?AccessKeyId=40C80D0B51471CD86975&disposition=0&alloworigin=1

Kalinowski, M. B., and L. C. Colschen. 1995. "International Control of Tritium to Prevent Horizontal Proliferation and to Foster Nuclear Disarmament." Science and Global Security 5: 147. [Taylor & Francis Online], [Google Scholar]. . Crossref.

Khan, B. 2017. "Pakistan Officially Unveils Extended Range Ra'ad 2 Air-Launched Cruise Missile." Quwa Defence News & Analysis Group, March 23. https://quwa.org/2017/03/23/pakistan-officially-unveils-extended-range-raad-2-air-launched-cruise-missile/ [Google Scholar]

Khan, B. 2019a. "Profile: Pakistan's New Hangor Submarine." Quwa, November 11. https://quwa.org/2019/11/11/profile-pakistans-new-hangor-submarine/

Khan, F. H. 2015. "Going Tactical: Pakistan's Nuclear Posture and Implications for Stability." Proliferation Papers. No. 53, Institut Français des Relations Internationales (IFRI), September. 41. https://www.ifri.org/sites/default/files/atoms/files/pp53khan_0.pdf [Google Scholar]

Khan, F. H. 2019b. "Nuclear Command, Control and Communications (NC3): The Case of Pakistan." NAPSNet Special Reports, September 26. https://nautilus.org/napsnet/napsnet-special-reports/nuclear-command-control-and-communications-nc3-the-case-of-pakistan/

Kidwai, K. 2015. "A Conversation with Gen. Khalid Kidwai." Carnegie Endowment for International Peace, March 23. <https://carnegieendowment.org/files/02_230315carnegieKIDWAI.pdf>

Kidwai, K. 2020. "Deterrence, Nuclear Weapons and Arms Control." Keynote Address, "Workshop on South Asian Strategic Stability." International Institute for Strategic Studies and Centre for International Strategic Studies, February 6. <https://www.youtube.com/watch?v=bInVdvk39e0&ab_channel=TheInternationalInstituteforStrategicStudies>

Kristensen, H. M. 2007. "Pakistani Nuclear Forces, 2007." FAS Strategic Security Blog, May 9. http://fas.org/blogs/security/2007/05/article_pakistani_nuclear_forc/ [Google Scholar]

Kristensen, H. M. 2009. "Pakistani Nuclear Forces, 2009." FAS Strategic Security Blog, August 28. http://fas.org/blogs/security/2009/08/pakistan2009/ [Google Scholar]

Kristensen, H. M. 2016. "Pakistan's Evolving Nuclear Missile Infrastructure." FAS Strategic Security Blog, November 1. https://fas.org/blogs/security/2016/11/pakistan-nuclear-infrastructure/ [Google Scholar]

Laskar, R. H. 2021. "Pakistan PM Imran Khan Again Seeks US Intervention on Kashmir." The Hindustan Times, June 21. <https://www.hindustantimes.com/india-news/pakistan-pm-imran-khan-again-seeks-us-intervention-on-kashmir-101624274376335.html>

National Air and Space Intelligence Center. 2013. Ballistic and Cruise Missile Threat. http://fas.org/programs/ssp/nukes/nuclearweapons/NASIC2013_050813.pdf [Google Scholar]

National Air and Space Intelligence Center. 2020. Ballistic and Cruise Missile Threat. <https://media.defense.gov/2021/Jan/11/2002563190/-1/-1/1/2020%20BALLISTIC%20AND%20CRUISE%20MISSILE%%20 20THREAT_FINAL_2OCT_REDUCEDFILE.PDF>

Nayyar, A. H., and Z. Mian. 2010. The Limited Military Utility of Pakistan's Battlefield Use of Nuclear Weapons in Response to Large Scale Indian Conventional Attack, Pakistan Security Research Unit (PSRU), Brief Number 61, November 11. http://spaces.brad.ac.uk:8080/download/attachments/748/Brief61doc.pdf [Google Scholar]

Panda, A. 2016. "Pakistan's Shaheen-III Ballistic Missile May Use Chinese Transporter." The Diplomat, July 1. <https://thediplomat.com/2016/07/pakistans-shaheen-iii-ballistic-missile-may-use-chinese-transporter>

Quwa. 2021. "Pakistan Aeronautical Complex Delivers New JF-17B Batch." January 2. <https://quwa.org/2021/01/02/pakistan-aeronautical-complex-delivers-new-jf-17b-batch-2/>

Rahmat, R. 2019. "Pakistan Navy Flexes Land Attack Capabilities in Arabian Sea." Janes, April 24. <https://www.janes.com/defence-news/news-detail/pakistan-navy-flexes-land-attack-capabilities-in-arabian-sea>

Reed, T. C., and D. B. Stillman. 2009. The Nuclear Express: A Political History of the Bomb and Its Proliferation. Minneapolis: Zenith Press. [Google Scholar]

Schaffer, T. 1989. "Deputy Assistant Secretary of State for South Asia. U.S. Department of State." Proposed Sale of F-16s to Pakistan: Hearings before the Committee on Foreign Relations. Washington, DC: U.S. Senate Committee on Foreign Affairs, August 2. [Google Scholar]

Scroll. 2016. "No, Pakistan's Defence Minister Did Not Threaten Nuclear Strikes after the Uri Attacks." September 19. Available at: https://scroll.in/video/816903/no-pakistans-defence-minister-did-not-threaten-nuclear-strikes-after-the-uri-attacks [Google Scholar]

Senate Committee on National Defense. 2016. "Pakistan & China's JF-17 Fighter Program." n.d. accessed September 8. http://www.senatedefencecommittee.com.pk/production-detail.php?pageid=news-detail&pid=MTc= [Google Scholar]

Siddique, F., and M. Faisal. 2016. "Pakistan's Strategic Nuclear Policy and Implications for Deterrence Stability." CISS Insight: Quarterly News and Views IV (1): 1–17. Center for International Strategic Studies, March. [Google Scholar]. http://ciss.org.pk/wp-content/uploads/2016/05/1-Article-Farzana-Faisal.pdf

Tasleem, S. 2017. "No Indian BMD for No Pakistani MIRVS." Stimson Center, Off Ramps Initiative, Paper, October 2. [Google Scholar]

Tasleem, S., and T. Dalton 2019. "Nuclear Emulation: Pakistan's Nuclear Trajectory." The Washington Quaterly, January 22, 135–155. https://carnegieendowment.org/2019/01/22/nuclear-emulation-pakistan-s-nuclear-trajectory-pub-78215 Crossref.

The White House. 2017. "Remarks by President Trump on the Strategy in Afghanistan and South Asia." August 21. Available at: https://www.whitehouse.gov/briefings-statements/remarks-president-trump-strategy-afghanistan-south-asia/ [Google Scholar]

US Defense Intelligence Agency. 1999. The Decades Ahead: 1999-2020, A Primer on the Future Threat. In (2004) Rumsfeld's War: The Untold Story of America's Anti-Terrorist Commander, edited by R Scarborough, 194–223. Washington, DC: Regnery. [Google Scholar].

US NATO Mission. 2008. "Subject: Allies Find Briefing on Afghanistan NIE 'Gloomy.'" USNATO 000453, December 5, paragraph 12. http://www.theguardian.com/world/us-embassy-cables-documents/181529 [Google Scholar]

Warnes, A. 2020. "PAC Kamra Rolls Out Final 14 JF-17B Fighters for Pakistan Air Force." Janes, December 30. <https://www.janes.com/defence-news/news-detail/pac-kamra-rolls-out-final-14-jf-17b-fighters-for-pakistan-air-force>.

World Bulletin. 2013. "Pakistan Refutes Saudi Funding, Weapons Claims." November 9. [Google Scholar]

Chapter 7: India-China Friction and the South China Sea

1. Richard Purcell. 28 January 2020-Global Security Review

2. behind the US–China Trade War: The Race for Global Technological Leadership, Marianne Schneider-Petsinger.

3. Richard Purcell 28 January 2020-Global Security Review

4. Analyst Marianne Schneider-Petsinger highlighted aspects of trade war and technological competition between China and the United States

5. Ravi Agrawal paper

6. June 6, 2015, Pajhwok News

7. Mir Sajad Modern diplomacy 29 May 2020

8. Haris Bilal Malik, Modern Diplomacy 28 May 2020

9 George PerKovich and Toby Dalton, 2015

10. Bilal Malik Modern Diplomacy 28 May 2020

Chapter 8: The US–China Rivalry in the Emerging Bipolar World: Hostility, Alignment, and Power Balance. Suisheng Zhao

1. Cliff Kupchan, 'US–China: The Cool War', Eurasia Live, September 4, 2019, accessed May 1, 2021, https://www.eurasiagroup.net/ live-post/us-china-cool-war; Andrew A. Michta, 'Bipolarity Is Back', The American Interest, January 17, 2020, accessed May 1, 2021, https://www.the-american-interest.com/2020/01/17/bipolarity-is-back/; Richard Maher, 'Bipolarity and the Future of US– China Relations', Political Science Quarterly 133(3), (2018), pp. 497–525; Lin Linim and Wang Xuan, 'The US and China: A New Bipolar World', Contemporary International Relations 30(1), (2020), pp. 1–8; 阎学通 [Yan Xuetong], '2019开启了世界两极格 局' ['2019 opened the bipolar world'], 现代国际关系 [Contemporary International Relations] (1), (2020), pp. 6–8.

2. 金灿荣 [Jin Canrong], "展望未来十年国际格局'两超多强'与'双文明冲突'" ['Looking forward to the next ten years, the international pattern of "two superpowers, multiple powers" and "dual civilization conflicts'], South China urbanity, September 29, 2019, accessed May 1, 2021, http://www.sinotf.com/GB/Person/134/2017-09-29/4NMDAwMDI3NjE4Nw.html.

3. Robert D. Kaplan, 'A New Cold War Has Begun', Foreign Policy, January 7, 2019, accessed May 1, 2021, https://foreignpolicy.com/ 2019/01/07/a-new-cold-war-has-begun/; Lawrence J. Haas, 'US must prepare for cold war with China', The Hill, March 27, 2021, accessed May 1, 2021, https://thehill.com/opinion/international/545215-us-must-prepare-for-cold-war-with-china;

Alan Dupont, 'The US–China Cold War Has Already Started', Th Diplomat, July 8, 2020, accessed May 1, 2021, https://thediplomat. com/2020/07/the-US–China-cold-war-has-already-started/; Michael Lind, 'Cold War II', National Review, May 10, 2018, accessed May 1, 2021, https://www.nationalreview.com/magazine/2018/05/28/US–China-relations-cold-war-ii/

4. John Mearsheimer, The Tragedy of Great Power Politics (New York: W. W. Norton & Company, 2014).

5. Graham Allison, Destined for War, Can America and China Escape Thucydides' Trap? (New York: Houghton Miflin Harcourt, 2017).

6. Kori Schake, 'How International Hegemony Changes Hands', Cato Unbound, March 5, 2018, accessed May 1, 2021, https://www. cato-unbound.org/2018/03/05/kori-schake/how-international-hegemony-changes-hands; Robert D. Kaplan, 'A New Cold War has Begun', Foreign Affairs, January 29, 2019, accessed May 1, 2021, https://foreignpolicy.com/2019/01/07/a-new-cold-war-has- begun/.

7. Thomas J. Christensen, 'There Will Not Be a New Cold War', Foreign Affairs, March 24, 2021, accessed May 1, 2021, https://www. foreignaffairs.com/articles/united-states/2021-03-24/there-will-not-be-new-cold-war;   Michael Mcfaul, 'Cold War Lessons and Fallacies for US–China Relations Today', Washington Quarterly 43(4), (2021), pp. 7–39; Ian Bremmer, 'No, the U.S. and China Are Not Heading Towards a New Cold War', Time, December 28, 2020, accessed May 1, 2021, https://time.com/5920725/us-china- competition/.

8. Michael R. Pompeo, Secretary of State, 'Communist China and the Free World's Future', July 23, 2020, accessed May 27, 2021, https://www.state.gov/communist-china-and-the-free-worlds-future/

9. Press Briefing by Press Secretary Jen Psaki and National Security Advisor Jake Sullivan, The White House, March 12, 2021, accessed May 1, 2021, https://www.whitehouse.gov/briefing-room/press-briefings/2021/03/12/press-briefing-by-press-secretary-jen- psaki-march-12-2021/.

10. 钟声 [Zhong Sheng], '冷战思维当休矣' ['The Cold War mentality should stop'], People's Daily, July 10, 2020, accessed May 1, 2021, http://theory.people.com.cn/n1/2020/0710/c40531-31778024.html; Editorial, 'China urges U.S. to discard Cold War mentality', Xinhua, July 21, 2020, accessed May 1, 2021, http://www.xinhuanet.com/english/2020-07/21/c_139227316.htm.

11. 'Xi Jinping's speech at the virtual Davos Agenda event', CGTN, January 26, 2021, accessed May 1, 2021,https://news.cgtn.com/news/2021-01-25/Full-text-Xi-Jinping-s-speech-at-the-virtual-Davos-Agenda-event-Xln4hwjO2Q/index.html.

12. Chas W. Freeman, Jr, 'The Struggle with China is not a Replay of the Cold War', Remarks to the Asia American Forum, September 25, 2020, accessed

June 8, 2021, https://chasfreeman.net/the-struggle-with-china-is-not-a-re-play-of-the-cold-war/

13. Suisheng Zhao, 'Rhetoric and Reality of China's Global Leadership in the Context of COVID-19: Implications for the US-led World Order and Liberal Globalization', the Journal of Contemporary China 30 (128), pp. 245–247.

14. Paul Heer, 'Understanding U.S.-China Strategic Competition', National Interest, October 20, 2020, accessed May 1, 2021, https:// nationalinterest.org/feature/understanding-US–China-strategic-competition-171014.

15. Kerry A. Dolan, 'Forbes 35th Annual World Billionaires List: Facts and Figures2021', Forbes, April 6, 2021, accessed May 1, 2021, https://www.forbes.com/sites/kerryadolan/2021/04/06/forbes-35th-annual-worlds-billionaires-list-facts-and-figures-2021/?sh= 3385e89d5e58.

16. Pankaj Mishra, 'U.S.-China Cold War Will Have More Than Two Sides', Bloomberg Opinion, April 3, 2021, accessed May 1, 2021, https://www.bloomberg.com/opinion/articles/2021-04-04/u-s-china-cold-war-will-have-more-than-two-sides.

17. James T. Areddy, 'Americans' Views on China went from Bad to Worse', Wall Street Journal, March 4, 2021, accessed May 11, 2021, https://www.wsj.com/articles/americans-negative-views-on-china-spike-polls-show-11614870001

18. Zbigniew Brzezinski, The Grand Chessboard: American Primacy and Its Geostrategic Imperatives (New York: Basic Books, 1998), p. 54.

19. Shan Jie and Yang Sheng, 'China, Russia reaffirm mutual support on core interests, sovereignty', Global Times, July 8, 2020, accessed May 1, 2021, https://www.globaltimes.cn/content/1193952.shtml.

20. Yaroslav Trofimov, 'The New Beijing-Moscow Axis', Wall Street Journal, February 1, 2019, accessed May 1, 2021, https://www. wsj.com/articles/the-new-beijing-moscow-axis-11549036661.

21. Editor, 'Xi and Putin, best friends forever?' Foreign Affairs, June 6, 2019, accessed May 27, 2021, https://foreignpolicy.com/2019/ 06/06/xi-and-putin-best-friends-forever/

22. 'China-Russia ties deepen while US and allies flail', Global Times, March 21, 2021, accessed May 1, 2021, https://www. globaltimes.cn/page/202103/1219002.shtml.

23. Eduardo Baptista, 'Why Russia's Vladivostok celebration promoted backlash in China' South China Morning Post, July 2, 2020, accessed May 1, 2021, https://www.scmp.com/news/china/diplomacy/article/3091611/why-russias-vladivostok-celebration- prompted-nationalist.

24. Robert Sutter, 'How the United States Influences Russia-China Relations', The National Bureau of Asian Research, February 27, 2018, accessed May 1, 2021, http://www.nbr.org/research/activity.aspx?id=848.

25. Worldwide Threat Assessment by the U.S. intelligence community to Senator Select Committee on Intelligence, Office of the Director of National Intelligence, May 11, 2017, accessed May 1, 2021, https://www.dni.gov/files/documents/Newsroom/ Testimonies/SSCI%20Unclassified%20SFR%20-%20Final.pdf.

26. Ivo Daalder, 'Commentary: Trump's epic fail: His gambit with Iran drives Tehran toward China', Chicago Tribune, July 16, 2020, accessed May 27, 2021, https://www.chicagotribune.com/opinion/commentary/ct-opinion-iran-china-pact-trump-daalder -20200716-ftdlnqts6zaplerban2zwtzzn4-story.html

27. Philippe Le Corre and Erik Brattberg, 'How the Coronavirus Pandemic Shattered Europe's Illusions of China', Carnegie Endowment for International Peace, July 9, 2020, accessed May 1, 2021, https://carnegieendowment.org/2020/07/09/how- coronavirus-pandemic-shattered-europe-s-illusions-of-china-pub-82265.

28. Theresa Fallon, 'China and the EU: A Tale of Two Summits, COVID-19 has accelerated shifting dynamics in EU-China relations', The Diplomat, September 1, 2020, accessed May 1, 2021, https://thediplomat.com/2020/08/china-and-the-eu-a-tale-of-two- summits/.

29. Editorial, 'Anti-dumping on Aussie wine not "trade war," but Canberra urged to "grow up" or face more pain', Global Times, November 27, 2020, accessed May 1, 2021, https://www.globaltimes.cn/content/1208273.shtml.

30. Editorial, 'Canberra only has itself to blame', China Daily, November 5, 2020, accessed May 1, 2021, https://enapp.chinadaily. com.cn/a/202011/05/AP-5fa3e92ea310b0a661bf3fc5.html.

31. Joint Statement on Australia-U.S. Ministerial Consultations (AUSMIN), US Department of Defense, July 28, 2020, accessed May 1, 2021, https://www.defense.gov/Newsroom/Releases/Release/Article/2290911/joint-statement-on-australia-us-ministerial- consultations-ausmin-2020/.

32. Wajahat Khan And Alex Fang, 'US and Australia propose "network of alliances" to curb China', Nikkei Asian review, July 29, 2020, accessed May 1, 2021, https://asia.nikkei.com/Politics/International-relations/US–China-tensions/US-and-Australia-propose- network-of-alliances-to-curb-China.

33. Katrina Mansion, 'Australia treads careful line on China in US meeting', Financial Times, July 28, 2020, accessed May 1, 2021, https://www.ft.com/content/43c65abc-748e-4854-84e8-6aee70d793c2.

34. Stephen Dziedzic, 'Scott Morrison calls on United States and China to dial down hostilities in speech at UK think tank Policy Exchange', ABC News Australia Broadcast, November 23, 2020, accessed May 1, 2021, https://www.abc.net.au/news/2020-11- 24/scott-morrison-calls-on-us-and-china-to-dial-down-hostilities/12913062.

35. Lee Hisen Loong, 'The Endangered Asian Century, America, China, and the Perils of Confrontation', Foreign Affairs, June 4, 2020, accessed May 1, 2021, https://www.foreignaffairs.com/articles/asia/2020-06-04/lee-hsien-loong-endangered-asian-century.

36. Fumiaki Kubo, 'Japan–US relations in a post-COVID-19 world', East Asia Forum, June 6, 2020, accessed May 1, 2021, https:// www.eastasiaforum.org/2020/06/06/japan-us-relations-in-a-post-covid-19-world/.

37. 'Suga Denies Possible Military Involvement over Taiwan', Nippon, April 2, 2021, accessed May 1, 2021, https://www.nippon.com/ en/news/yjj2021042000731/

38. 吴正龙 [Wu Zhenglong], '解读当今世界百年未有之大变局' ['Interpretation of the Profound Changes Unseen in a Century'], Huanqiu net, September 25, 2018, accessed May 1, 2021, https://opinion.huanqiu.com/article/9CaKrnKcZDj.

39. 'How it happened: Transcript of the US–China opening remarks in Alaska', Nikkei Asia, March 19, 2021, accessed May 1, 2021, https://asia.nikkei.com/Politics/International-relations/US-China-tensions/How-it-happened-Transcript-of-the-US-China- opening-remarks-in-Alaska.

40. Zhou Xin, ' Is China rich or poor? Nation's wealth debate muddied by conflicting government data', South China Morning Post, May 29, 2020, accessed May 1, 2021, https://www.scmp.com/economy/china-economy/article/3086678/china-rich-or-poor- nations-wealth-debate-muddied-conflicting.

41. David F. Gordon, 'A trade opportunity Washington shouldn't pass up', Washington Post, November 10, 2011, accessed May 1, 2021, http://www.washingtonpost.com/opinions/a-trade-opportunity-washington-shouldnt-pass-up/2011/11/10/ gIQA1K3t9M_story.html?sub=AR.

42. Basilio Sepe and Froilan Gallardo, 'Philippines Delays Decision on Defense Pact with US by Another 6 Months', Benar News, November 11, 2020, accessed May 1, 2021, https://www.benarnews.org/english/news/philippine/ph-us-military-pact -11112020132859.html.

43. Steven Stashwich, 'Chinese Militia Vessels Departing Contested South China Sea Reef', The Diplomat, April 15, 2021, accessed May 1, 2021, https://thediplomat.com/2021/04/chinese-militia-vessels-departing-contested-south-china-sea-reef/.

44. Jeff M. Smith, 'Strategic Autonomy and US-India Relations', War on the Rocks, November 6, 2020, accessed May 1, 2021, https:// warontherocks.com/2020/11/strategic-autonomy-and-u-s-indian-relations/.

45. Yan Xuetong, 'Alliances can present greater conflicts between China, US', Global Times, March 31, 2016, accessed May 11, 2021, https://www.globaltimes.cn/page/201603/976746.shtml

46. Alex Lo, 'Beijing must prepare for a drastic reversal ahead of China's rise and America's fall', South China Morning Post, April 30, 2021, accessed May 11, 2021, https://www.scmp.com/comment/opinion/article/3131690/beijing-must-prepare-drastic-reversal -ahead-chinas-rise-and

47. Paul Heer, 'Understanding U.S.-China Strategic Competition', National Interest, October 20, 2020, accessed May 1, 2021, https:// nationalinterest.org/feature/understanding-US–China-strategic-competition-171014.

48. Fu Ying, 'Cooperative Competition Is Possible Between China and the U.S.', New York Times, November 24, 2020, accessed May 22, 2021, https://www.nytimes.com/2020/11/24/opinion/china-us-biden.html

49. Robert B. Zoellick, 'Trump is losing his new "Cold War" with China', Washington Post, October 7, 2020, accessed May 1, 2021, https://www.washingtonpost.com/opinions/2020/10/07/trump-is-losing-his-new-cold-war-with-china/.

50. Jordan Schneider, 'China Talk: China's True Tech Ambitions', Lawfare, October 16, 2020, accessed May 1, 2021, https://www. lawfareblog.com/chinatalk-chinas-true-tech-ambitions.

51. '习近平在中国科学院第十九次院士大会、中国工程院第十四次院士大会上的讲话' ['Xi speech at the China Academy of Sciences'], Xinhua, May 28, 2018, accessed May 1, 2021, http://www.xinhuanet.com/politics/2018-05/28/c_1122901308.htm.

52. 李晓华 [Li Xiaohua], '推进产业链现代化要坚持独立自主和开发合作相促进' ['The modernization of the industrial chain must adhere to the promotion of independence and development cooperation'], Guangmin Daily, April 10, 2020, p. 11

53. '我国是全世界唯一拥有全部工业门类的国家' ['China is the only country in the world with all industrial categories'], Xinhua, September 20, 2019, accessed May 1, 2021, http://www.xinhuanet.com/politics/2019-09/20/c_1125020250.htm.

54. Staff writers, 'Chinese tech companies topple Japan, chase US in market share', Nikkei, August 12, 2020, accessed May 1, 2021, https://asia.nikkei.com/Business/China-tech/Chinese-tech-companies-topple-Japan-chase-US-in-market-share.

55. Eric Schmidt and Graham Allison, 'Is China Winning the AI Race?' Project Syndicate, August 4, 2020, accessed May 1, 2021, https://www.project-syndicate.org/commentary/china-versus-america-ai-race-pandemic-by-eric-schmidt-and-graham- allison-2020-08.

56. Amrita Jash, 'Will Covid-19 Cost China its "World's Factory" Title?', Pacific Forum PacNet #55, October 6, 2020, accessed May 1, 2021, https://mailchi.mp/pacforum/pacnet-55-will-covid19-cost-china-its-worlds-factory-title-1170474?e=19e05c85a8.

57. Arthur Kroeber, 'Don't Bet against China's Investment-led Growth model', Financial Times, May 20, 2021, https://www.ft.com/ content/1e71be2e-0e6e-4af8-a703-1c92066065c7

58. Lei Guang, Margaret Roberts, Yiqing Xu and Jiannan Zhao, 'Pandemic Sees Increase In Chinese Support For Regime, Decrease In Views Towards The US', UC San Diego China Data Lab, July, 2020, accessed May 1, 2021, http://china-datalab.ucsd.edu/viz-blog /pandemic-sees-increase-in-chinese-support-for-regime-decrease-in-views-towards-us/.

59. 习近平 [Xi Jinping], "在纪念中国人民抗日战争暨世界反法西斯战争胜利75周年座谈会上的讲话['Speech at the Symposium to Commemorate the 75th Anniversary of the Victory of the Chinese People's Anti-Japanese War and the World Anti-Fascist War'] Xinhua, September 3, 2020, accessed May 1, 2021, http://cpc.people.com.cn/n1/2020/0904/c64094- 31848723.html.

60. Andrew Erickson, 'Make China Great Again: Xi's Truly Grand Strategy', War on Rock, October 30, 2019, accessed May 1, 2021, https://warontherocks.com/2019/10/make-china-great-again-xis-truly-grand-strategy/.

61. Chas W. Freeman, Jr, 'The Struggle with China is not a Replay of the Cold War', Remarks to the Asia American Forum, September 25, 2020, accessed June 8, 2021, https://chasfreeman.net/the-struggle-with-china-is-not-a-re-play-of-the-cold-war/

62. Sarah Repucci and Amy Slipowitz, 'Freedom in the World 2021: Democracy under Siege', Freedom House, accessed May 1, 2021, https://freedomhouse.org/report/freedom-world/2021/democracy-under-siege.

63. Eli Yokley, 'Biden's Early Tenure Has Improved America's Image Abroad', Morning Consult, April 27, 2021, accessed May 1, 2021, https://morningcon-sult.com/2021/04/27/biden-100-days-global-views-america/

64. Lee Hisen Loong, 'The Endangered Asian Century, America, China, and the Perils of Confrontation', Foreign Affairs, June 4, 2020, accessed May 1, 2021, https://www.foreignaffairs.com/articles/asia/2020-06-04/lee-hsien-loong-endangered-asian-century.

Chapter 9: Combating nuclear smuggling? Exploring drivers and challenges to detecting nuclear and radiological materials at maritime facilities. Robert Downes, Christopher Hobbs, and Daniel Salisbury

1   ITDB, IAEA, <www-ns.iaea.org/security/itdb.asp>.

2   "IAEA Incident and Trafficking Database: Incidents of Nuclear and Other Radioactive Material out of Regulatory Control—2017 Fact Sheet," IAEA, December 31, 2016, <www.iaea.org/sites/default/files/17/12/itdb-factsheet-2017.pdf>, p. 3.

3   See, for instance, J.A. Azuara, "Main issues in the Acerinox Event," in IAEA, Safety of Radiation Sources and Security of Radioactive Materials, Proceedings of an international Conference, Dijon, France, September 14–18, 1998, pp. 45–51; IAEA, The Radiological Accident in Lilo (Vienna, 2000).

4   "IAEA Incident and Trafficking Database," p. 2.

5   There is wide variation in terms of impact across the different weapon types and scenarios in which radiological and nuclear materials could be used. For a detailed discussion, see Charles D. Ferguson and William C. Potter, The Four Faces of Nuclear Terrorism (London: Routledge, 2005).

6   "Measures to Improve the Security of Nuclear Materials and Other Radioactive Materials," IAEA Board of Governors General Conference, GOV/2001/37-GC(45)/20, August 14, 2001; Miles A. Pomper, Ferenc Dalnoki-Veress, and George M. Moore, "Treatment, Not Terror: Strategies to Enhance External Beam Cancer Therapy in Developing Countries while Permanently Reducing the Risk of Radiological Terrorism," Stanley Foundation, February 2016, <www.stanleyfoundation.org/publications/report/TreatmentNotTerror212. pdf>; Emily S. Ewell, "NIS Nuclear Smuggling since 1995: A Lull in Significant Cases?" Nonproliferation Review, Vol. 5 (1998), pp. 120–23.

7   Tyson Gustafson, "Radiological and Nuclear Detection Devices," Nuclear Threat Initiative, April 19, 2017, <www.nti.org/analysis/articles/radiological-nuclear-detection-devices>.

8   Jeffrey W. Knopf, "Wrestling with Deterrence: Bush Administration Strategy after 9/11," Contemporary Security Policy, Vol. 29, No. 2 (2008), p. 241

9   See, for example, US Government Accountability Office (GAO), "Combatting Nuclear Smuggling: NNSA's Detection and Deterrence Program Is Addressing Challenges but Should Improve Its Program Plan," GAO-16-460, June 2016, pp. 9–10, 21–22; Oak Ridge National Laboratory, "Nuclear Smuggling Detection and Deterrence FY2016: Data Analysis Annual Report," January 2017, pp. 13–14.

10 These interviews are drawn upon in this article in a non-attributable manner.

11 Richard T. Kouzes, "Detecting Illicit Nuclear Materials: The Installation of Radiological Monitoring Equipment in the United States and Overseas Is Helping Thwart Nuclear Terrorism," American Scientist, Vol. 93, No. 5 (2005), p. 425.

12 Kay Bird, "The First Line against Terrorism," Washington Post, December 12, 2001, <www.washingtonpost.com/archive/opinions/2001/12/12/the-first-line-against-terrorism/4a53ee41-f528-4a4f-9f9b-64d38353a03c/?utm_term=.ae16fd1a0f95>.

13 Jerome I. Friedman and William A. Little, "Robert Hofstadter," Biographical Memoirs, Vol. 79 <www.nap.edu/read/10169/chapter/11#175>, p.175.

14 Wolfgang K.H. Panofsky, "Radiation Detectors," New Yorker, April 9, 2007, <www.newyorker.com/magazine/2007/04/09/mail>.

15 Ibid.

16 Jeffrey T. Richelson, Defusing Armageddon: Inside Nest, America's Secret Nuclear Bomb Squad (New York: W.W. Norton, 2009), p. 1.

17 Central Intelligence Agency, "The Clandestine Introduction of Nuclear Weapons into the US," TS 190512, July 1970, <www.cia.gov/library/readingroom/docs/DOC_0001211144.pdf> p. 4.

18 Ibid., pp. 4–5.

19 Richelson, Defusing Armageddon, pp. 236–40.

20 Cameron Reed, "The Nuclear Emergency Support Team (NEST)," Physics and Society, Vol. 42, No. 1 (2013), <www.aps.org/units/fps/newsletters/201301/reed.cfm>.

21 Walter Laqueur, "Postmodern Terrorism: New Rules for an Old Game," Foreign Affairs, September/October 1996, <www.foreignaffairs.com/articles/1996-09-01/postmodern-terrorism-new-rules-old-game>.

22 John H. Nuckolls, "Post-Cold War Nuclear Dangers: Proliferation and Terrorism,"Science, Vol. 267, No. 5201 (1995), pp. 1112–14.

23 William C. Potter, "Before the Deluge? Assessing the Threat of Nuclear Leakage from the Post-Soviet States," Arms Control Today, Vol. 25, No. 8 (1995), pp. 9–16.

24 Lyudmila Zaitseva and Friedrich Steinhäusler, "Nuclear Trafficking Issues in the Black Sea Region," Non-proliferation Papers No. 39, Stockholm International Peace Research Institute, April 2014, <www.sipri.org/publications/2014/eu-non-proliferation-papers/nuclear-trafficking-issues-black-sea-region>, p. 3.

25 G. Smagala, "Measures to Detect and Control Radioactive Contaminated Metallurgical Scrap at Border Checkpoints in Poland," in Workshop on Radioactive Contaminated Metallurgical Scrap (New York and Geneva: United Nations Economic Commission for Europe), pp. 123–30; M. Fabretto, "Monitoring of Scrap Loads at Gorzia Border Checkpoints: A Thirty Months Experience and Some Suggestions," Ibid., pp. 31–42.

26 GAO, "Report to the Ranking Minority Member, Subcommittee on Emerging Threats and Capabilities," GAO-02-426, <www.gao.gov/assets/240/234392.pdf#page=36>, p. 36

27 IAEA General Conference, GC(38)/RES/15, "Measures against Illicit Trafficking in Nuclear Material," September 1994, <www-legacy.iaea.org/About/Policy/GC/GC38/GC38Resolutions/English/gc38res-15_en.pdf>.

28 38th IAEA General Conference, "Secondary Plenary Meeting," September 1994, <www.iaea.org/About/Policy/GC/GC38/GC38Records/English/gc38or-2_en.pdf>, p. 6.

29 P. Beck, K. Duftschmid, and C. Schmitzer, "ITRAP: The Illicit Trafficking Radiation Assessment Program," in Safety of Radiation Sources and Security of Radioactive Materials, pp. 265–69.

30 Ibid.

31 Three technical guidance documents were produced: IAEA, "Prevention of the Inadvertent Movement and Illicit Trafficking of Radioactive Materials," IAEA-TECDOC-1311, September 2002, <www-pub.iaea.org/MTCD/Publications/PDF/te_1311_web.pdf>; IAEA, "Detection of Radioactive Materials At Borders," IAEA-TECDOC-1312, September 2002, <www-pub.iaea.org/MTCD/Publications/PDF/te_1312_web.pdf>; IAEA, "Response to Events Involving the Inadvertent Movement or Illicit Trafficking of Radioactive Materials," IAEA-TECDOC-1313, September 2002, <www-pub.iaea.org/MTCD/Publications/PDF/te_1313_web.pdf>.

32 As just one example, funding provided to the US Export Control and Related Border Security Assistance program expanded from $3 million in fiscal year 1998 to $40.1 million in fiscal year 2001. GAO, "U.S. Efforts to Help Other Countries Combat Nuclear Smuggling Need Strengthened Coordination and Planning," GAO-02-426, <www.gao.gov/assets/240/234392.pdf>, p. 10

33 US agencies involved in counter-illicit smuggling efforts included the Department of Energy (DoE), Department of State (DoS), Department of Defence (DoD), the US Customs Service, the Federal Bureau of Investigation, and the US Coast Guard. Radiation-detection equipment was provided through the Office of the Second Line of Defence (SLD) program in the DoE, the Nonproliferation and Disarmament Fund (DoS), the Export Control and Related Border Security Assistance program in the DoS, the Georgia Border Security and Law Enforcement program in the DoS, and the Cooperative Threat Reduction Programme and International Counterproliferation program in the DoD. GAO, "Report to the Ranking Minority Member, Subcommittee on Emerging Threats and Capabilities," GAO-02-426, <www.gao.gov/assets/240/234392.pdf#page=5>, p. 6–8.

34 Ibid., p. 11.

35 Ibid.

36 Brian M. Jenkins, "The New Age of Terrorism," in Brian M. Jenkins, ed., McGraw-Hill Homeland Security Handbook (Santa Monica, CA: RAND, 2006).

37 UN Security Council Resolution (UNSCR) 1540, for example, placed a legal obligation on all UN member states to put in place "appropriate effective border controls" to prevent the trafficking of weapons-of-mass-destruction-(WMD)-related goods. United Nations, Security Council Resolution 1540, April 28,

2004,   <www.un.org/ga/search/view_doc.asp?symbol=S/RES/1540%20 (2004)>.

38 GAO, "Report to the Ranking Minority Member, Subcommittee on Emerging Threats and Capabilities," GAO-02-426, May 2002, <www.gao.gov/assets/240/234392.pdf#page=5>, p. 2; GAO, "Combating Nuclear Smuggling: Efforts to Deploy Radiation Detection Equipment in the United States and in Other Countries," GAO-05-840T, June 21, 2005, <www.gao.gov/assets/120/111799.pdf>, p. 2.

39 The Telegraph, "Ports Equipped to Deter Nuclear Attack," May 14, 2003, <www.telegraph.co.uk/news/1430029/Ports-equipped-to-deter-nuclear-attack.html>.

40 UK Parliament, "Memorandum Submitted by the Home Office," Select Committee on Defence, <https://publications.parliament.uk/pa/cm200304/cmselect/cmdfence/417/417we02.htm>; David Blunkett, speech to the House of Commons, June 10, 2004, Parliamentary Debates, Commons, Vol. 422 (2004), Cols. 525–26.

41 Richard T. Kouzes, "Detecting Illicit Nuclear Materials: The Installation of Radiological Monitoring Equipment in the United States and Overseas Is Helping Thwart Nuclear Terrorism," American Scientist, Vol. 93, No. 5 (2005), p. 442.

42 GAO, "Combating Nuclear Smuggling: Megaports Initiative Faces Funding and Sustainability Challenges," GAO-13-37, October 2012, <www.gao.gov/assets/650/649759.pdf>.

43 Ibid. p. 9; GAO, "Combating Nuclear Smuggling: NNSA's Detection and Deterrence Program Is Addressing Challenges but Should Improve Its Program Plan," GAO-16-460, June 2016, <www.gao.gov/assets/680/677895.pdf>, p. 8.

44 "Joint Statement on Maritime Supply Chain Security," Nuclear Security Summit, April 5, 2016, <www.nss2016.org/document-center-docs/2016/4/1/joint-statement-on-maritime-supply-chain-security>.

45 "Nuclear Security Summit Enhancing the Security of the Maritime Supply Chain Gift Basket: Best Practice Guide for Removing Nuclear and Radiological Materials that Are out of Regulatory Control from the Global Maritime Supply Chain," Nuclear Security Summit, March 2016, <https://static1.squarespace.com/static/568be36505f8e2af8023adf7/t/57051237859fd04c9f dd0699/1459950136051/Joint±Statement±on±Maritime±Supply±Chain±Sec urity±Best±Practices.pdf>.

46 The Act noted that "A container that was loaded on a vessel in a foreign port shall not enter the United States (either directly or via a foreign port) unless the container was scanned by nonintrusive imaging equipment and radiation detection equipment at a foreign port before it was loaded on a vessel."

See "Implementing Recommendations of the 9/11 Commission Act of 2007," Public Law 110–53, 110th Congress, August 3, 2007.

47   A two-year extension was passed in 2012, 2014, 2016, and seemingly 2018. See section 1701 (b) (4) of the Act.

48   Dimitrios Anagnostakis, "Securing the Transatlantic Maritime Supply Chains from Counterterrorism: EU–U.S. Cooperation and the Emergence of a Transatlantic Customs Security Regime," Studies in Conflict & Terrorism, Vol. 39, No. 5 (2016), p. 463.

49   "Shipping and World Trade—Overview," International Chamber of Shipping, <www.ics-shipping.org/shipping-facts/shipping-and-world-trade>.

50   "How Many Shipping Containers Are There in the World?" Budget Shipping Containers, <www.budgetshippingcontainers.co.uk/info/how-many-shipping-containers-are-there-in-the-world/>.

51   "Top 50 World Container Ports," World Shipping Council, <www.worldshipping.org/about-the-industry/global-trade/top-50-world-container-ports>.

52   John Frittelli and Jennifer E. Lake, "Terminal Operators and Their Role in U.S. Port and Maritime Security," CRS Report for Congress, January 19, 2007, p. 2.

53   In this context, materials of particular concern (threat materials) include fissile materials such as plutonium and HEU and strong radioactive sources (IAEA Category 1, 2, and 3). For a discussion on the destructive and disruptive potential of different nuclear and radiological materials please see Charles D. Ferguson and William C. Potter, The Four Faces of Nuclear Terrorism (New York: Routledge, 2005).

54   Hugh Griffiths and Michael Jenks, "Maritime Transport and Destabilizing Commodity Flows," SIPRI Policy Paper 32, 2012, <www.sipri.org/sites/default/files/files/PP/SIPRIPP32.pdf>, p. 1.

55   This delicate balance occasionally manifests in the public domain; see Daniel Boffey, "'Dirty Bombs' May Have Been Missed by Private Border Staff as Games Approach," The Guardian, July 7, 2012 <www.theguardian.com/uk/2012/jul/07/border-agency-terrorism-games-dirty-bombs>.

56   "Revised KYOTO Convention," World Customs Organization, 2006, <www.wcoomd.org/en/topics/facilitation/instrument-and-tools/conventions/pf_revised_kyoto_conv.aspx>.

57   GAO, "Supply Chain Security: CBP Needs to Conduct Regular Assessments of Its Cargo Targeting System," October 2012, <www.gao.gov/assets/650/649695.pdf>.

58   Ibid.

59   Gary M. Gaukler, Chenhua Li, Yu Ding, and Sunil S. Chirayath, "Detecting Nuclear Materials Smuggling: Performance Evaluation of Container Inspection Policies," Risk Analysis, November 1, 2011, pp. 505–16.

60 Jonathan Medalia, "Detection of Nuclear Weapons and Materials: Science, Technologies, Observations," Congressional Research Service, June 4, 2010, <https://fas.org/sgp/crs/nuke/R40154.pdf>.

61 Ibid., p. 105.

62 World Nuclear Association, "Naturally-Occurring Radioactive Materials (NORM)," December 2016, <www.world-nuclear.org/information-library/safety-and-security/radiation-and-health/naturally-occurring-radioactive-materials-norm.aspx>.

63 For examples of differences in background radiation levels, see "Nuclear Smuggling Detection and Deterrence FY2016: Data Analysis Annual Report," Oak Ridge National Laboratory, January 2017, pp.13–14; Tom Burr, James R. Gattiker, Kary Myers, and George Tompkins, "Alarm Criteria in Radiation Portal Monitoring," Applied Radiation and Isotopes, No. 65 (2007), p. 580.

64 La Fonda Sutton-Burke, "Detection Instruments: Operation and Maintenance Challenges," Technical Meeting on Radiation Detection Instruments for Nuclear Security," IAEA, Division of Nuclear Security, Vienna, April 4, 2016.

65 Gary M. Gaukler, Chenhua Li, Yu Ding, and Sunil S. Chirayath, "Detecting Nuclear Materials Smuggling: Performance Evaluation of Container Inspection Policies," Risk Analysis, November 1, 2011, p. 534.

66 Radiation-detection expert at international organization, personal interview with one of the authors, July 12, 2018.

67 IAEA, "Nuclear Security Systems and Measures for the Detection of Nuclear and Other Radioactive Material out of Regulatory Control," IAEA Nuclear Security Series No. 21, 2013, p. 37

68 Radiation readings are taken at fractions of a second as the container passes through the RPM. These can be used to construct a radiation profile of counts versus container occupancy time.

69 "International Maritime Dangerous Goods (IMDG) Code, 2016 Edition," International Maritime Organization, <www.imo.org/en/Publications/Documents/IMDG%20Code/IMDG%20Code%202016%20Edition/QK200E_122017.pdf>.

70 Radiation-detection expert at international organization, personal interview with one of the authors, July 12, 2018.

71 "Evaluating Testing, Costs, and Benefits of Advanced Spectroscopic Portals for Screening Cargo at Ports of Entry Interim Report (Abbreviated Version)," National Academy of Sciences, 2009, p. 3.

72 Nitin Bakshi, Stephen E. Flynn, and Noah Gans, "Estimating the Operational Impact of Container Inspections at International Ports," Management Science, Vol. 57, No. 1 (2011), p. 10.

73 GAO, "Combating Nuclear Smuggling: Lessons Learned from Cancelled Radiation Portal Monitor Program Could Help Future Acquisitions," GAO-13-256, May 2013, pp. 10–11.

74 Stephen E. Flynn, "America the Vulnerable," Foreign Affairs, Vol. 81, No. 1 (2002), <www.foreignaffairs.com/articles/2002-01-01/america-vulnerable>.

75 For more details on the survey that underpins this study, please refer to the Appendix at the end of this article.

76 IAEA, "Nuclear Security Systems and Measures for the Detection of Nuclear and Other Radioactive Material out of Regulatory Control."

77 Fifteen of twenty-four respondents had national guidance in place.

78 Quoted from a single survey respondent.

79 Four of twenty-four did not have national-level guidance, and five were unsure about it.

80 Of thirteen respondents to this question, six reported that over 80 percent was scanned; four reported less than 20 percent; two reported 40–59 percent; one reported 60–79 percent.

81 Note that seaports are selected for participation in the Megaports Initiative based on a number of factors including shipping volume but also threat factors, container export destimations, and proximity to facilities with special nuclear materials. See GAO, "Combating Nuclear Smuggling: Megaports Initiative Faces Funding and Sustainability Challenges," GAO-13-37, October 2012, p. 2.

82 Phil Williams, "Transnational Criminal Networks," in John Arquilla and David Ronfeldt, eds., Networks and Netwars (Santa Monica, CA: RAND, 2001), p. 71.

83 Twenty-four respondents claimed that their system scanned imports, and twenty-one suggested that exports were scanned.

84 Fourteen respondents claimed that their system scanned transshipments.

85 Paola Papa, "US and EU Strategies for Maritime Transport Security: A Comparative Perspective," Transport Policy, No. 28 (2013), p. 79.

86 Former public health official, personal interview with one of the authors, July 19, 2017.

87 M.-A. Descalle, D. Manatt, and D. Slaughter, "Analysis of Recent Manifests for Goods Imported through US Ports," Lawrence Livermore National Laboratory Report, UCRL-TR-225708, October 2006, <https://e-reports-ext.llnl.gov/pdf/339093.pdf>.

88 "Nuclear Smuggling Detection and Deterrence FY2016: Data Analysis Annual Report," Oak Ridge National Laboratory, January 2017, p.12.

89 Eleven respondents had found orphaned or disused sources; seventeen, contaminated goods; six, radiological sources mislabeled on the manifest; six, nuclear material; and six, special nuclear materials. One respondent also found "medical isotopes in waste."

90 One known example involving the detection of HEU by border-monitoring equipment occurred in Georgia in 2000. Please see GAO, "Nuclear Nonproliferation: US Efforts to Help Other Countries Combat Nuclear Smuggling Need Strengthened Coordination and Planning," GAO-02-426, May 2002, <www.gao.gov/assets/240/234392.pdf#page=36>, p. 33.

91 Gary M. Gaukler, Chenhua Li, Yu Ding, and Sunil S. Chirayath, "Detecting Nuclear Materials Smuggling: Performance Evaluation of Container Inspection Policies," Risk Analysis, November 1, 2011, p. 549

92 Given sensitivities around the interception of HEU and plutonium, it was not possible to obtain more information on how and in what quantities special nuclear material was detected.

93 Nine of twenty-one respondents placed innocent alarms at over 10 percent of cargo; three of twenty-one respondents placed innocent alarms at less than 1 percent of cargo.

94 Given sensitivities, respondents were not asked to identify alarming thresholds for RPMs.

95 Four of twenty-one respondents suggested that secondary inspections were undertaken in less than 1 percent of cases; five of twenty-one suggested 1–10 percent of cases; two of twenty-one suggested that they were undertaken in 11–50 percent of cases; three of twenty-one suggested they were undertaken in more than 90 percent of cases and seven of twenty-one responded to the question by selecting "unknown."

96 Twenty of twenty-three respondents suggested they had RPMs; eighteen of twenty-three had handheld detectors; and seven of twenty-three had vehicle-based systems. Five of twenty-three respondents suggested they had access to all three types. Seth Van Liew, William Bertozzi, Nathan D'Olympia, Wilbur A. Franklin, Stephen E. Korbly, Robert J. Ledoux, and Cody M. Wilson, "Identification and Imaging of Special Nuclear Materials and Contraband Using Active X-ray Interrogation," Physics Procedia, Vol. 90 (2017), p. 314.

97 More importance was placed by respondents on informing national rather than international bodies.

98 Representative of global shipping company, personal interview with two of the authors, September 15, 2015.

99 Ibid.

100 Designated as International Maritime Dangerous Goods Code Class 7.

101 See, for instance, IAEA, "Strengthening Control over Radioactive Sources in Authorized Use and Regaining Control over Orphan Sources," IAEA-TEC-DOC-1388, <www-pub.iaea.org/MTCD/Publications/PDF/te_1388_web.pdf>, p. 10

102 Eighteen of thirty-six respondents indicated that international partnership had been involved in initiating their radiation detection programs.

103 Sixteen of twenty-four respondents suggested that their system was to detect all MORC; five suggested that theirs focused on health and safety risks alone.

104 B. Wilson and K. Van Haperen, Soft Systems Thinking, Methodology and the Management of Change (London, UK: Macmillan, 2015), p. 107.

105 Renate Sefzig, Bejoy Saha, and Gisela Stoppa, "Co-60 contaminated stainless steels in Germany experiences and first steps," presentation delivered at the International Conference on Control and Management of Inadvertent Radioactive Material in Scrap Metal, Tarragona, Spain, February 23–27, 2009, pp. 87, 265–67, 323.

106 Wenkai Li, Colin Jones, and Mark Goh, Planning and Scheduling for Maritime Container Yards (Heidelberg, Germany: Springer, 2015), pp. 15–16.

107 Cimen Karatas-Cetin, "Port and Logistic Chains: Changes in Organizational Effectiveness," in Dong-Wook Song, Photis Panayides, eds., Maritime Logistics, 2nd edn, (London, UK: Kogan Page, 2015), pp. 343–72.

108 Twelve of twenty-five respondents noted that target alarm rate was the most important factor in determining alarm thresholds.

109 Only eight of twenty-five indicated that it was based on the material that the system was seeking to detect.

110 Radiation-detection expert at international organization, personal interview with one of the authors, July 12, 2018.

111 Comments by several survey respondents.

112 Seventeen of twenty-one respondents felt their organization was able to manage the number of innocent alarms produced by NORM.

113 Four of twenty-three respondents noted that detaining containers in order to carry out secondary and tertiary inspections was the greatest challenge they faced.

114 Eight respondents of twenty-three selected sustainability costs as the greatest challenge; fourteen respondents selected cost-related issues as the greatest challenge (sustainability costs, inspection costs, staffing shortages, and equipment malfunction).

115 Radiation-detection expert at international organization, personal interview with one of the authors, July 12, 2018.

116 Seven observe training once a year, five observe training two to three times a year, two had never been trained, three were trained less than once a year, and two reported training for only new officers.

117 GAO, "Combating Nuclear Smuggling: Megaports Initiative Faces Funding and Sustainability Challenges," GAO-13-37, October 2012, pp. 28–35.

118 For example, 85 percent of Megaports program funding was cut in 2012. "Obama Slashes Funding for Megaports Program," Nuclear Threat Initiative, December 11, 2012; Russia, accounting for 45 percent of the US Second Line of Defense program's sites, halted much cooperation in the area of nuclear security in 2014. See GAO, "Combatting Nuclear Smuggling: NNSA's Detection and Deterrence Program Is Addressing Challenges but Should Improve Its Program Plan," p. 3.

119 Sixteen out of twenty-one respondents supported the development of new technical international scanning guidelines or requirements.

120 IAEA, "Technical and Functional Specifications for Border Monitoring Equipment," Nuclear Security Series No. 1, 2006; IAEA, "Nuclear Security Recommendations on Nuclear and Other Radioactive Material out of Regulatory Control," Nuclear Security Series No. 2, 2011; IAEA, "Combating Illicit Trafficking in Nuclear and Other Radioactive Material," Nuclear Security Series No. 6, 2007; IAEA, "Nuclear Security Systems and Measures for the Detection of Nuclear and Other Radioactive Material out of Regulatory Control," Nuclear Security Series No. 21, 2013.

121 <www-pub.iaea.org/books/IAEABooks/7400/Technical-and-Functional-Specifications-for-Border-Monitoring-Equipment##description>.

122 Suggested by eleven of twenty-one respondents.

123 Wyn Q. Bowen and Christopher Hobbs, "Sensitive Nuclear Information: Challenges and Options for Control," Strategic Analysis, Vol. 38, No. 2 (2014), pp. 225–26.

124 IAEA, "Improved Assessment of Initial Alarms from Radiation Detection Instruments," CRP-J02005, and "Advancing Radiation Detection Equipment for Detecting Nuclear and Other Radioactive out of Material out of Regulatory Control," CRP-J02012, <http://cra.iaea.org/cra/explore-crps/all-active-by-programme.html>.

125 Ibid.

126 Note there currently exists a technical document for "Monitoring for Radioactive Material in International Mail Transported by Public Postal Operators" (NSS No. 3).

127 "Nuclear Smuggling Detection and Deterrence FY2016: Data Analysis Annual Report," Oak Ridge National Laboratory, January 2017, p. 12.

128 IAEA, "IAEA Launches Mobile Application Tool for Radiation Alarm and Commodity Evaluation," June 9, 2017, <www.iaea.org/newscenter/news/iaea-launches-mobile-application-tool-for-radiation-alarm-and-commodity-evaluation>.

129 "IAEA's Mobile App Helps Sri Lanka to Fight Smuggling of Radioactive Materials," Nuclear Asia, June 13, 2018, <www.nuclearasia.com/gallery/iaeas-mobile-app-helps-sri-lanka-fight-smuggling-radioactive-materials/2331/>.

130 "Nuclear Smuggling Detection and Deterrence FY2016: Data Analysis Annual Report," Oak Ridge National Laboratory, January 2017, pp. 8, 26.

131 There is a host of data-science techniques such as dynamic time warping, random forest, and neural networks that could potentially be applied to RPM data in support of the alarm assessment process.

132 GAO, "Combatting Nuclear Smuggling: NNSA's Detection and Deterrence Program is Addressing Challenges but Should Improve Its Program Plan," GAO-16-460, June 2016, p. 17

Chapter 10: Not by NPT alone: The future of the global nuclear order. Jeffrey W. Knopf

1. Adler, E. (1992). The emergence of cooperation: National epistemic communities and the international evolution of the idea of nuclear arms control. International Organization, 46(1), 101–145. https://doi.org/10.1017/S0020818300001466 [Crossref], [Web of Science ®], [Google Scholar]

2. Ahmed, M. (2016, June 30). Pakistan's tactical nuclear weapons and their impact on stability. Carnegie Endowment for International Peace. http://carnegieendowment.org/2016/06/30/pakistan-s-tactical-nuclear-weapons-and-their-impact-on-stability-pub-63911 [Crossref], [Google Scholar]

3. Arms Control Association. (2017a, updated July). Nuclear Weapon Free Zones (NWFZ) at a glance. Fact Sheet. https://www.armscontrol.org/factsheets/nwfz [Google Scholar]

4. Arms Control Association. (2017b, updated August). Nuclear Suppliers Group (NSG) at a glance. Fact Sheet. https://www.armscontrol.org/factsheets/NSG [Google Scholar]

5. Baker, P., & Tackett, M. (2018, January 2). Trump says his 'nuclear button' is 'much bigger' than North Korea's. New York Times. https://www.nytimes.com/2018/01/02/us/politics/trump-tweet-north-korea.html [Google Scholar]

6. Baklitskiy, A., Bidgood, S., & Meier, O. (2020). Russian-U.S. strategic stability talks: Where they are and where they should go. Deep Cuts Issue Brief #13. https://deepcuts.org/files/pdf/Deep_Cuts_Issue_Brief_13-Russian_US_Strategic_Stability_Talks.pdf [Google Scholar]

7. BBC News. (2018, March 1). Russia's Putin unveils 'invincible' nuclear weapons. http://www.bbc.com/news/world-europe-43239331 [Google Scholar]

8. Berger, A. (2015, May 27). Gangs of New York: The 2015 NPT RevCon. European Leadership Network. https://www.europeanleadershipnetwork.org/commentary/gangs-of-new-york-the-2015-npt-revcon/ [Google Scholar]

9. Bino, T. (2020). A Middle Eastern WMD-free zone: Are we any closer now? Arms Control Today, 50(7), 11–16. [Google Scholar]

10. Blair, B., & Wolfsthal, J. (2019, August 1). We still can't 'win' a nuclear war. Pretending we could is a dangerous fantasy. Washington Post. https://www.washingtonpost.com/outlook/2019/08/01/we-still-cant-win-nuclear-war-pretending-we-could-is-dangerous-fantasy/ [Google Scholar]

11. Bleek, P. C. (2002). Nuclear Posture Review leaks; outlines targets, contingencies. Arms Control Today, 32(3), 20–21. [Google Scholar]

12. Broad, W. J. (2021, January 15). Hypersonic weapons are a mirage, new analysis says. New York Times. https://www.nytimes.com/2021/01/15/science/hypersonic-missile-weapons.html [Google Scholar]

13. Broad, W. J., & Sanger, D. E. (2021, July 26). A 2nd new nuclear missile base for China, and many questions about strategy. New York Times. https://www.nytimes.com/2021/07/26/us/politics/china-nuclear-weapons.html [Google Scholar]

14. Broom, F. (2019, April 10). Making a murderer: the assassination of Kim Jong-nam. Lowy Institute. https://www.lowyinstitute.org/the-interpreter/making-murderer-assassination-kim-jong-nam [Google Scholar]

15. Brown, H., & Deutch, J. (2007, November 19). The nuclear disarmament fantasy. Wall Street Journal, A19. [Google Scholar]

16. Bunn, M., Malin, M. B., Roth, N., & Tobey, W. H. (2016). Preventing nuclear terrorism: Continuous improvement or dangerous decline? Project on Managing the Atom, Belfer Center for International Affairs, Harvard Kennedy School. [Crossref], [Google Scholar]

17. Burns, R. (2020, February 3). US adds new 'low-yield' nuclear weapon to its submarine arsenal. AP News. https://apnews.com/article/john-rood-ap-top-news-wa-state-wire-nuclear-weapons-politics-b910d5f4f-2076d558416ae021b511517 [Google Scholar]

18. Bush, G., & Scowcroft, B. (1998). A world transformed. Alfred A. Knopf. [Google Scholar]

19. Colby, E. A., & Gerson, M. S. (2013). Strategic stability: Contending interpretations. U.S. Army War College Press. [Crossref], [Google Scholar]

20. Cranes For Our Future. (n.d.). A joint project of the Hiroshima Prefecture, Nagasaki Prefecture, Nuclear Threat Initiative, and Hiroshima Organization for Global Peace. https://www.cranesforourfuture.org/ [Google Scholar]

21. Defense Threat Reduction Agency (DTRA). (n.d.). The history of cooperative threat reduction. https://www.dtra.mil/Portals/61/Documents/History%20 of%20CTR.pdf?ver=2019-04-25-140558-733 [Google Scholar]

22. Dunn, L., & Potter, W. (2020). Time to renew the Reagan-Gorbachev principle. Arms Control Today, 50(2), 18–23. [Google Scholar]

23. Dvorkin, V. (2019, February 8). Preserving strategic stability amid U.S.-Russian confrontation. Carnegie Moscow Center. https://carnegieendowment. org/files/2-8_Dvorkin_Strategic_Stability.pdf [Google Scholar]

24. Egeland, K. (2021). The ideology of nuclear order. New Political Science, 43(2), 208–230. https://doi.org/10.1080/07393148.2021.1886772 [Taylor & Francis Online], [Web of Science ®], [Google Scholar]

25. Egeland, K. (2022). A theory of nuclear disarmament: Cases, analogies, and the role of the non-proliferation regime. Contemporary Security Policy, Advance online publication. https://doi.org/10.1080/13523260.2021.1978159 [Web of Science ®], [Google Scholar]

26. European Leadership Network. (2019, December 13). Policy recommendations: Options for P5 cooperation. https://www.europeanleadershipnetwork. org/policy-intervention/policy-recommendations-options-for-p5-cooperation/ [Google Scholar]

27. Freedman, L. (2003). The evolution of nuclear strategy (3rd ed.). Palgrave Macmillan. [Crossref], [Google Scholar]

28. Freedman, L. (2013). Disarmament and other nuclear norms. Washington Quarterly, 36(2), 93–108. https://doi.org/10.1080/0163660X.2013.791085 [Taylor & Francis Online], [Web of Science ®], [Google Scholar]

29. Futter, A., & Zala, B. (2021). Strategic non-nuclear weapons and the onset of a third nuclear age. European Journal of International Security, 6(3), 257–277. https://doi.org/10.1017/eis.2021.2 [Crossref], [Web of Science ®], [Google Scholar]

30. Gaddis, J. L. (1986). The long peace: Elements of stability in the postwar international system. International Security, 10(4), 99–142. https://doi. org/10.2307/2538951 [Crossref], [Web of Science ®], [Google Scholar]

31. Gault, M. (2015, February 19). This TV movie about nuclear war depressed Ronald Reagan. War Is Boring. https://medium.com/war-is-boring/this-tv-movie-about-nuclear-war-depressed-ronald-reagan-fb4c25a50044 [Google Scholar]

32. Gellman, B. (1998, June 21). U.S. and China nearly came to blows in '96. Washington Post. https://www.washingtonpost.com/archive/politics/1998/06/21/us-and-china-nearly-came-to-blows-in-96/926d105f-1fd8-404c-9995-90984f86a613/ [Google Scholar]

33. Gheorghe, E. (2019, July 12). Iran's nuclear program seems to be accelerating. Will Saudi Arabia take a similar path? Washington Post Monkey Cage blog. https://www.washingtonpost.com/politics/2019/07/12/irans-nuclear-weapons-program-seems-be-accelerating-will-saudi-arabia-take-similar-path/ [Google Scholar]

34. Gibbons, R. D. (2018). The humanitarian turn in nuclear disarmament and the treaty on the Prohibition of Nuclear weapons. Nonproliferation Review, 25(1-2), 11–36. https://doi.org/10.1080/10736700.2018.1486960 [Taylor & Francis Online], [Google Scholar]

35. Gibbons, R. D., & Herzog, S. (2022). Durable institution under fire? The NPT confronts emerging multipolarity. Contemporary Security Policy, Forthcoming. [Google Scholar]

36. Hanson, M. (2022). The NPT: The limits of a treaty based on a "power over" model. Contemporary Security Policy, Forthcoming. [Google Scholar]

37. Harrington de Santana, A. (2011). The strategy of non-proliferation: Maintaining the credibility of an incredible pledge to disarm. Millennium, 40(1), 3–19. https://doi.org/10.1177%2F0305829811413312 [Crossref], [Web of Science °], [Google Scholar]

38. Horsburgh, N. (2015). China and global nuclear order: From estrangement to active engagement. Oxford University Press. [Crossref], [Google Scholar]

39. Jervis, R. (1989). The meaning of the nuclear revolution: Statecraft and the prospect of armageddon. Cornell University Press. [Google Scholar]

40. Khan, H. (1965). On escalation: Metaphors and scenarios. Frederick A. Praeger. [Google Scholar]

41. Kheel, R. (2021, June 16). Overnight defense. The Hill. https://thehill.com/policy/defense/overnights/558850-overnight-defense-biden-putin-agree-to-launch-arms-control-talks-at [Google Scholar]

42. Kimball, D. G., & Thielmann, G. (2010). Obama's NPR: Transitional, not transformational. Arms Control Today, 40(4), 19–23. [Google Scholar]

43. Klimas, J. (2018, February 2). Trump plan calls for new nuclear weapons. Politico. https://www.politico.com/story/2018/02/02/trump-plan-nuclear-weapons-386087 [Google Scholar]

44. Knopf, J. W. (2012/13). Nuclear disarmament and nonproliferation: Examining the linkage argument. International Security, 37(3), 92–132. https://doi.org/10.1162/ISEC_a_00109 [Crossref], [Web of Science °], [Google Scholar]

45. Knopf, J. W. (2012). The concept of nuclear learning. Nonproliferation Review, 19(1), 79–93. https://doi.org/10.1080/10736700.2012.655088 [Taylor & Francis Online], [Google Scholar]

46. Knopf, J. W. (ed.). (2016). International cooperation on WMD nonproliferation. University of Georgia Press. [Google Scholar]

47. Kristensen, H. M., & Korda, M. (2020). Russian nuclear forces, 2020. Nuclear notebook. Bulletin of the Atomic Scientists, 76(2), 102–117. https://doi.org/ 10.1080/00963402.2020.1728985 [Taylor & Francis Online], [Web of Science ®], [Google Scholar]

48. Kroenig, M. (2016). US nuclear weapons and nonproliferation: Is there a link? Journal of Peace Research, 53(2), 166–179. https://doi. org/10.1177%2F0022343315626770 [Crossref], [Web of Science ®], [Google Scholar]

49. Kutchesfahani, S. Z. (2019). Global nuclear order. Routledge. [Google Scholar]

50. Kutchesfahani, S. Z., Davenport, K., & Connolly, E. (2018). The Nuclear Security Summits: An overview of state actions to curb nuclear terrorism, 2010–2016. Report, Arms Control Association and Fissile Materials Working Group. [Google Scholar]

51. Landler, M., & Cooper, H. (2018, February 1). White House wants Pentagon to offer more options on North Korea. New York Times. https://www.ny-times.com/2018/02/01/us/politics/white-house-pentagon-north-korea.html [Google Scholar]

52. Lavoy, P. R. (ed.). (2009). Asymmetric warfare in South Asia: The causes and consequences of the Kargil conflict. Cambridge University Press. [Crossref], [Google Scholar]

53. Lewis, J. (2018). The 2020 commission report on the North Korean nuclear attacks against the United States: A speculative novel. Mariner Books. [Google Scholar]

54. Mandelbaum, M. (1979). The nuclear question: The United States and nuclear weapons, 1946–1976. Cambridge University Press. [Google Scholar]

55. Meyer, P. (2011). The NPT Review Conference: an assessment of outcome and outlook. Simons papers in Security and development, No. 11/2011, School for International studies, Simon Fraser University. [Google Scholar]

56. Narang, V. (2009/10). Posturing for peace? Pakistan's nuclear postures and South asian stability. International Security, 34(3), 38–78. https://doi. org/10.1162/isec.2010.34.3.38 [Crossref], [Web of Science ®], [Google Scholar]

57. Nebehay, S., & Landay, J. (2021, July 28). U.S., Russia hold nuclear talks in Geneva after summit push. Reuters. https://www.reuters.com/world/us-russia-hold-nuclear-talks-geneva-after-summit-push-2021-07-28/ [Google Scholar]

58. Noda, O. (2022). A wolf in sheep's clothing? The NPT and symbolic proliferation. Contemporary Security Policy, Forthcoming. [Google Scholar]

59. N Square. (n.d.). https://nsquare.org/ [Google Scholar]

60. NTI. (n.d.). The hair trigger game. https://hairtriggergame.org/ [Google Scholar]

61. Nuclear Threat Initiative (NTI). (2018, updated May 1). Global Partnership Against the Spread of Weapons and Materials of Mass Destruction ("10 plus 10 over 10 program"). https://www.nti.org/learn/treaties-and-regimes/global-partnership-against-spread-weapons-and-materials-mass-destruction-10-plus-10-over-10-program/ [Google Scholar]

62. Onderco, M., & Zutt, M. (2021). Emerging technology and nuclear security: What does the wisdom of the crowd tell us? Contemporary Security Policy, 42(3), 286–311. https://doi.org/10.1080/13523260.2021.1928963 [Taylor & Francis Online], [Web of Science °], [Google Scholar]

63. Panda, A., & Narang, V. (2021, February 22). Sole purpose is not no first use: Nuclear weapons and declaratory policy. War on the Rocks. https://waron-therocks.com/2021/02/sole-purpose-is-not-no-first-use-nuclear-weapons-and-declaratory-policy/ [Google Scholar]

64. Pant, H. V., & Joshi, Y. (2020, October 23). Is India overturning decades of nuclear doctrine? Foreign Policy. https://foreignpolicy.com/2020/10/23/in-dia-nuclear-no-first-use-strike-china-pakistan/ [Google Scholar]

65. Paul, T. V. (2009). The tradition of non-use of nuclear weapons. Stanford University Press. [Crossref], [Google Scholar]

66. Potter, W. C. (2017). Disarmament diplomacy and the nuclear ban treaty. Survival, 59(4), 75–108. https://doi.org/10.1080/00396338.2017.1349786 [Taylor & Francis Online], [Web of Science °], [Google Scholar]

67. Press, D. G., Sagan, S. D., & Valentino, B. A. (2013). Atomic aversion: Experimental evidence on taboos, traditions, and the non-use of nuclear weapons. American Political Science Review, 107(1), 188–206. https://doi.org/10.1017/S0003055412000597 [Crossref], [Web of Science °], [Google Scholar]

68. Pretorius, J., & Sauer, T. (2022). When is it legitimate to abandon the NPT? Withdrawal as a political tool to move nuclear disarmament forward. Contemporary Security Policy, Forthcoming. [Google Scholar]

69. Ritchie, N. (2019). A hegemonic nuclear order: Understanding the Ban treaty and the power politics of nuclear weapons. Contemporary Security Policy, 40(4), 409–434. https://doi.org/10.1080/13523260.2019.1571852 [Taylor & Francis Online], [Web of Science °], [Google Scholar]

70. Rydell, R. (2005). Looking back: The 1995 nuclear nonproliferation treaty review and extension conference. Arms Control Today, 35(3), 47–48. [Google Scholar]

71. Sagan, S. D. (2000). The commitment trap: Why the United States should not use nuclear threats to deter biological and chemical weapon attacks. Inter-

national Security, 24(4), 85–115. https://doi.org/10.1162/016228800560318 [Crossref], [Web of Science ®], [Google Scholar]

72. Sagan, S. D. (2004). Realism, ethics, and weapons of mass destruction. In S. Hashmi, & S. Lee (Eds.), Ethics and weapons of mass destruction (pp. 73–95). Cambridge University Press. [Crossref], [Google Scholar]

73. Sagan, S. D., & Valentino, B. A. (2017). Revisiting Hiroshima in Iran: What Americans really think about using nuclear weapons and killing non-combatants. International Security, 42(1), 41–79. https://doi.org/10.1162/ISEC_a_00284 [Crossref], [Web of Science ®], [Google Scholar]

74. Sanger, D. E., Jakes, L., & Fassihi, F. (2021, July 31). Biden promised to restore the Iran nuclear deal. now it risks derailment. New York Times. https://www.nytimes.com/2021/07/31/us/politics/biden-iran-nuclear-deal.html [Google Scholar]

75. Sanger, D. E., & Sang-Hun, C. (2020, June 12). Two years after Trump-Kim meeting, little to show for personal diplomacy. New York Times. https://www.nytimes.com/2020/06/12/world/asia/korea-nuclear-trump-kim.html [Google Scholar]

76. Sasikumar, K. (2019). India-Pakistan crises under the nuclear shadow: The role of reassurance. Journal for Peace and Nuclear Disarmament, 2(1), 151–169. https://doi.org/10.1080/25751654.2019.1619229 [Taylor & Francis Online], [Web of Science ®], [Google Scholar]

77. Schmemann, S. (1993, November 4). Russia drops pledge of no first use of atom arms. New York Times, A8. [Google Scholar]

78. Seligman, L., Bender, B., & O'Brien, C. (2021, June 2). Biden goes 'full steam ahead' on Trump's nuclear expansion despite campaign rhetoric. Politico. https://www.politico.com/news/2021/06/02/biden-trump-nuclear-weap-ons-491631 [Google Scholar]

79. Shankar, M., & Paul, T. V. (2016). Nuclear doctrines and stable strategic rela-tionships: The case of South Asia. International Affairs, 92(1), 1–20. https://doi.org/10.1111/1468-2346.12503 [Crossref], [Web of Science ®], [Google Scholar]

80. Smetana, M., & O'Mahoney, J. (2022). NPT as an antifragile system: How contestation improves the nonproliferation regime. Contemporary Security Policy, Forthcoming. [Web of Science ®], [Google Scholar]

81. Smetana, M., & Wunderlich, C. eds. (2021). Forum: Nonuse of nuclear weap-ons in world politics: Toward the third generation of 'nuclear taboo' research. International Studies Review. https://doi.org/10.1093/isr/viab002 [Crossref], [Web of Science ®], [Google Scholar]

82. Sonne, P. (2021, February 3). United States extends nuclear treaty with Russia for five years. Washington Post. https://www.washingtonpost.com/

national-security/us-russia-new-start-nuclear-treaty/2021/02/03/4293d0fa-6638-11eb-bf81-c618c88ed605_story.html [Google Scholar]

83. Stockholm International Peace Research Institute (SIPRI). (2015). World nuclear forces. In SIPRI yearbook 2015 (pp. 459–520). Oxford University Press. [Google Scholar]

84. Tannenwald, N. (2007). The nuclear taboo: The United States and the non-use of nuclear weapons since 1945. Cambridge University Press. [Crossref], [Google Scholar]

85. Tannenwald, N. (2018a). The great unravelling: The future of the nuclear normative order. In N. Tannenwald & J. M. Acton (Eds.), Meeting the challenges of the new nuclear age: Emerging risks and declining norms in the age of technological innovation and changing nuclear doctrines (pp. 6–31). American Academy of Arts & Sciences. [Google Scholar]

86. Tannenwald, N. (2018b). The vanishing nuclear taboo? Foreign Affairs, 97(6), 16–24. [Web of Science], [Google Scholar]

87. Trinkunas, H. A., Lin, H., & Loehrke, B. (eds.). (2020). Three tweets to midnight: Effects of the global information ecosystem on the risk of nuclear conflict. Hoover Institution Press. [Google Scholar]

88. UN Office for Disarmament Affairs. (n.d.). Treaty on the Non-Proliferation of Nuclear Weapons. https://www.un.org/disarmament/wmd/nuclear/npt/text/ [Google Scholar]

89. Ven Bruusgaard, K. (2017, September 22). The myth of Russia's lowered nuclear threshold. War on the Rocks. https://warontherocks.com/2017/09/the-myth-of-russias-lowered-nuclear-threshold/ [Google Scholar]

90. Walker, W. (2000). Nuclear order and disorder. International Affairs, 76(4), 703–724. https://doi.org/10.1111/1468-2346.00160 [Crossref], [Web of Science *], [Google Scholar]

91. Walker, W. (2012). A perpetual menace: Nuclear weapons and international order. Routledge. [Google Scholar]

92. Wenger, A., & Wilner, A. (eds.). (2012). Deterring Terrorism: Theory and practice. Stanford University Press. [Crossref], [Google Scholar]

93. Wheeler, T. (2016, May 18). China's MIRVs: Separating fact from fiction. The Diplomat. https://thediplomat.com/2016/05/chinas-mirvs-separating-fact-from-fiction/ [Crossref], [Google Scholar]

94. Wilkening, D. (2019). Hypersonic weapons and strategic stability. Survival, 61(5), 129–148. https://doi.org/10.1080/00396338.2019.1662125 [Taylor & Francis Online], [Web of Science *], [Google Scholar]

95. Williams, H., & Drew, A. (2020). Escalation by tweet: Managing the new nuclear diplomacy. Centre for Science & Security Studies, King's College London. [Google Scholar]

96. Woolf, A. F. (2017, December 6). Russian compliance with the Intermediate Range Nuclear Forces (INF) Treaty. Congressional Research Service Report R43832. [Google Scholar]

97. Yusuf, M. W. (2019). The Pulwama crisis: Flirting with war in a nuclear environment. Arms Control Today, 49(4), 6–11. [Google Scholar]

Index

About the Author

Musa Khan Jalalzai is a journalist and research scholar. He has written extensively on Afghanistan, terrorism, nuclear and biological terrorism, human trafficking, drug trafficking, and intelligence research and analysis. He was an Executive Editor of the Daily Outlook Afghanistan from 2005-2011, and a permanent contributor in Pakistan's daily *The Post, Daily Times,* and *The Nation, Weekly the Nation,* (London). However, in 2004, US Library of Congress in its report for South Asia mentioned him as the biggest and prolific writer. He received Masters in English literature, Diploma in Geospatial Intelligence, University of Maryland, Washington DC, certificate in Surveillance Law from the University of Stanford, USA, and diploma in Counter terrorism from Pennsylvania State University, California, the United States.